Welcome to
Photoshop®
for Beginners

Welcome to the fourth revised edition of Photoshop for Beginners, your essential guide to using all versions of Photoshop. Whether you have Photoshop CS2 or CS6, or even Elements 11, this updated book will take you through all the key tools and commands step by step. Suitable for new Creative Cloud users too, the introductory feature explains what the Creative Cloud actually is, exploring its top features. Then delve into the tutorial sections, whether it's basic corrections and retouching that you want to learn more about, or adjustments and selections. All this and more is covered in-depth. There is also a selection of creative projects so you can practise the skills you've learned on creating something wonderful. And if that wasn't enough, the book also comes with a free disc, which has some great resources to help you on your Photoshop journey, from tutorial files and fonts to bonus video tuition and more.

Photoshop for Beginners

Imagine Publishing Ltd
Richmond House
33 Richmond Hill
Bournemouth
Dorset BH2 6EZ
☎ +44 (0) 1202 586200
Website: www.imagine-publishing.co.uk
Twitter: @Books_Imagine
Facebook: www.facebook.com/ImagineBookazines

Head of Publishing
Aaron Asadi

Head of Design
Ross Andrews

Production Editor
Sarah Harrison

Senior Art Editor
Greg Whitaker

Designer
Ali Innes

Photographer
James Sheppard

Printed by
William Gibbons, 26 Planetary Road, Willenhall, West Midlands, WV13 3XT

Distributed in the UK & Eire by
Imagine Publishing Ltd, www.imagineshop.co.uk. Tel 01202 586200

Distributed in Australia by
Gordon & Gotch, Equinox Centre, 18 Rodborough Road, Frenchs Forest,
NSW 2086. Tel + 61 2 9972 8800

Distributed in the Rest of the World by
Marketforce, Blue Fin Building, 110 Southwark Street, London, SE1 0SU

Part of the

Photoshop® creative
bookazine series

IMAGINE
PUBLISHING

Contents

118

"Once you've learned all the basics put them to the test"

Ultimate guide

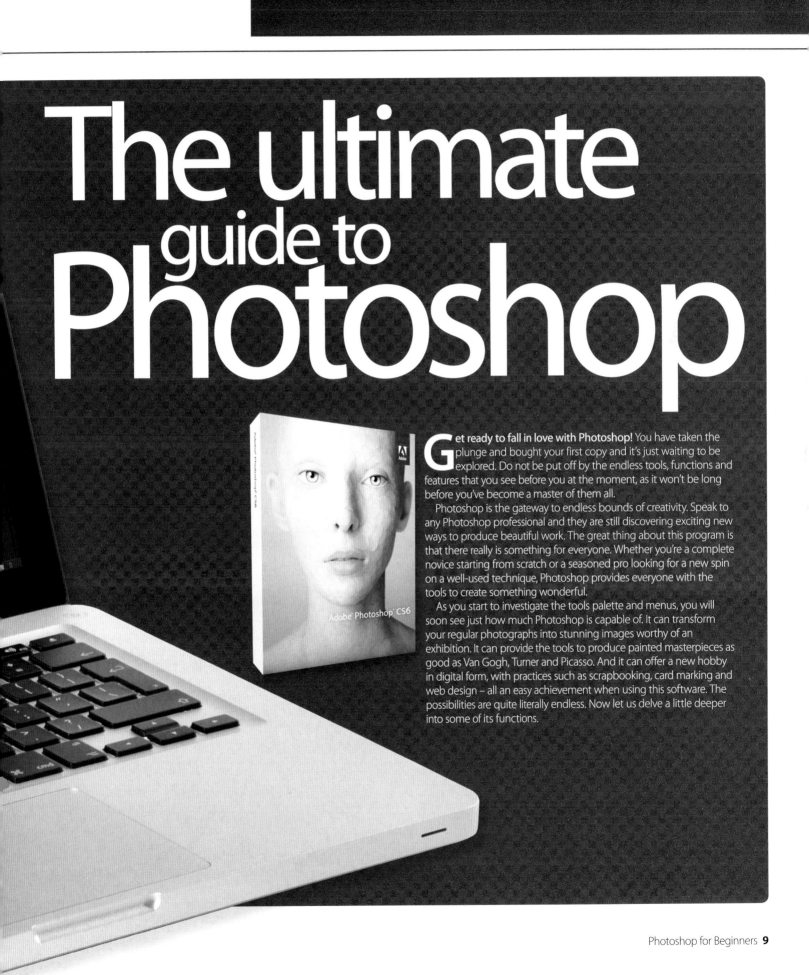

The ultimate guide to Photoshop

Get ready to fall in love with Photoshop! You have taken the plunge and bought your first copy and it's just waiting to be explored. Do not be put off by the endless tools, functions and features that you see before you at the moment, as it won't be long before you've become a master of them all.

Photoshop is the gateway to endless bounds of creativity. Speak to any Photoshop professional and they are still discovering exciting new ways to produce beautiful work. The great thing about this program is that there really is something for everyone. Whether you're a complete novice starting from scratch or a seasoned pro looking for a new spin on a well-used technique, Photoshop provides everyone with the tools to create something wonderful.

As you start to investigate the tools palette and menus, you will soon see just how much Photoshop is capable of. It can transform your regular photographs into stunning images worthy of an exhibition. It can provide the tools to produce painted masterpieces as good as Van Gogh, Turner and Picasso. And it can offer a new hobby in digital form, with practices such as scrapbooking, card marking and web design – all an easy achievement when using this software. The possibilities are quite literally endless. Now let us delve a little deeper into some of its functions.

Editing photos

Tweak your images to perfection

As the name suggests, one of the main uses of Photoshop is editing your photos. In a world where we are always snapping our friends, families, pets and surroundings, we all have plenty of images to get creative with in Photoshop. Whether you rely on your iPhone or other smartphone to capture a moment, or prefer to have a compact camera or digital SLR with you at all times, Photoshop can tweak your images to perfection. It makes no difference what the subject matter is or what device you used to capture the shot, there is always a way to improve the image with a little help from Photoshop.

For landscape lovers, your first task will be to learn how to straighten your pictures in order to achieve a perfect horizon. A wonky photo is an obvious sign of an amateur shot, so it's a good technique to master from the start. You will call upon items such as the Crop tool and the Transform tool to achieve a poker-straight shot – Photoshop CS6 has a dedicated Straighten option built into the Crop tool. Photoshop also enables you to use rulers and guides to help you line up your images perfectly.

Landscapes will often benefit from a colour and contrast boost before you print them off, which is an easy task using one of the many image-adjustment features. You will find Levels and Curves will become frequent friends to help boost your photos and give them extra pop. As your skills progress, you can introduce adjustment layers, which allow you to make alterations to specific areas of your photo as opposed to the whole scene.

Photoshop is an essential ally when it comes to fixing your portraits, and once you've mastered a few simple retouching skills, you'll be hounded by family and friends asking for their teeth whitened, wrinkles decreased and double chins removed. All these tasks are easy to achieve in Photoshop, mainly due to features such as the Clone tool, which can hide blemishes and wrinkles.

You can employ Masks to help smooth the skin, while keeping the eyes and lips perfectly sharp. You can also get creative with your image editing by altering the colour of eyes and hair to give your friends an entirely different look. These skills are easily achievable with a little practice.

There are plenty of other fantastic ways to improve your images in Photoshop. By using the Dodge and Burn tools you can lighten and darken areas of your shot, which is ideal if you find your image is slightly over or under exposed. You can also enhance the colour of the scene by adding a Photo Filter, ideal for boosting the warm tones of a sunset for example.

No matter what you choose to do to your shot in Photoshop, there is one task that is vital before you hit that print button. That is to learn how to sharpen your images. Every photographer should master this quick and easy editing skill to ensure their photos are full of punch when you hang them on the wall. With this skill under your belt, your photos will really shine.

Experiment with selective colour and black and white when editing

Add creative effects, such as a vignette

5 PHOTO-EDITING METHODS

01 Fix the exposure

You'll often find your photographs appear too dark or too light. This can be fixed in Photoshop by a number of methods. First of all you can head to the Image menu in the top toolbar and select Adjustments. Here you will find an Exposure slider, which you can use to lighten or darken a shot. Alternatively, use the Dodge and Burn tools to lighten and darken specific areas of an image for a more localised correction.

02 Straighten the horizon

A wonky horizon is a common photographic error that can be easily fixed in Photoshop. Pre-CS6, open up your image and select the Crop tool. Now draw a rectangle shape over your image and head to one of the top corners. A curved arrow will appear, which enables you to move your image to straighten it up. In CS6, there is a dedicated Straighten button, which lets you draw a line where the horizon should lie and you Photoshop will straighten and crop for you.

03 Convert to black and white

It's really easy to change a picture to black and white to add a fantastic documentary feel to your images. Simply open your photo in Photoshop and go to Image>Adjustments and select either Black and White or Hue/Saturation. The latter option provides more tonal control. Add a Curves adjustment to boost the contrast.

04 Add a photo filter

There are plenty of photo filters that emulate the real-life filters used in photography. These are perfect for changing the atmosphere of a picture. Here we have added a Warming filter to a cool blue shot to add warmth and a feeling of sunset tones. Use the sliders to intensify or reduce the effect.

05 Selective colour your shots

Selective colouring is a technique used to accentuate a particular part of your shot. Go to Image>Adjustments>Selective Color to adjust a specific colour without affecting the rest of the hues in the image. You can turn the rest black and white, keeping your chosen colours vivid.

Manipulating photos
Transform your shots into something new

Create abstract scenes by manipulating your images

Photomanipulation is quite different from image editing, as it involves taking a photo and transforming it into something new. This is where things start to get really interesting.

You will have undoubtedly heard a lot about layers in Photoshop, but may not be aware of what they actually do. In their most basic sense, they enable you to build up a sandwich of images and effects. Each layer of the sandwich interacts with the other fillings until you have a whole new sandwich, or image. For example, you may start with a portrait photo and then add a new background onto a new layer. You can add some text on a different layer and then an illustration on another. Before you know it, all these layers have added up to create a brand-new image full of details.

You'll find that the Selection tools are useful for photomanipulation, as they enable you to cut out parts of your image. You can then use these cutouts in other designs, move them about the page, or simply discard them. By getting to know some of the Selection tools (the Pen tool and Lasso tool being two of the most called upon) you'll soon see your creative opportunities opening up.

You will be able to select the outline of a person and add them to a completely new background in a few simple steps. Add in a few more new skills, such as lighting effects, and you will be able to make your person and background look as if they had always been together.

By exploring the Filter menu, you will be able to transform your photos in exciting new ways. Completely change the weather by adding a rain effect, or turn a dull sky into a bright backdrop. By using layers, you can form composites, which are images made up of lots of different parts. This is a great technique if you want to create new and interesting landscapes, sci-fi scenes or fairytale glades. These are made by combining different images and textures that result in a whole new world.

For an abstract touch, how about creating scenes within scenes? You can literally make a storm in a teacup by adding a raging sea to a regular-looking cup of tea for a fantastic visual play on words.

Another great photo-manipulation technique is to create wonderful tricks for the eye. You can call upon the Liquify tool to bend and shape your photographs in Dali-esque creations dripping across the screen, which has been massively improved in Photoshop CS6 to make it faster and easier to use. Alternatively, you can use Lens Blur and masks to transform a shot of a city scene into a miniature toy town.

The only limit is your imagination when it comes to photo manipulation. Photoshop provides all the tools you need to make your ideas come to life on screen. The tricky bit is deciding which is the best method to use. Often there are multiple ways of doing the same thing using various tool combinations – you just have to figure out your preferred way of working.

5 PHOTOMANIPULATION TECHNIQUES

01 Get creative with a single shot

By using a multitude of repeated layers and the Crop tool, you can transform a single shot into a multidimensional image reminiscent of David Hockney's famous creations. You can control how many portions you divide the image into. Use the Transform tools to slightly angle each frame to give the impression they are piled up on top of each other. Adding Blend modes to some frames alters the intensity of colour for each shot.

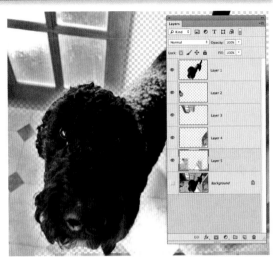

02 Change the weather

Photoshop is a fantastic tool to help change the background and add dramatic effects such as weather conditions. By exploring the extensive Filter Gallery, you can produce convincing rain effects. Adding Blur can give the impression of driving rain or soften the effect for a light shower. This can entirely alter the atmosphere of an image and, in this instance, add mood and drama. Snow and ice effects are also easily achievable in Photoshop.

03 Lighting effects

Play tricks on the eye by introducing creative text effects to your images. Add completely new signatures to walls and buildings by applying a careful and considered use of the Lighting effects filter. This will take some practice, but the results are very convincing and can transform a regular, bland image into something extremely engaging. Blurring the outline can create a fall-off of light onto the surrounding areas to help your image look even more realistic.

04 Get creative with textures

A simple way of manipulating images is by introducing new textures and backgrounds to the shot. Textures can be added by using the Texturizer filter, or you can head online and source hundreds of free textures, which can be imported into Photoshop. Whether you are looking for paper textures, stone textures or even animal textures, you will find an overwhelming supply with a quick internet search.

05 Change the seasons

Photoshop is such a powerful tool that you can quite literally control the seasons at the touch of a button. By using a combination of Photoshop brushes, filters and blending modes you can produce distinguishable changes to a single image. Use gradients to alter the sky colour, and the opacity sliders to determine the strength of the effect on your photograph. You will be amazed by the power that's at your fingertips.

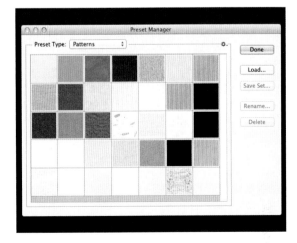

Digital art

Create visual masterpieces

Consider Photoshop an artist's treasure trove of tools, paints and media. Even if your artistic skills are limited to stick men, Photoshop can provide all the features to help you realise your inner Van Gogh.

Unlike traditional drawing and painting, Photoshop makes it as easy as tracing over an image. You can literally sketch or paint over any photograph to create a stunning masterpiece. By using layer masks, you can create a host of drawing and painting styles.

On the drawing side of things, you will discover there are far more options than a simple pencil sketch. Open your eyes to the world of chalk and charcoal drawing, sketching in watercolour, and pen and ink effects. By carefully selecting the right type of brush and combining it with the right kind of filter, you can create realistic artwork of which you can be proud. Photoshop CS5 and CS6 both introduced new brush types which are even more like their real-life counterparts, making it easier than ever to get realistic results.

You can choose from a wide range of paper types too. Work on canvas, rough paper, smooth paper, chalkboard, rag paper, and so on – any surface is possible. Some can be simulated using Photoshop's default textures and others can be downloaded as texture libraries online, and imported into Photoshop.

If traditional painting styles are more your thing, then get ready to delve into the endless supply of brushes, paint swatches and blending modes. Photoshop provides a wealth of painting tools and if you use a graphics tablet, these can be further extended by setting the Pen Pressure settings to emulate the pressure of a paintbrush. You can create light, feathery paint strokes or strong, bold strokes depending on the style you want to achieve. You can also create custom brushes depending on the style you have chosen, and there are plenty of free brushes you can use from the internet too.

You are not limited to painting with brushes either. In fact, the Filter menu is capable of producing plenty of painting effects of its own. Experiment with Dry Brush and Pointillize filters to create a rough textured effect which, when layered over a start photo, can create something rather beautiful. CS6's new Oil Paint filter is also a powerful way to turn photos into paintings with little effort.

Digital painting in Photoshop is one of the most satisfying activities. Granted, it takes time and patience, but you'll find that the results can be truly awe-inspiring and well worth the effort.

Use words and images to create impressive pieces of art

5 GREAT DIGITAL ART PROJECTS

01 Vector art

Vector art is a modern trend and popular with many digital artists for its clean, bold impact. The effect is achieved predominantly by using the Pen tool, which enables you to cut out specific parties of your image. The tool is very precise and lets you trace around both curved and straight edges. After a little practise, this tool becomes second nature and will open up a wealth of creative opportunities to you.

Utilise the extensive range of brushes and textures

02 Print effects

Any real-world artistic effect can be reproduced in Photoshop. The Shape tools can create colourful characters. You can then call upon Blending modes to experiment with the intensity of your colours and the way each layer interacts with one another. There are many Blending modes to choose from, and then discover which works best in each creative situation.

03 Get creative with brushes

You can create a Van Gogh masterpiece thanks to the extensive range of brushes and brush options. You can alter your brush shape, intensity, width and pressure, which helps recreate works like this. You also have an endless supply of colour swatches so you can find the right shade of paint you're looking for. Add in a canvas texture and you're ready to start painting your incredible work of art.

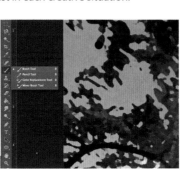

Use your own photographs to create awe-inspiring results

04 Retro effects

In Photoshop CS6 there are many new Airbrush options to play which you can customise to vary the intensity and the area of spray. There are presets for common brush setups too. A graphics tablet and pen can alter the pressure settings so you can press hard for a saturated spray or press softly for a light smattering – just as if you were using a real-life airbrush.

05 Learn to shade

The key to successful digital art relies on the same principles as traditional methods, which is building up the shading and toning gradually. This particularly applies to areas such as the hair and skin, which normally features a wide range of tones instead of one base colour. By introducing a number of similar shades you will easily add depth and realism to your lacklustre images that look one dimensional.

Ultimate guide

What's new with the Creative Cloud?

Photoshop has changed, but has it been for the better? We reveal ten top new features

Photoshop Creative Cloud is the new name for Adobe's Creative Suite. Photoshop and the entire collection of Creative Suite programs are now available under an annual or monthly subscription to the Creative Cloud. With this link to the Creative Cloud, Photoshop CC will update as and when new features are released, which is very useful. For digital artists, this latest version has a number of impressive new features. Some of these include the ability to remove blurriness from an image, apply the powerful Camera Raw plug-in to any layer and create Conditional Actions for telling Photoshop exactly what you want it to do.

> "Photoshop Creative Cloud will update as and when new features are released, which is very useful"

TOP 10 NEW FEATURES

01 Say goodbye to blurry photos
With the Camera Shake Reduction filter, what was once deemed impossible is now reality. Blurry images can be deblurred inside this incredible new filter, with Photoshop tracking the movement of the lens and retracing its steps to show you how it would look if in focus.

02 Play what you want
Actions are great for telling Photoshop what to do. But unlike in previous versions, they can now have conditions applied to what task you record. Actions can be told to just edit the size or style of the image being handled, such as only images with a landscape orientation.

03 Edit with Camera RAW
Adobe's Camera RAW software is now kept in the Filter menu, meaning it can be applied to any layer at any stage in the editing process. This powerful software (designed to improve camera RAW images) has a vast arrangement of adjustments for tweaking exposure, retouching blemishes and improving colour.

04 Connect to the Cloud
If you plan on using multiple applications within the Creative Cloud, you can make sure your favourite presets, styles, brushes, Actions and more are accessible wherever you go. See all the options by going to Preferences and then Sync Settings.

Camera RAW editing You can find Camera Raw inside the Filter menu. The software lets you apply targeted adjustments and retouching to make images look their best.

Smart Sharpen

☑ Preview

Preset: Default

Amount: 200 %

Radius: 1.0 px

Reduce Noise: 10 %

Remove: Lens Blur   0

▼ Shadows

Fade Amount: 0 %

Tonal Width: 50 %

Radius: 1 px

Highlights

Fade Amount: 0 %

Tonal Width: 50 %

Radius: 1 px

Cancel   OK

100%

05 Network with Behance

Behance is a network and community for digital artists to collaborate and
share ideas. With Photoshop CC, Behance is just a click away. So if you're
wondering what your next big project might be, simply head over to www.
behance.net for lots of inspiration.

06 Rounder corners

Add finesse to your images with a stylish frame, now made even easier
with the Properties palette. The palette has new features for controlling the
roundness of corners when using the Rectangle tool. Other aspects of the
frame can be adapted as well, for example adding an outline colour and
changing its overall size.

07 Visualise your image

The Image Size menu has been redesigned to show how your image will
look while it's being resized. This is incredibly handy when it comes to
increasing the dimensions and resolution of your image, lowering pixel
dimensions, and compressing images for uploading online or saving after
editing.

08 A sharper view

The Smart Sharpen filter has been redesigned to give you a closer look at
your image. This window is resizable and its sliders have been rearranged
to make the whole thing look and feel friendlier.

09 Liquify magic

Not only does the Liquify filter contain a new Smooth tool for getting rid of
sharp edges, it can also be applied as a Smart Filter. What this means is that
you'll be able to hop back into the filter at any point.

10 Think big

Now when you make an image larger (upsample) using the Image Size
menu, you no longer have to worry about dramatic changes to quality. The
new Preserve Details (Enlargement) setting, along with the Reduce Noise
slider, will make sure definition doesn't disappear.

Frame styles Handy for applying frames to your image, the corners can be rounded off with a
stroke outline. These can be applied inside the Properties palette in Photoshop CC.

Getting started

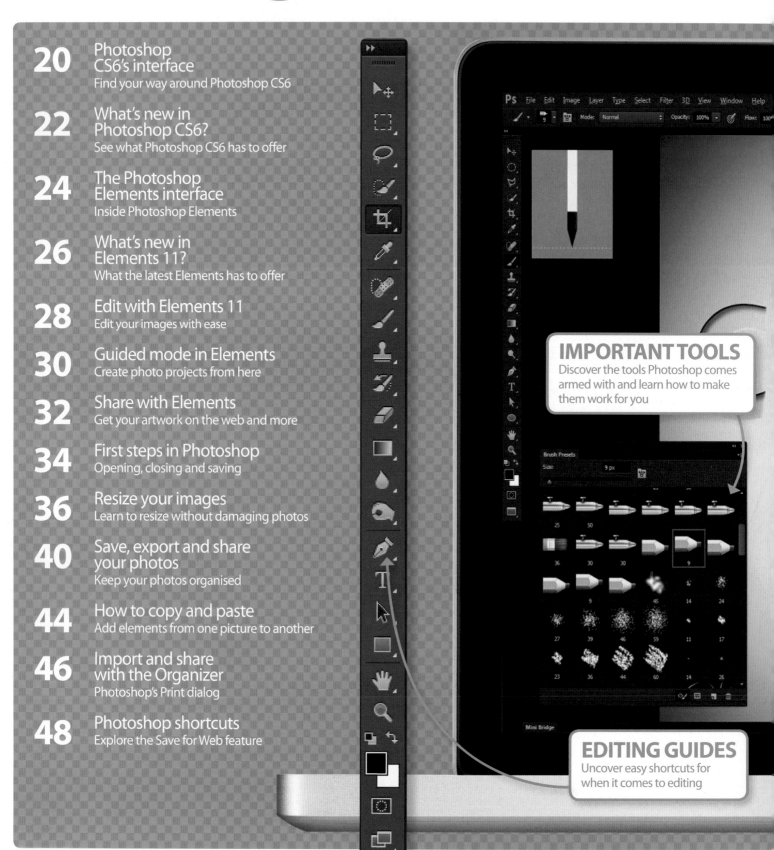

IMPORTANT TOOLS
Discover the tools Photoshop comes armed with and learn how to make them work for you

EDITING GUIDES
Uncover easy shortcuts for when it comes to editing

CS6 INTERFACE EXPLAINED
Find your way around the Photoshop interface before you get started

MacBook Pro

Photoshop CS6's interface

A look at the new palettes and features

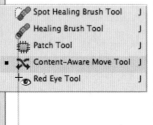

The interface has a number of new palettes, tools and options for changing how it all works. The brand new Content-Aware Move tool is helpful for moving objects across the canvas, and the Crop tool has been improved too. Here's a pick of the top changes in this new version and what you can expect to see.

New tools

The new Content-Aware Move tool is found with the Healing Brush and Red Eye tools. Draw around the subject that you want to move and then drag it to a new position. Blank pixels are filled in with similar pixels straightaway.

Timeline palette

Both Photoshop CS6 and CS6 Extended come with the Timeline palette. Edit and create videos using your layers for some interesting visual effects and transitions.

Color Range

When you're selecting skin, tick Detect Faces in the Color Range menu. Set this to Skin Tones and Color Range finds and highlights skin. Keep Fuzziness low to begin with and gradually increase until all skin is white in the preview.

QUICK TIP

New in CS6

There are even more features in the Photoshop CS6 Beta than we've mentioned here. To see all of the additions to the program in one go, head to the top-right corner of your interface and open the drop-down menu containing the various view modes. In this list is the option New in CS6, which replaces your current setup of palettes and tools with the complete collection of updated ones. Have a peek at the menus too, as the newest options are highlighted blue.

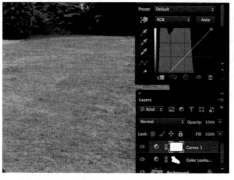

Interface colours

Photoshop CS6 has four colour options for its interface. The white interface, which is what's been used since day one, can be changed to a darker shade of grey or even black. To change the interface's colour, go to the Preferences>Interface. A darker interface, akin to the Elements backdrop, keeps eyes focused more on your artwork, but this really depends on what you're used to.

Lighting Effects filter

In Photoshop CS6, the Lighting Effects filter has been greatly improved. The interface of the filter is easier to use and the bigger preview window means that it's much quicker to adapt the effect. The sliders have been reduced and the perimeter of the lighting effect is larger. These changes have turned what used to be a good filter into one of the best. We highly recommend checking it out.

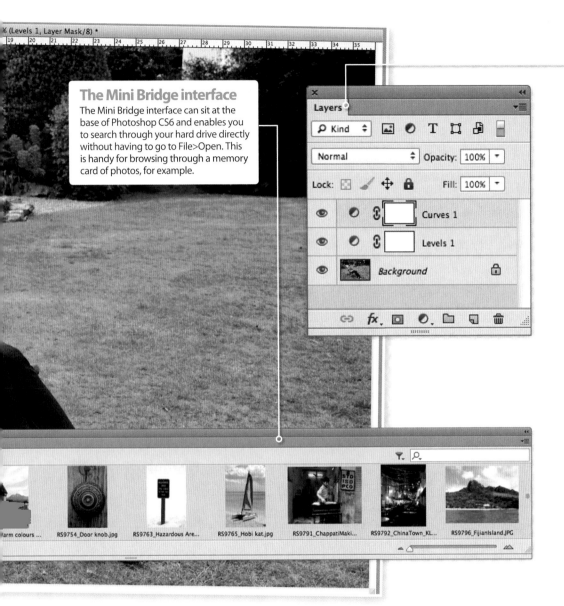

The Mini Bridge interface
The Mini Bridge interface can sit at the base of Photoshop CS6 and enables you to search through your hard drive directly without having to go to File>Open. This is handy for browsing through a memory card of photos, for example.

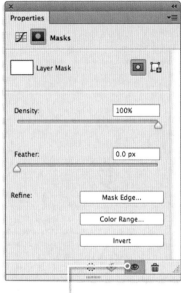

Layers palette
Layers can be sorted by type, name, mode or colour using the options at the top of the palette. For multi-layered compositions, this will do the searching and filtering for you, saving those precious minutes.

Adjustment layers
Adjustment layers and their masks are controlled in the Properties palette. Cycle between the two and lower the Density slider to make the adjustment fainter in appearance. Apply Feather to soften the edges if you're working with selections.

Using the Crop tool
Select the Crop tool and head to the Options bar for the new features, changing the View setting for various guides. These include the Golden Spiral, Rule of Thirds, Diagonal or Triangle, and line up the subjects where the various lines intersect. Photoshop keeps the image centred as you move the cropping area. This can be switched off using the Classic Mode option by clicking on the cog.

Adaptive Wide Angle
The Adaptive Wide Angle filter corrects distortion, which can occur when using a wide-angle lens. This will straighten out an image back to a more natural composition. When you open the filter, draw lines across what should be a straight edge. The filter will detect the curvature of the image by what lens was used, and adjust it to level everything out.

What's new in Photoshop CS6?

With CS6, Adobe has given us great improvements in performance as well as significant and powerful new features

CS6 is the thirteenth version release of Photoshop and comes nearly 23 years after its 1.0 release back in 1990. The CS6 version is significant in several ways. One of the most significant changes isn't even readily visible, it's under the hood. The performance and stability of the program is greatly enhanced by the addition of new Mercury Graphics Engine that makes the program operate smoother and snappier than ever before. Even processor-intensive features like the Liquify filter are more responsive. This increases production while decreasing user frustration.

On the face Photoshop looks dramatically different. The interface itself has changed from the well-known slate grey to a very dark grey. While this change may seem simply cosmetic, it's surprisingly deep. Every icon in every dialog box has been redesigned to work within the new colour scheme. This move puts Photoshop visibly in line with other programs in the Creative Suite.

Adobe continues to build on the amazing new Content Aware technology. This groundbreaking feature made famous in CS5 through the Edit>Fill command, now gets its own tool in the tool box. The Content Aware Move tool is in the same tool set as the Spot Healing Brush, which also sports a Content-Aware option. The Content Aware Move tool can automatically fill in the gaps left behind when moving a selection on an image, and works to seamlessly blend the subject in with the new location.

This upgrade of Photoshop is known by some as the "User's Upgrade" because of the great number of changes implemented directly due to users' requests. Things like a larger preview window for the Lighting Effects filter to applying true Dashed Strokes to vector shapes. CS6 proves that Adobe really does listen to its user base, and it shows!

"One of the most significant changes isn't even readily visible"

NEW FEATURES OF CS6

Darker interface
Photoshop goes dark with CS6. The new darker interface aligns with the other applications in the Creative Suite. The dimmer tone is less distracting and helps you to focus on your image.

Erodible Tip brushes
CS6 offers some new Erodible Brush tips that wear away like a real media drawing tool to simulate the look and feel of graphite or charcoal.

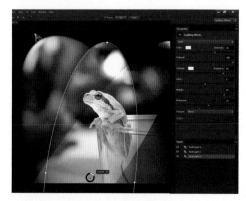

Larger Lighting Effects
Thankfully, the Lighting Effects Filter preview is now full screen and many of the light settings can be adjusted by using an on-canvas adjustment widget.

Content Aware Move
The Content Aware technology now goes beyond the Fill command. The new Content Aware Move can relocate objects in an image and automatically fill in the holes and seams.

Better Crop
Adobe completely revamped the Crop tool for CS6. The image to mouse movement is more flexible and intuitive. There's also a new ability to retain the cropped pixels.

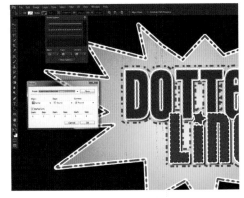

Properties Panel

The new Properties Panel reduces the number of pop-up dialog boxes and allows greater visibility of your work while adjusting controls like curves or levels.

Character styles

New Character and Paragraph styles make it easy to capture text formatting and apply it to other text or to quickly change the formatting for several text areas at once.

Dotted lines

CS6 also features some brand-new vector tools including the ability to add live strokes without a layer style. These strokes have their own properties such as style and colour.

Oil Paint filter

The new Oil Paint filter makes great strides forward in easily creating a hand-painted appearance by adjusting the settings on a filter. A great addition that will save a lot of time.

Blur Gallery

The new Blur Gallery features three new Blur types: Field Blur, Iris Blur, and Tilt-Shift Blur. All have on-canvas adjustment widgets for easy adjustments with live previews.

Getting started

The Photoshop Elements interface

Elements 11 offers the photo-editing power of a Photoshop product in a user-friendly, affordable package

The main Photoshop product can seem very intimidating and unwieldy for the student photographer or hobbyist. The price tag for the full package can be even more difficult to overcome. Photoshop Elements 11 is Adobe's greatest effort to reach a user base who wants the power of Photoshop, but not the price tag or learning curve that goes along with it. People who want to take great pictures of their families and create their own memories with lasting photos of their own. The target audience isn't trying to launch their own photography studio so they are not looking for the highest professional level equipment, but they still want to capture the cherished life moments and share them with other loved ones.

Photoshop Elements 11 is a perfect solution for the amateur shutterbugs who are looking to hone their photography skills and spend more time behind the lens than behind the monitor. With three different editing environments, users of any skill or experience level can find the tools they need to make their photos as perfect as possible. The new Organizer helps keep track of the best shots so users don't need to swim through hundreds of files to find that one special photo.

The Elements 11 interface is designed to be welcoming, without undercutting the powerful feature set. Both new users and experienced pros can get to work quickly and efficiently with an assortment of new guided edits and filter settings for great effects. Photoshop Elements 11 allows users to correct and enhance photos with ease and quickly share or store them so you can get back to shooting more great photos!

"The Photoshop Elements 11 interface is designed to be welcoming and unintimidating"

Quick Edit
The Quick Edit environment provides several one-click fixes, such as Smart Fix, where Photoshop Elements 11 uses automated tools to correct common problems found in photographs. The slider and grid controls regulate the amount of applied correction.

Guided Edit
The Guided Edit mode features several step-by-step guides for a variety of edits. These walk-throughs provide detailed instructions and buttons that activate the tools you need.

Expert
The Expert Mode editing environment allows access to more tools, effects, filters and styles. These additional features offer more freedom and control than the other editing environments.

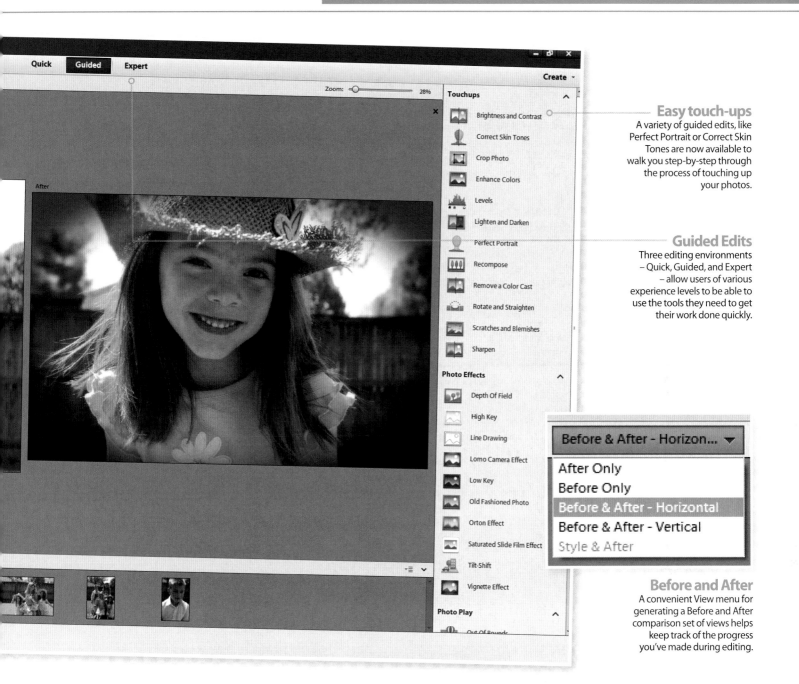

Easy touch-ups
A variety of guided edits, like Perfect Portrait or Correct Skin Tones are now available to walk you step-by-step through the process of touching up your photos.

Guided Edits
Three editing environments – Quick, Guided, and Expert – allow users of various experience levels to be able to use the tools they need to get their work done quickly.

Before and After
A convenient View menu for generating a Before and After comparison set of views helps keep track of the progress you've made during editing.

Organizer
The new Organizer is invaluable for sorting and managing your photos. There's even facial recognition technology that can automatically sort photos by person.

Photo Play
Some fun and easy options are available under the Photo Play section of the Guided Edit environment. Out of Bounds and Picture Stack are just two examples of the fun effects.

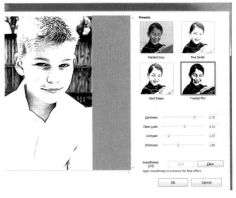

New filters
Photoshop Elements 11 now includes a host of fun new filters like new Graphic Novel filter. Use it with some distinctive presets or custom controls to get a unique effect.

What's new in Elements 11?

Elements 11 has many new features such as a redesigned interface and powerful new filters to help you in a number of ways

The first thing you noticed when open Photoshop Elements 11 is a totally new intuitive user interface. Depending on your skill level, you can select from three different editing environments; Quick, Guided and the Expert Mode.

The Quick Mode is simple and easy to use, you can correct the exposure, levels, colour, balance, and sharpness of images. Each option displays a grid of nine thumbnails with various settings applied. Hover the mouse over each thumbnail and see how the settings will change your image.

Jumping in the Guided Mode, you will find three groups, the Touchups, Photo Effects and Photo Play. Each display step-by-step instructions on how to apply a particular effect to your photos. Under the Photo effect group you will find some amazing new effects such as the High/Low-Key, Vignette, and Tilt-Shift to produce a professional-grade photo

However, if you are already familiar with photo editing the Expert Mode is for you. It gives you a full pallet of tools and lets you work with layers, colour correction, filters, styles, and effects. There is a new refine edge feature to make it easy to select complex elements in your photo such as hair. There are also three new Sketch filters – Comic, Graphic Novel, and Pen Ink – to help transform your photos into illustrations.

The new intuitive Organizer makes it easier to navigate through, view and manage your pictures based on people, places and events. The Smart Tag feature automatically analyses your photos to make finding them even faster. You can share your images, via print, the web, and mobile devices, as well as create online albums, cards, and scrapbooks.

"The intuitive Organizer makes it easier to navigate your pictures"

ELEMENTS 11

Nested tools
To access the other tools nested together, click on the tool and you will see the other tools nested within.

New interface
The new interface is brighter and the Tool Option is now on the taskbar at the bottom. The toolbar on the left is rearranged and labelled into categories.

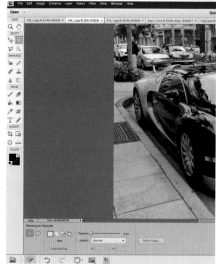

Tilt-Shift
Create a miniature world in three simple steps. Open your image into the Guided Mode, under the Photo Effects group choose Tilt-Shift, follow the instructions to create this popular effect.

Vignette effect
Create a nice portrait photo using the new Vignette effect. Open the Guided Mode and select the Vignette effect, choose the colour, the intensity and apply the effect.

Comic Filter
Turn your photos in illustrations using the new Graphic Novel Filter. You can locate the filter under the Sketch filter menu which you'll find in the Expert Mode.

Panels
Click on the big icons on the taskbar to open the correspondent panel. If you want to customise or open more panels click on the More icon.

Create button
Click on the Create button in the top-right corner to get quick access and create greeting cards, photo books, photo prints, slideshows and much more.

Comic effect
You can have some fun in Photoshop Elements 11 with the all-new Comic Filter. Choose one of the presets and use the sliders to adjust the effect even further.

High Key effect
Add a beautifully dramatic look to your photographs using a High Key effect. Head into the Guided Mode, click High Key and then choose the Color or B&W presets.

Pen/ Ink
The Pen and Ink filter works like the Comic and Graphic Novel effect. Choose the preset that you like and use the controls to edit different details like colour, and so on.

Edit with Elements 11

Learn the different Editing Modes in Elements 11 to quickly edit, enhance and create professional-looking images

There are three different editing environments in Photoshop Elements 11; Quick, Guided and the Expert Mode (known as Full Mode in the previous versions).

In Quick Editing Mode, you will find six basics photo fixing tools: Smart Fix, Exposure, Levels, Color, Balance, and Sharpen. You can use the slider controls to adjust the settings or hover the mouse over the thumbnails to preview and apply the adjustment on the photo. If your image just requires a simple quick fix, the Quick Editing mode is the easiest way to improve your images with just a click.

The Guided Editing Mode will walk you through step-by-step instructions for more detailed fixes for your images. Some of the newest features of Photoshop Elements are in the Guided Mode, the Vignette effects helps you to create a nice portrait, the High/Low key can be used to add drama to your photos, and the Tilt-Shift effect makes your photos look like a miniature scene. There are 25 Guided edits with detailed instructions to help you to achieve the desired effect. Once you've finished the tutorial in Guided Mode, you can jump into Expert Mode to see how Photoshop Elements creates all the layers and adjustments, so you can fine-tune it manually.

In the Expert Mode, you are in charge of everything. You have total control over your editing and have at your disposal a full range of tools, filters, effects, and adjustments to work with your photos. You have a new Refine edge dialog for more precise control over complex selections. There are even four new filters – Lens Blur, Comic, Pen & Ink, and Graphic Novels – for you to create unique effects.

"Quick Editing mode is the easiest way to improve your images"

THE EDIT MENU IN ELEMENTS

Color Cast
In the Guided Mode click 'Remove a Color Cast'. Click on the Color Cast Selection and using the Color eyedropper, click on a part of the image that should be white.

Enhance Colors
Click on the Enhance Colors and click Auto to balance the colours and contrast in the image. Increase the Saturation to add a more vivid colour.

ORIGINAL

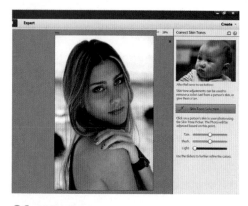

01 Skin Tones
In the Guided Mode click on Correct Skin Tones, and then click on the person's skin using the Skin Tone Picker. This command will bring out more natural skin tones.

02 Brightness/ Contrast
To add warmth, click on the Brightness and Contrast command and increase the Brightness to 25 and the Contrast to 10 by dragging the slider control then click Done.

03 High Key
Click on the High Key option and click once on the B&W preset to create the High key Effect. Click once on Add Diffuse Glow to intensify the effect and click Done when you're happy.

Crop Photo

Click on Crop Photo and Elements creates a crop box around the image. From the drop-down menu, choose the crop box size or drag the handles to the desired size.

Brightness/Contrast

Click on the Brightness and Contrast command. Increase the Contrast by dragging the slider control. This will bring more detail to the image, and then click Done.

04 Expert editing

Select the Expert Editing Mode. Here you are able to see the settings used to create certain effects, allowing you to practise and perfect the skills all by yourself.

05 Fix issues

If you find that the Diffuse Glow has left the image a little over exposed, click on the Background copy layer and turn off the visibility by clicking on the eye icon.

06 Adjust levels

On the levels Adjustment Layer click on the Output Levels and drag the slider control to the left, now you can add more details by dragging the level sliders.

Guided mode in Elements

Photoshop Elements has a dedicated interface for all kinds of photo projects, so you can do more with your pics

It's so easy to build up a massive collection of photos that sit on your desktop and do nothing, gathering digital dust and forgotten about. As we have mentioned, there are a number of different interfaces within Photoshop Elements, which each deal with different tasks. Here we are taking a look at the Quick interface, which promises to give a new lease of life to these photographs.

This enables you to create exciting photo projects from within Photoshop Elements, including books, calendars and more. Each project guides you through step by step, and you can pick templates, add text, upload images and more, without any prior knowledge. You can select images to add to your projects from the Elements Organizer, or from your computer, and then it's time for the fun part – experimenting!

You can keep trying out new ideas again and again, as nothing is set in stone. When you are done, you can use the dedicated Adobe Photoshop Services to get your project printed professionally. There are also online suppliers for some of the categories that you can choose from, including Kodak Gallery. You can even use the Create interface to order prints from your photo library.

This is a real plus point of the Elements software, and it is not something that you will find in the standard Photoshop version. There is a big emphasis on creating, sharing and doing more with your photos.

"Create exciting photo projects from within Elements, including books, calendars and more"

Photo Book
The classic presentation method, the Photo Book, is as popular as ever. Design the book through Elements, then prepare for printing.

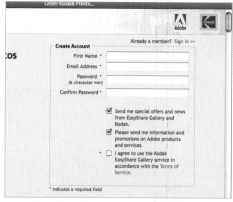

Photo Prints
Order prints using Kodak Printing service. Photos are uploaded to your Kodak Gallery account, offering storage online.

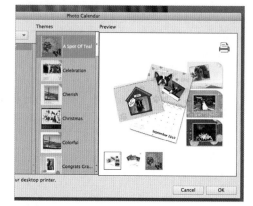

Photo Calendar
Print your own calendars using this effective step-by-step guide. Tick the Autofill box in order to get started with the layout.

Zoom: 25%

Touchups

Brightness and Contrast

Correct Skin Tones

Crop Photo

Enhance Colors

Levels

Lighten and Darken

Perfect Portrait

Recompose

Remove a Color Cast

Rotate and Straighten

Scratches and Blemishes

Sharpen

Photo Effects

Depth Of Field

High Key

Line Drawing

Lomo Camera Effect

Low Key

Old Fashioned Photo

Orton Effect

Creative options
Down the right-hand side are all of the options for what you can create using Photoshop Elements, which are all easy-to-follow guides.

Open image
Your open images are here in the Project Bin, but when you choose to start a new photo project, you will be able to go back in and select more images to use.

Templates
Each project gives you a choice of templates that you can use as you create your product, and you can customise these with text and images.

Photo Collage
A lovely way to show off lots of your images in one go, you can have a lot of fun with your collage projects and get creative with text too.

CD Jacket
This is a fantastic way to design and personalise your own CD jackets in order to store collections onto for future use.

DVD Labels
As well as jackets, you can use photos from Collection for printing your own DVD labels. This is a great gift and decorative finishing touch.

Share with Elements

Don't keep your images to yourself; let everyone see and enjoy them with Elements' built-in Share options

We are living in a digital world, where sharing ideas, images, text and, well, anything, is easily done via the web. Photoshop Elements has obviously been following this trend and has incorporated the sharing options into the main interface.

There are the classic options here, such as sending images via email to friends and relatives. However, there are some more modern integrations, such as direct upload to Facebook and Flickr. Photoshop Elements will prepare your images for upload and then post them to your account. The engine that Elements uses is faster than the one on Facebook, for example, as it does the compression using your computer's power so that when it uploads to Facebook it does so in a flash. There are other options here too, but we have focused on the ones that are the most popular.

Sharing images is great if you have family and friends spread around the country, or the world, as it lets them instantly see what you have been up to. Even better, if you have organised your images with the Organizer and tagged people in your pictures, these tags are automatically added to Facebook – a real timesaver.

We'll have a closer look at some of the built-in Share options over the following two pages.

"There are some more modern integrations, such as direct upload to Facebook and Flickr – a real timesaver"

LEARN TO SHARE

Facebook tagging
Tag your photos using the Elements Organizer, which even does a lot of the hard work for you by tagging familiar subjects for you, and these will be translated straight into Facebook – clever stuff!

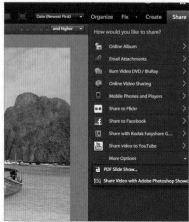

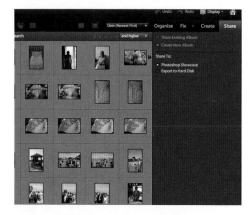

Online Album
Use this option if you want to upload a set of pictures to your own web page, so that you can share your images with your friends.

Email
You can instantly attach a picture to an email via your desktop account by using this option. It's super-simple and it's quicker too.

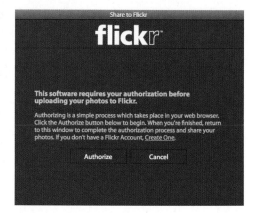

Flickr
The world's best-known photo-sharing site is at your fingerprints. Once you have an account, then you can quickly add images to your albums.

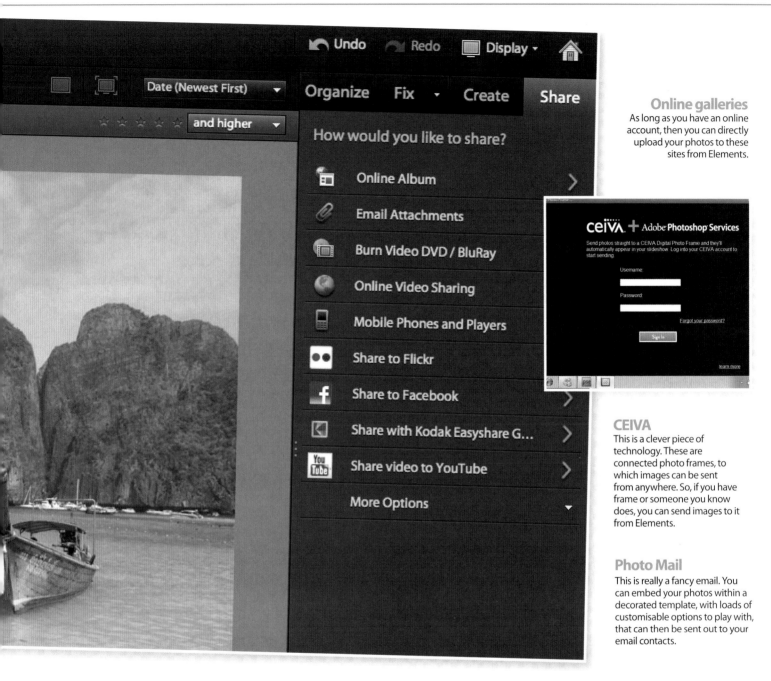

Online galleries

As long as you have an online account, then you can directly upload your photos to these sites from Elements.

CEIVA

This is a clever piece of technology. These are connected photo frames, to which images can be sent from anywhere. So, if you have frame or someone you know does, you can send images to it from Elements.

Photo Mail

This is really a fancy email. You can embed your photos within a decorated template, with loads of customisable options to play with, that can then be sent out to your email contacts.

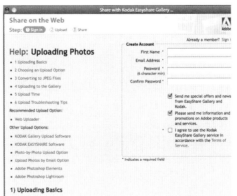

Facebook

If Facebook is your choice of sharing platform, images are compressed and sent directly from within the Adobe interface.

Kodak

Upload and share images with the Kodak Easyshare Gallery. A handy step-by-step guide is avalible to help you start uploading your images with ease.

You Tube

Organise video files and, at a click of a button, share them on a worldwide scale. YouTube allows you to upload and enjoy your clips with others.

First steps in Photoshop

First time in Photoshop? Use this primer to get up to speed with the basics in our essential guide

The first time you open Photoshop, it can seem a bewildering mess of icons, menus and palettes. You no doubt realise that there are two flavours of Photoshop – Photoshop CS and Photoshop Elements. It is generally thought that Photoshop is for professionals and that Elements is purely for beginners. The interface of Elements is a bit more intuitive than Photoshop, and features such as the Quick Edit mode mean that it's incredibly easy to make your first edit. But Elements still has a lot of the same tools as Photoshop so don't dismiss it is 'Photoshop Lite'. It might be that the tool is called something slightly different or that it's in a different place, but there's generally a workaround to give Elements users the same wealth of editing options as Photoshop users. In places where there is a difference between Photoshop and Elements, we've included the Elements way of carrying out a technique. If you don't see an alternative way, then it's the same.

There are three core skills that you need when you first start using Photoshop. You need to be able to load a file, open a new file and also save a file. These three tasks all require extra knowledge, such as understanding resolution and file formats.

The other essential ability that you need is to get access to all of the tools. If you think the Photoshop interface is confusing as it is, it would cause your brain to explode if all of the tools were on display at once! To avoid this, a lot of tools are grouped together and hidden behind a major tool.

One other thing that is worth mentioning is shortcuts. We always give the menu commands for performing tasks as it's a good way to get used to where things are and how things are organised. But once you get more comfortable with moving around the interface, you can start to use your keyboard to carry out the most common commands.

01 Open a file
To load an image, go to File>Open and then use the window browser to navigate to the file you want. Once found, simply click Open.

02 Create a file
To open a new file, go to File>New and enter a name, a size and a resolution. Click OK to create it. In Elements, go to File>New>Blank File.

03 Save a file
Saving is also a straightforward affair. Go to File>Save As. You can rename the file if you want and, more importantly, set the file format.

04 File formats
Adobe has supplied a lot of different file formats for you to save your image in and we'll be looking at this in more detail throughout this book.

05 Selecting tools
Adobe has bundled similar tools together. If you see a small arrow in the bottom-right corner of a tool, then there are other tools hidden behind.

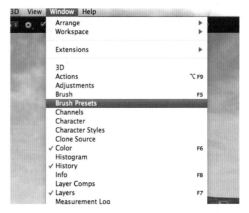

06 Options
Tools and commands are found in a series of palettes. You can set which palettes are seen using the Window menu.

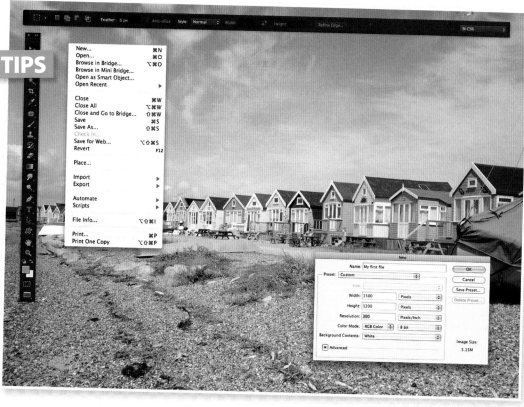

QUICK PHOTOSHOP TIPS

Quick save

The first time that you save a new file, use the Save As command as we have described, so that you can set the file name and format. Then, if you continue working on the image, you can just use File>Save instead, which saves your progress to the same file. It can be easier to get used to the keyboard shortcut, which is the Apple/Cmd key if you're using a Mac, or the Ctrl key if you're using a PC, plus the 'S' key at the same time.

File sizes

When you are creating a new file from scratch, you can use the Preset menu to see different pre-defined sizes. International Paper offers you A4 and A5, for example, for quick setup of new documents to the right dimensions.

Common file types

JPEG is the most common file format. It is used because it offers smaller file sizes but that can lead to loss of quality. When you choose to save in JPEG, you are given a slider to set the quality. PSD is a Photoshop document and is needed if you are saving a multi-layered document. TIFF results in larger but in good quality files. Use this when you need the optimum quality.

Resolution Get it right the first time

What is resolution?

All images are made up of square pixels. These pixels control how detailed an image is – put simply the more pixels the better the image.

Start with 72ppi

Photoshop measures pixels in inches (or ppi). Our screens work in 72ppi, so if you are doing something that will never be printed, 72ppi is fine.

Go 300ppi for quality

If you need quality or you want to print an image, work in 300ppi. The extra pixels mean that an image has more information.

Resize your images

Discover the tools and tricks that enable you to control the size of your shots

When it comes to resizing images, the most important task is understanding how images are constructed. Open up an image, zoom all the way in and you'll see that all the detail is constructed from small squares called pixels. Photoshop handles these pixels on a pixel-per-inch basis (ppi). This is as it sounds – the number of pixels contained in an inch. The rule is simple: the more pixels there are, the more detailed the image will be. When we talk about the pixels in an image, we are referring to its resolution. A resolution of 300ppi is a general goal, as it's high enough for most uses and is certainly fine for printing.

When resizing images you have to be aware of resolution, because this will dictate your end result. Going smaller is no problem whatsoever, however, once you start to go larger, you will start to see some quality issues. This is because pixels have to be generated and added to the image in order to make it larger.

Most resizing is done within the Image Size dialog. From here you can alter an image's physical size as well as its resolution. However, the Save For Web function is a useful tool for trimming images down. Here we're going to look at both of these, explaining how they work, in addition to showing a good way of enlarging images.

> "Most resizing is done within the Image Size dialog. From here you can alter an image's physical size as well as its resolution"

ALTER SIZE AND RESOLUTION

Edit an image with the Image Size dialog box

For anything related to an image's size and resolution, the Image Size dialog should be your first port of call. Photoshop users can find this under the Image menu, while Elements users will have to navigate to Image>Resize.

Once open, you can check the size of your image and then move to editing the resolution and/or dimensions. There are various dropdown menus that can make things seem confusing, but we'll explain what they all do below.

Document Size
You can use this to view the physical size and resolution of your image. You can alter the units of measurement from the dropdown menu on the right.

Pixel Dimensions
This area reveals the number of pixels, along the width and height of your image.

Constrain Proportions
Enable this option to keep the proportions of your image. If you edit the width, for example, the height will follow suit.

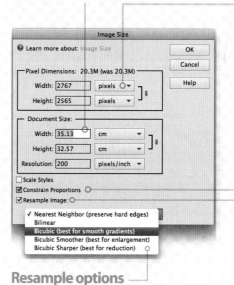

Resample options
When resampling you can use this menu to access options for achieving the best results.

Resample Image
Choose this option to alter the resolution of your image. Once altered, the size of the image will also change.

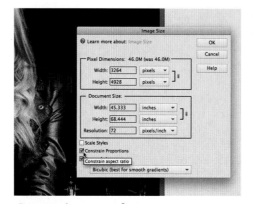

Physical size
Open up the Image Size dialog. Professionals will use pixels to measure an image but the rest of us can get by with the physical dimensions. Look at the Document Size area and use the dropdown menu next to Width to select the unit you want to work in. Here we've picked Inches.

Constrain your elements
If you want to alter the size of your image, chances are you will want to keep the proportions. You can do this by ensuring the Constrain Proportions box is checked. If it isn't activated, check the Resample Image box, select Constrain Proportions and then deselect Resample Image.

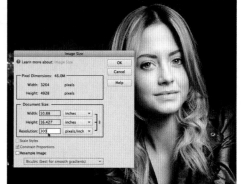

Alter the resolution
There is a dance between the resolution of an image and its physical size. You can increase the resolution, but to keep the quality you have to make do with a physically smaller image. Here we have a large 72ppi image. We need 300ppi for printing, so type this into the Resolution box.

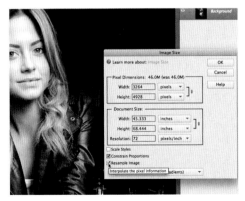

Resample images

When you would like to keep an image's resolution the same, but alter its size slightly, you need to resample that image. It is always advisable to make an image smaller, as this still keeps the image quality high. To get started, click the Resample Image box.

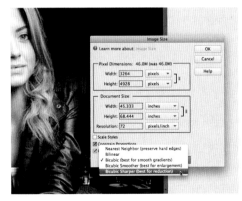

The resampling options

Once you've checked the Resample Image box you'll be able to get to the dropdown menu below it, which holds different resampling options. We are going to be reducing the size, so pick the Bicubic Sharper option, as it automatically applies sharpening to keep the image looking good.

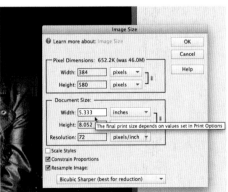

Make the change

You can alter the number of pixels or the physical size of the image by first entering a new width in inches. As Constrain Proportions is ticked, the height will alter and you'll see the new file size up in the Pixel Dimensions area. Hit OK to confirm, or Opt/Alt-click on the Cancel button to reset.

Getting started

Save an image for the web
Quickly reduce an image's size with the Save for Web command

The Save for Web dialog used to be essential in the early days of the web, when a large image would bring a modem to its knees. While the connections are much improved now, it's still good practise to shave file sizes down when posting images online or sharing via email. The Save for Web command makes light work of this.

Easy options
This dropdown menu gives you a choice of preset edits based on image quality. You can also manually enter a quality value in the Quality area.

Alter the pixel size
If you want to alter the amount of pixels along the width or height of an image, enter a value here.

Zoom in and refine detail
To properly assess the quality of the edited image, use this area to click and zoom in or enter a Zoom value.

Before and after
You can instantly see the results of any edit in the main window, including the new file size and loading time underneath the image. Click the arrow to pick different Download options.

Reduce the file size of an image
Make a photo that's lean, mean and ready for the web

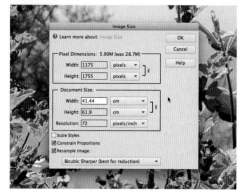

01 Prepare your work
The Save for Web command isn't meant to shrink huge images, so if yours is a mammoth, use the Image Size dialog to reduce either the resolution or the physical size.

02 Adjust the view
You will now see two versions of your image. Go down to the bottom-left and use the plus (+) icon to zoom in on an area. Click and drag on the image to move to a specific point.

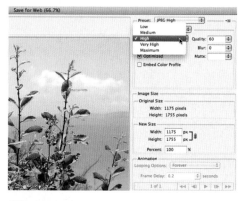

03 Reduce the size
Use the dropdown menu on the right panel to set the quality. The higher the quality, the larger the file size, so keep an eye on the numbers underneath the preview and pick the size you want.

Enlarge an image

Keep quality when you go bigger

Ideally you should never force an image to go beyond its means, but there are times when this is unavoidable. This is especially true when it comes to old photos that have been scanned in. You won't get the perfect result, but there is a way to get pretty close.

New size

When you resample any image, you will see the new size as well as the old one. Because we have increased the size and resolution, our pixel dimensions (and file size) have also increased.

Resolution

When you are scanning images, always do so at 600ppi so you have lots of options for altering the physical size. If the image is to be printed, you will need 300ppi as a minimum.

Smooth edges

There are various edits that can help fix any problems from the enlarging process, but the first one is the Bicubic Smoother resampling option.

01 Good scanning practice

A trip to the Image Size menu reveals that this was scanned at 180ppi and is physically small. As a rule, you should scan images in at 600ppi to get decent-sized results by lowering the resolution.

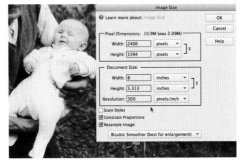

02 Take things larger

A professional printer would demand the image be 300ppi. With Image Size open and Resample Image checked, pick the Bicubic Smoother option, enter 300 in the Resolution area.

03 Smooth problems

A downside of forcing an image to be a higher resolution is that areas can become blocky. The Bicubic Smoother option helps this, but you can go to Filter> Noise>Despeckle to smooth edges.

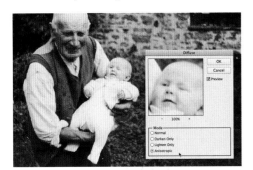

04 Sharpen the edges

To counteract smoothing the edges, you now need to sharpen them. Go to Filter>Stylize>Diffuse and pick the Anisotropic option. Zoom in close to an edge to see the results and, if happy, click OK.

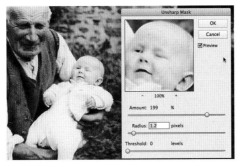

05 Use the Unsharp Mask

It's time to go to Enhance>Unsharp Mask (or Filter>Sharpen>Unsharp Mask if in Photoshop). Generally a high Amount, small Radius and small to zero Threshold tends to work well.

06 Final Touches

To finish we can add noise, as this makes the image seem more uniform. Go to Filter>Noise>Add Noise and enter a small amount. Go to View>Print Size to see what the image will look like when printed.

Save

Hit File>Save, or use the shortcut Cmd/Ctrl+S, to save your work as you go. Photoshop CS6 automatically saves recovery information in case you lose your edits.

Create PDF

To make a PDF, go to File at the top menu bar and select Print. Instead of selecting a printer, choose Adobe PDF and hit print.

Name and Save

From the dialog box choose Save As PDF, click the print button, and then name your file and choose Save.

Print Settings

Print directly from Photoshop by choosing your printer from the Print Settings menu. Your image will print in its original size, but check out the preview to see how big the image will appear on the page.

Save As

Use File>Save As to give your image a name for the first time, or to create a new type of file from the one that you're working on.

Save, export and share your photos

Get your images ready for the web or as a printed masterpiece

The process used to save an image changes depending on what it'll be used for.

Size really does matter when you're printing a photograph or a piece of artwork, as you want to include as much image information as possible. This helps the image come out bright and clear when on a large canvas, but also means saving large, high-resolution files.

On the other hand, when saving an image for the internet you will want to do away with any information that isn't necessary so that it will load up quickly on a page. Emailing images to friends and family also becomes easier when you work with smaller file sizes. Photoshop gives you the option to save in 23 different file formats, but luckily most users will just need a handful of these for their everyday editing. One format to take note of is the Photoshop file, or PSD for short. This is a layered file that saves all adjustments made when you edit your image. It's always a good idea to save a layered copy of any image that you're working on, as going back to make changes to the photo later on will be much easier.

"Size really does matter when you're printing a photograph or a piece of artwork"

Save photos for uploading online

Take your photos out of Photoshop and on to the web

The smaller an image is, the better it behaves when displayed online. Photoshop's Save For Web feature guides you through the process of trimming your image of all unnecessary information. This makes it a pleasure to upload to web galleries or to share with friends and on a blog. The menu is dauntingly large, but here are a few simple settings to get your image ready for the web.

Image Size
Image size tells you how big your image is in pixels. The larger these values are, the more time it will take load up once it's online.

GIF files
The GIF file format is very popular for the web because it is small. It's best suited for graphics and is rarely used to save photos.

Quality
Lowering the quality of your image means getting rid of unnecessary information. The file size will become much smaller too and will load up quicker.

Preview
The preview screen shows what your image will look like after saving it. Use the plus and minus buttons to zoom in and out and check the final image quality.

Back out
If you change your mind while saving your image, hit Cancel and this will take you back to your original image.

Save for web
Prepare your images with Photoshop's Save for Web feature

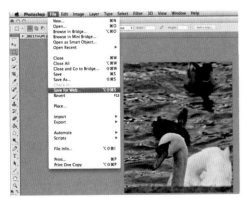

01 Load up menu
Once you've made the final adjustments to your image, and you're ready to save, click File in the top menu bar and find the Save for Web option. This will take you into a completely different menu for setting up your image.

02 Select file type
From the box menu, change the file format from the default GIF to the JPEG format. From the Compression Quality option below choose Small. Leave all other settings as they are. Hit Save once these are all set in place.

03 Name and Save
At the top of the Save As menu, type the name you would like to give your photo. Choose a location on your computer where you would like to save your file to, such as the Desktop, and then hit Save. This image is now set up and ready for uploading online.

Getting started

Printing artwork
Prepare your image for print

A chieving outstanding results when printing artwork requires a little bit of know-how.

Printers look at individual pixels in an image, which means that with more detail and a high number of pixels the printout will look better.

If your image has a small resolution, with little detail, then it's quite possible you might be disappointed with the final print. First decide whether you're going to print the image yourself or whether you're going to use a service. If you're using a service then don't worry about setting up the image's size. Just follow on from step five, where we discuss a file format for printers.

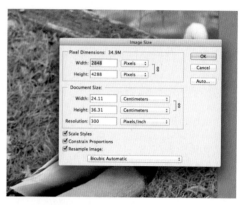

01 Image Size
From the top menu select Image>Image Size. This will show you how large your image is. Printing any larger than this size will reduce the quality.

02 Check DPI
Check that your image has a Pixels/Inch setting of 300. If its value is below this amount then feel free to change it to 300, but note that this will make your image size a lot smaller.

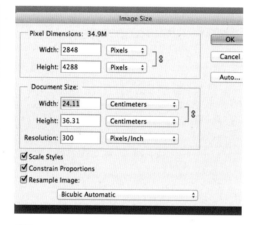

03 Stick to original size
If you plan on printing smaller than the original image size, you won't need to adjust the size options in Photoshop. Simply specify the print size in your printer's settings when you come to that important final stage.

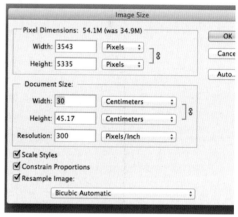

04 Printing bigger
It is possible to print an image larger by entering a new value in the Height and Width columns. Unfortunately, the printout will lose quality, so this is not recommended, but there is room for enlargement up to a point.

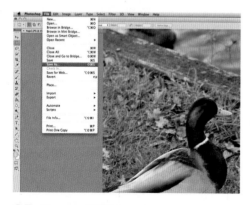

05 Choose TIFF
When you're happy with your image, head over to File>Save As from the top menu. Then choose TIFF from the Format options. This is an uncompressed format which means it will keep your image's size large for printing.

06 Name your file
At the top of the Save As dialog box, name your file and select a location on your computer. Hit Save to complete the process of formatting your image, which should now be ready for printing.

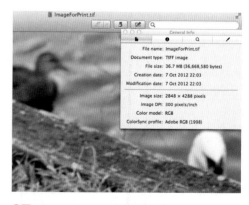

07 Working with the file
Your photo can now be printed and, as it's high resolution and uncompressed, it is very large in size. If you're moving the file to another computer then use a device such as a memory stick, because it's not ideal to email an image at this size.

Save layered artwork or a flattened version

Keep your options open by saving a master copy

Photoshop works with layers, allowing you to edit and adjust images at any stage. When you save an image as a JPEG then the file is flattened and the layers are lost.

It's a good idea to keep both a layered and a flattened version of the image on your computer. If you want to make changes it's as simple as opening your master, layered copy and making the adjustments.

01 Make an adjustment

With your image open in Photoshop, add an Adjustment on a new layer, such as the Brightness/Contrast Adjustment (Layer>New Adjustment Layer>Brightness/Contrast). This could be to improve the lighting in your image if slightly under or overexposed.

Flattened images

JPEG is the file type most commonly used with photographic images, as it supports CMYK, RGB and Grayscale colour modes. This will, however, remove all layers and flatten the image.

Quality

JPEG files can be compressed selectively, which means that you can choose the final file size of your flattened image.

File size preview

Select the quality using the slider, depending on whether you want to output a small or large file. Keep an eye on your image behind this menu to see how the changes will look.

Save with layers

Layered files will be saved at their original quality, so you can always go back and use the Save As option to store your image at a different size using the JPEG options.

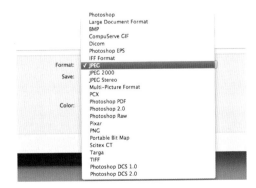

02 Save flattened file

Save your image as a flattened file by choosing File>Save As and selecting JPEG as the file format. Name your file, choose the JPEG quality you need and then save it. The High and Maximum options will increase the size of the file significantly.

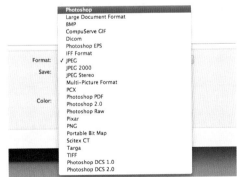

03 Keep a master copy

Choose File>Save As to save a layered copy of your image. Choose Photoshop under Format and then give your image a name. The file extension for this format is PSD – Photoshop Document – and it can be opened within all versions of Photoshop.

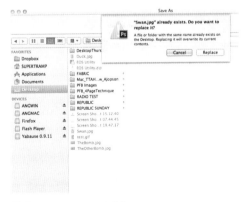

04 Update old files

To adjust an image, open the layered file to make the changes. Save your file as before and then choose Replace when prompted. This will update your previously saved image. Save the changes to your layered file and then you're safe to close it.

How to copy and paste

Discover the basis of composites by taking elements from one picture and adding them to another

ORIGINAL

The two words cut and paste describe very simple actions. You cut out (or copy) an object in one photo into an internal memory buffer called the clipboard and then paste it again in the same photo. Or, more usually, paste it into a different photo. However, it's the processes that lead up to the cut and what you do after the paste where all the work and complexity comes in, and with Photoshop it can be very complex indeed. But before you cut something out of a photo, you have to select it first either by using one of the selection tools: the Marquee tool, Lasso, Polygonal Lasso, Magnetic Lasso, Quick Selection, Pen tool, Magic Wand or the Quick Mask mode. After you paste an object it can need cleaning up or adjusting, so at this stage even more tools like masks and the Transform options come into play.

"From the most basic pasting to complicated, layered collages, copy and paste are Photoshop fundamentals"

How to copy Select one area to move to another

01 Get the right background
The most common example of cut and paste is to take someone from one photo and paste them into a more scenic one. This is made much easier if the person is stood against a plain background to start with. Start by loading the subject photo.

02 Magic Wand settings
Select the Magic Wand tool and set the Tolerance in the top Options bar to 30 so it picks up all of the white. Put ticks into the Anti-alias box for a soft edge and Contiguous so only the background is selected. Now click on the white area.

03 Refine and copy
Hold down the Shift key and click on any unselected areas. Go to Select>Inverse to select the figure, and then Select>Modify>Contract and enter a value of 1px. Finally, use either Edit>Copy or press the shortcut combination Ctrl/Cmd+C.

Paste a subject How to retrieve your copied selection

01 Tackle the pasting
Close your subject image and don't save it. Load the scenic picture and go to Edit>Paste or press Ctrl/Cmd+V. She has appeared but is floating in midair. Select the Move tool and tick Show Transform Controls.

02 Position carefully
If you click on the subject and hold the mouse down, you can drag it around the screen. In this case her head should be no further than halfway up the screen, so we move her down to a more realistic position.

03 Rescale
The model is so close we've now lost part of the subject. Click and hold the corner gadget of the Transform box then move the mouse left and down. Click on the Aspect Lock button between W and H then apply.

Clean up your copied image Integrate the elements

01 Refine the edges
To clean up the pasted object, make sure you are on its layer and click the New Layer Mask icon in the Layers palette. Select the Brush tool with a black Foreground colour. Start to brush over any untidy areas carefully.

02 Color balance
To match colours between the two images, work on the subject layer and go to Image> Adjustments>Color Balance. Move the sliders to adjust the tone. In our case, we removed the yellow hue.

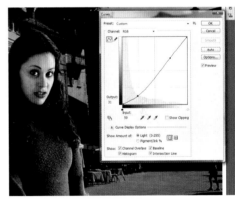

03 Brightness reduction
Go to Image>Adjustments>Curves. Create two control points by clicking on the curve. One should darken the shadow areas and the other the highlights. You could also add grain or use the Lens Correction filter.

MISMATCHED RESOLUTIONS

If picture A is a low-resolution image and picture B high resolution, when you copy the object from picture A and paste it into B it will appear to be too small. If you use the Transform tool to make it bigger, the quality will suffer as a result. There are only two things solutions to this fairly common problem. The first is to increase the size of picture A using specialised plug-in software like Alien Skin's Blow Up 3 or onOne's Perfect Resize 7 rather than Photoshop's tools. The second is that you could find pictures that are the same kind of resolution. However, if picture A is higher resolution than picture B the problem is easily solved. Now that the object being pasted appears too large, simply use the Transform tools to scale it down to the right size!

Import and share with the Organizer

Keep your photo collection in order with this essential extra that comes with Photoshop Elements

The Organize function in Elements is handy for arranging all of your photos and videos in one place. Due to the thumbnail displays, which can be customised to suit how you prefer to view images, it is easy and quick to locate just the photos you want to work with and arrange them accordingly. This even includes automatic People Recognition that cleverly detects the faces of people in your photos.

This technology analyses your people shots and brings up a window with all of the faces highlighted. You can then tag these people so that searching for photos with them in becomes an easy task later on.

You can even add a simple star rating to images. There are five stars underneath each image and you can click on them to light them up. Later you can scroll through your highest-rated photos, or select a star rating to display. You can then choose to filter your images based on their star rating – a good way to find all your best shots, or even the bad ones that need to be edited even further.

Your images can be keyworded, which means that you can add personal tags that identify your images. There is a preset selection of tags, such as people, location and so on, and each of these can be used as search criteria.

The Organizer is available for PCs and Mac users. If you have Premiere Elements for video-editing too, then you can use the same Organizer for both still and moving images, helping to keep your entire media collection in one place and happily sorted.

> "It is easy and quick to locate just the photos you want to work with"

01 Add images
The first thing that you need to do is add images to the Organizer, which you can easily do from the File menu.

02 Import options
When you are importing pictures you can ask Elements to correct red eye as it goes, or to suggest photo stacks of similar images.

03 Sort the view
By default, you will see the last images imported, however if you want to change this, you can pick a different album to view.

04 Show all
Hit the Show All button to see all of your images in one go. Using the stars underneath you can set individual ratings for your images too..

05 Filter by rating
When you have rated all your images, you can then use the rating filter to isolate just the images that you want to use.

06 Large view
Click on any image in the Organizer and you can see it bigger in the central screen, where you can add a caption, for example.

Quick save

The first time that you save a new file, use the Save As command as we have described, so that you can set the file name and format. Then, if you continue working on the image, you can just use File>Save instead, which saves your progress to the same file. It can be easier to get used to the keyboard shortcut, which is the Apple/ Cmd key if you're using a Mac, or the Ctrl key if you're using a PC, plus the 'S' key at the same time.

Thumbnail views

There are a number of ways you can choose to view your images which are selected. You can have thumbnails of various sizes and can filter by star rating to give a more accurate choice of photos. These features make viewing straightforward and far less time consuming.

Common file types

JPEG is the most common file format. It is used because it offers smaller file sizes but that can lead to loss of quality. When you choose to save in JPEG, you are given a slider to set the quality. PSD is a Photoshop document and is needed if you are saving a multi-layered document. TIFF results in larger but in good quality files. Use this when you need the optimum quality.

07 Tagging

Using the Keyword Tags panel, you can enter words like 'object', which you can use to sort your images at a later date.

08 Get tagging

If there are people in your shot, you can ask Photoshop Elements to use People Recognition, which searches a photo for faces.

09 Name game

When the face has been found, you can then add the name of the person underneath their picture in order to tag them.

Photoshop shortcuts

Dramatically speed up your workflow with these handy shortcuts

O nce you've got to grips with the basic Photoshop tools and features, it's a great idea to start practising some of the shortcuts.

Whether you are editing, retouching, creating or more, you can save loads of time by learning shortcuts. Over these two pages we've compiled an essential shortcut guide, which we've split into sections based on the type of tasks you perform. Make sure you have this cut-out-and-keep guide close to your computer and use it whenever you have a Photoshop project on the go. We're certain you will know these shortcuts off by heart in no time! We have given both Mac and PC commands, so Cmd/Ctrl means the Apple or Command key on a Mac, and Control on a PC.

Handy shortcuts for everyday tools

Crop Tool: C
Perspective Crop Tool: C
Slice Tool: C
Slice Select Tool: C

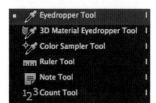

Eyedropper Tool: I
3D Material Eyedropper Tool: I
Color Sampler Tool: I
Ruler Tool: I
Note Tool: I
Count Tool: I

Eraser Tool: E
Background Eraser Tool: E
Magic Eraser Tool: E

Rectangle Tool: U
Rounded Rectangle Tool: U
Ellipse Tool: U
Polygon Tool: U
Line Tool: U
Custom Shape Tool: U

Hand Tool: H
Rotate View Tool: R

Zoom Tool: Z

Select and Selection tools

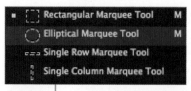

Rectangular Marquee Tool: M
Elliptical Marquee Tool: M
Single Row Marquee Tool: M
Single Column Marquee Tool: M

Lasso Tool: L
Polygonal Lasso Tool: L
Magnetic Lasso Tool: L

Quick Selection Tool: W
Magic Wand Tool: W

Toggle Standard/Quick Mask modes: Q
Cycle Path/Direct Selection tools: Shift+A
Toggle Slice/Slice Select tools: Shift+K
Cycle Lasso tools: Shift+L
Toggle Rectangular/Elliptical Marquee: Shift+M
Toggle Pen/Freeform Pen tools: Shift+P
Select All: Cmd/Ctrl+A
Select All Layers: Cmd+Opt+A/Ctrl+Alt+A
Deselect: Cmd/Ctrl+D
Feather: Cmd+Opt+D/Ctrl+Alt+D
Inverse: Cmd/Ctrl+Shift+I
Reselect: Cmd/Ctrl+Shift+D

Painting tools

Brush Tool: B
Pencil Tool: B
Color Replacement Tool: B
Mixer Brush Tool: B

Decrease/Increase Brush Size: [/]
Decrease/Increase Brush Hardness: {/}
Previous Brush: ,
Next Brush: .
First Brush: <
Last Brush: >
Brush tool: B
Pencil tool: B
Gradient tool: G
Paint Bucket tool: G
Sponge tool: O

History Brush Tool: Y
Art History Brush Tool: B
Tool Opacity 10%-100%: 1-0
Flow/Airbrush Opacity 10%-100%: Shift+ 1-0

Image-editing tools

Spot Healing Brush Tool: J
Healing Brush Tool: J
Patch Tool: J
Content-Aware Move Tool: J
Red Eye Tool: J

Clone Stamp Tool: S
Pattern Stamp Tool: S

Dodge Tool: O
Burn Tool: O
Sponge Tool: O

Toggle Clone/Pattern Stamp: Shift+S
Auto Color: Cmd/Ctrl+Shift+B
Auto Contrast: Cmd+Opt+Shift+L/Ctrl+Alt+Shift+L
Auto Levels: Cmd/Ctrl+Shift+L
Canvas Size: Cmd+Opt+C/Ctrl+Alt+C
Color Balance: Cmd/Ctrl+B
Color Balance (last settings): Cmd+Opt+M/Ctrl+Alt+M
Curves (last settings): Cmd+Opt+M/Ctrl+Alt+M
Curves: Cmd/Ctrl+M
Desaturate: Cmd/Ctrl+Shift+U
Hue/Saturation: Cmd/Ctrl+U
Hue/Saturation (last settings): Cmd+Opt+U/Ctrl+Alt+U
Image size: Cmd+Opt+I/Ctrl+Alt+I
Invert: Cmd/Ctrl+I
Levels: Cmd/Ctrl+L
Levels (last settings): Cmd+Opt+L/Ctrl+Alt+L

Foreground/Background colours
Default colours: D
Switch colours: X
Edit in Quick Mask Mode: Q

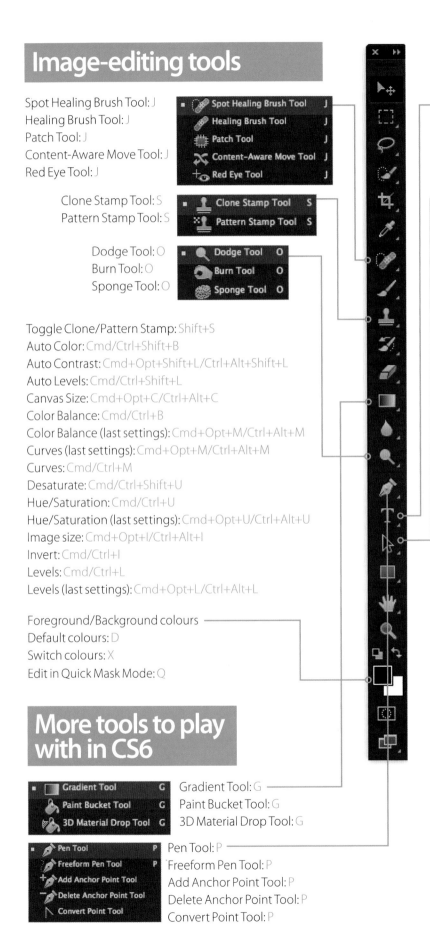

More tools to play with in CS6

Gradient Tool: G
Paint Bucket Tool: G
3D Material Drop Tool: G

Pen Tool: P
Freeform Pen Tool: P
Add Anchor Point Tool: P
Delete Anchor Point Tool: P
Convert Point Tool: P

Type tools

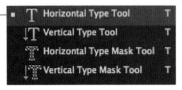

Horizontal Type Tool: T
Vertical Type Tool: T
Horizontal Type
Mask Tool: T
Vertical Type Mask Tool: T

Path Selection Tool: A
Direct Selection Tool: A

Align Left: Cmd/Ctrl+Shift+L
Align Right: Cmd/Ctrl+Shift+R
Bold (toggle): Cmd/Ctrl+Shift+B
Centre text: Cmd/Ctrl+Shift+C
Decrease/Increase Type Size by 10pt:
Cmd+Opt+ Shift+<, /Ctrl+Alt+Shift+<, >
Hyphenation (toggle): Cmd+Opt+Shift+H/
Ctrl+Alt+Shift+H
Italics (toggle): Cmd/Ctrl+Shift+I
Justify Paragraph (Force last line): Cmd/Ctrl+Shift+F
Justify Paragraph (Left align last line): Cmd/Ctrl+Shift+J
Underlining (toggle): Cmd/Ctrl+Shift+U
Uppercase (toggle): Cmd/Ctrl+Shift+K

Layers

Bring Forward: Cmd/Ctrl+]
Bring to Front: Cmd/Ctrl+Shift+]
Create/Release Clipping Mask (toggle): Cmd+Opt+G/
Ctrl+Alt+G
Group Layers: Cmd/Ctrl+G
Layer Opacity 10%-100%: 1-0
Layer Via Copy: Cmd+ Opt+J/Ctrl+Alt+J
Layer Via Copy (with dialog): Cmd/Ctrl+Shift+I
Merge Layers: Cmd/Ctrl+E Merge Visible: Cmd/Ctrl+Shift+E
New Layer: Cmd/Ctrl+Shift+N
New Layer (no dialog): Cmd+Opt+Shift+N/Ctrl+Alt+Shift+N
Next Layer: Opt/Alt+]
Previous Layer: Opt/Alt+[
Select Previous Layer: Opt/Alt+Shift+[
Select Next Layer: Opt/Alt+Shift+]
Send Backward: Cmd/Ctrl+[
Send to Back: Cmd/Ctrl+Shift+[
Stamp Down: Cmd+Opt+E/Ctrl+Alt+E
Stamp Visible: Cmd+Opt+Shift+E/Ctrl+Alt+Shift+E
Select Bottom Layer: Opt/Alt+, Select Top Layer: Opt/Alt+.

Basic corrections

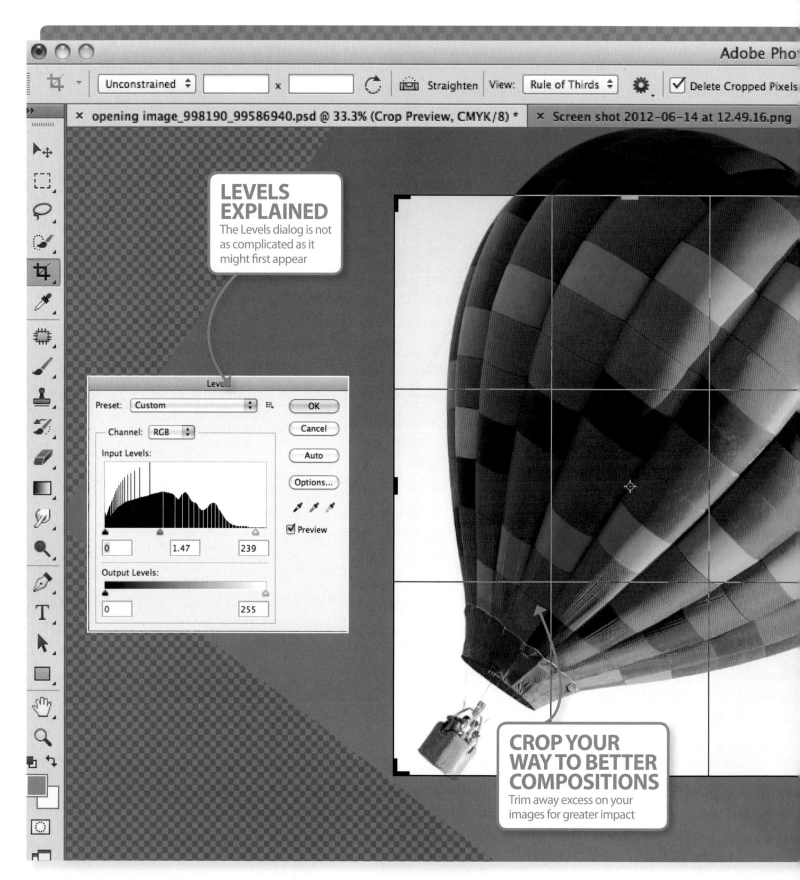

LEVELS EXPLAINED
The Levels dialog is not as complicated as it might first appear

CROP YOUR WAY TO BETTER COMPOSITIONS
Trim away excess on your images for greater impact

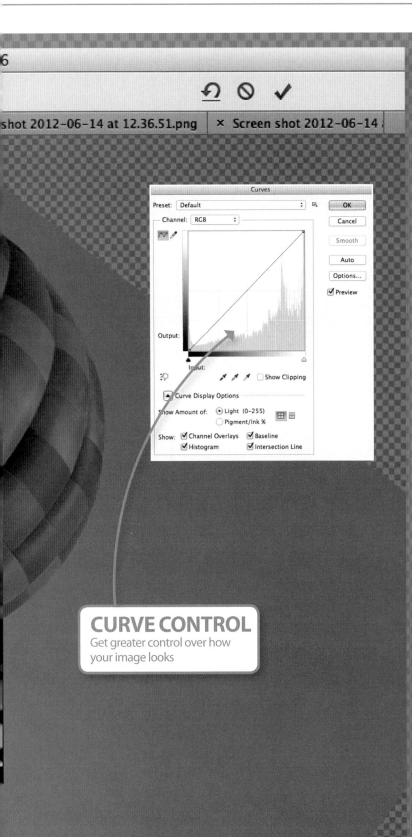

shot 2012-06-14 at 12.36.51.png | × Screen shot 2012-06-14 ...

Curves

Preset: Default

Channel: RGB

OK
Cancel
Smooth
Auto
Options...
☑ Preview

Output:

Input:

☐ Show Clipping

▲ Curve Display Options

Show Amount of: ● Light (0-255)
○ Pigment/Ink %

Show: ☑ Channel Overlays ☑ Baseline
☑ Histogram ☑ Intersection Line

CURVE CONTROL
Get greater control over how
your image looks

"The Levels dialog is probably the first you need to learn when correcting basic flaws in Photoshop"

Basic corrections

Perfect exposure with Auto Levels

Fix basic flaws and improve exposure across your photographs

The Levels dialog is probably the first one that you need to learn when it comes to correcting basic flaws in your images. Luckily, it is not as complex as it looks and it will fix and control the overall tonal and colour ranges in your images. There are various ways of applying Levels, from using the dialog box that comes up when you go to Image>Adjustments>Levels, or as an adjustment layer. For now, though, we are just looking at what happens when you use the Auto option.

As soon as you open an image in Photoshop, it is worth going straight into the Levels box and using the Auto option, as in many cases this will be all that an image needs, and it will certainly act as a good starting point for any further adjustments that you need to make. The Levels dialog analyses your image and creates a histogram with values for shadows and highlights in your photo. The Auto command levels out these values, so that the contrast is well balanced between both extremes of the tonal range.

ORIGINAL

"It will fix and control the overall tonal and colour ranges in your images"

SIMPLE LEVEL CONTROL

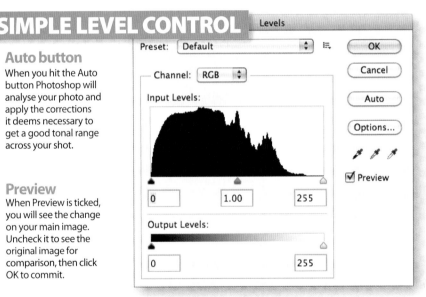

Auto button
When you hit the Auto button Photoshop will analyse your photo and apply the corrections it deems necessary to get a good tonal range across your shot.

Preview
When Preview is ticked, you will see the change on your main image. Uncheck it to see the original image for comparison, then click OK to commit.

01 Select your image
Our start image is a good composition with some nice colours, but you can see that the tonal range is a little on the dull side.

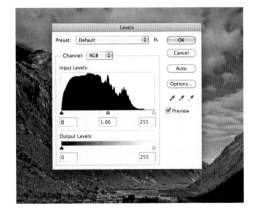

02 Open the Levels dialog
Go to Image>Adjustments>Levels and you will bring up this Levels dialog, with a histogram in the middle showing your tonal range.

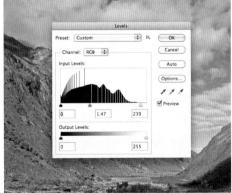

03 Auto it up
We will be looking in more detail about the other options in this box in the Colour & tone section, but for now, just hit Auto for a quick fix.

Basic corrections

Correct tone with Auto Curves

A simple one-click control that hides a very powerful editing tool

Curves and Levels are often talked about in the same sentence as they both affect the tonal range of your photos. However, though they do the same sort of thing, they do so in different ways.

With Levels, you can control the tonal range of the Highlights, Midpoints and Shadows, which is good for making global changes to your image as a whole. However, with Curves, you can pick literally any value in your whole image and tweak the tonal range at that point. This makes it an incredibly precise tool for getting perfect exposure and contrast. It can be a bit more intimidating though, as Curves is not something we see that often, whereas the histogram,

that is present in the Levels dialog is similar to the histogram that is often used by digital cameras to help you ensure even exposure when shooting.

Still, even a push of the Auto button in the Curves dialog can make a big difference to your image and you can worry about understanding the ins and outs of it at a later date.

ORIGINAL

"Pick any value in your image and tweak the tonal range at that point"

GET SOME CURVES

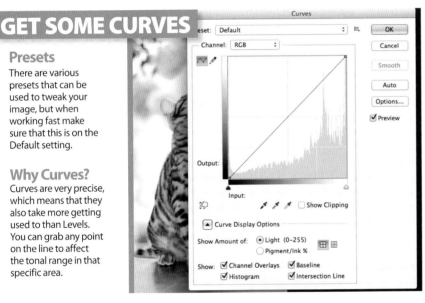

Presets
There are various presets that can be used to tweak your image, but when working fast make sure that this is on the Default setting.

Why Curves?
Curves are very precise, which means that they also take more getting used to than Levels. You can grab any point on the line to affect the tonal range in that specific area.

01 Open your image

Our image that we are going to work on is a little on the washed-out side. The greens aren't very vibrant and everything is blending together.

02 Access the Curves
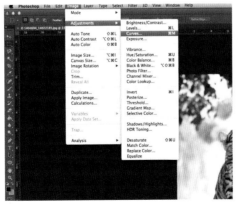
Go to Image>Adjustments>Curves and you will bring up the Curves window. This can also be opening by using the shortcut Cmd/Ctrl+M.

03 Automatic control
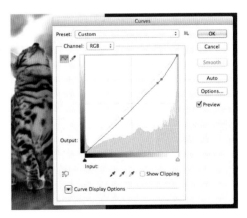
The Curves dialog maps the tones in your image using a curved line. For now, just hit Auto and you'll see the curve change and the tonal range fixed.

Basic corrections

Fix tone in seconds

A real one-click miracle control courtesy of Photoshop's Image menu

We've looked at Levels and Curves, and we'll come back to them later. But it you are looking for the ultimate quick fix for your photos, then we have a little trick for you.

While Photoshop Elements users have a whole host of automated controls to fix your images in a flash (we'll be looking at these further in the book), smart fix options aren't on display in Photoshop in your main interface.. However, take a visit to the Image menu from the top toolbar in Photoshop and you will find three completely automatic options. These use the power of Photoshop's more advanced colour and tone controls, like Levels and Curves, and improve the exposure and tonal range of your photos in literally seconds.

If you're unhappy with the result after applying you can also use the Undo command, which is easily found in the File menu, or by using the handy shortcut Cmd/Ctrl+Z. But even if you don't get the results you want, it's a good way to ensure you are editing on a well tonally balanced image.

> ## "Improve the exposure and tonal range of your photos in literally seconds"

GET TONED

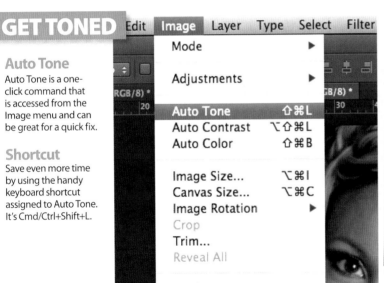

ORIGINAL

Auto Tone
Auto Tone is a one-click command that is accessed from the Image menu and can be great for a quick fix.

Shortcut
Save even more time by using the handy keyboard shortcut assigned to Auto Tone. It's Cmd/Ctrl+Shift+L.

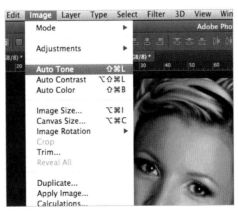

01 Analyse the image
When you open an image, have a look at the tone and contrast. Your eye can usually spot when something isn't quite right.

02 Try a tone up
Auto Tone is one of three automatic commands that reside within the Image menu. Click it once to affect your photo.

03 And you're done!
Without entering the Levels or Curves dialogs, we have brought out the multiple colours in our flowers and the greens leaves.

Basic corrections

Get great contrast in a click

Turn a so-so image into a keeper by using this handy automated command

Just as we have seen with Auto Tone in the last couple of pages, there is also a simple solution to alter the contrast in your image, ie the difference between the high and low tones in a photograph. If you have an image that is low contrast, tones will start to blend into one another and this can lead to a washed out effect.

Luckily we don't have to put up with these images as there is a really easy way to fix them. The Auto Contrast control will take your image and improve the contrast using powerful behind-the-scenes technology, which results in much better tone and colour across a scene.

The image that we are using here is a typical example of a low contrast image. The sun shining through the roots has made the overall image look rather washed out. By upping the contrast, more tones come through, such as the different shades of the roots, clearly defining the subject against its environment and transforming the image.

"It will fix and control the overall tonal and colour ranges in your images"

SEE THE CONTRAST

Contrast

The contrast in your image can have a massive effect on the final image. Our start image suffers from being low contrast, in that colours are not very defined from one another. One quick visit to the Image menu and suddenly we have a much stronger overall image.

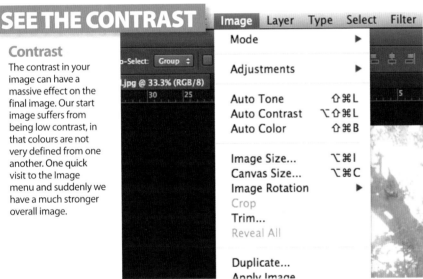

ORIGINAL

01 Wishy washy
This image is rather cool, but it is let down by the faded colours that appear washed out, stopping the detail of the roots from being prominent.

02 Auto Contrast
The Auto Contrast one-click solution is found under the Image menu in Photoshop and it will sort your image out super fast.

03 Final image
Our final image has much deeper tones, and the details and colour of the tree are a lot stronger, making it stand out far more.

Basic corrections

Fix colour casts with Auto Color

Get rid of common white balance problems with this auto option

The final automatic command of the three in the Image menu is Auto Color. This does not work on CMYK images, so if it is greyed out, then you cannot access it without changing the Image Mode to RGB. This simple command comes into its own if you have a colour cast over your image. This can be caused by a number of things when taking the photo, for example the lighting in which you are taking a shot. Different lights, like fluorescent or tungsten bulbs, will leave a cast over your photo, such as green or blue. Also, setting the wrong white balance setting can lead to an unwanted colour cast as well.

In our image we have a very noticeable green colour cast across our shot, the result of taking a photo by setting the wrong white balance option on our camera. However, one click on the Auto Color command gets rid of this, and restores the colours to a more natural state, giving us a great base to do further work on.

> "One click on the Auto Color command gets rid of our colour cast"

ORIGINAL

CAST YOUR SPELL

Mix your commands

Now that we have looked at all three automatic commands in the Image menu, don't be afraid to apply more than one to your photos. They each deal with a slightly different problem, so by using all three, you can perfect your image massively in just seconds.

01 Seeing green
We're pretty sure that this creature wasn't so green when we took the shot! But there is definitely a noticeable cast on our photograph.

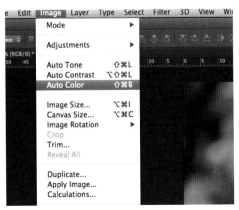

02 Locate your auto control
Go to Image>Auto Color in the Photoshop interface. This option will only be available if you are working in RGB.

03 That's better!
Our green cast is magically gone. However, the tones are still flat. Using the other auto options will give us a great final image.

Master the improved Crop tool

Exciting changes to the Crop tool make it easier and more fun to edit

The Crop tool has been one of Photoshop's most important tools from the very beginning.

It gives us the chance to increase the strength of an image by simply cutting out parts that distract the eye from the scene.

The tool has been given some exciting new options in CS6 that make using it easier than ever. The new features take some getting used to, as the tool is quite different from earlier versions.

Rather than focusing on just cropping out unwanted pixels, the Crop tool now makes it easier to create a pleasing overall composition. Take, for example,

the six new View options. There are a number of different ones (demonstrated across the page) that will let you position subjects along pre-defined lines of composition. This is massively useful and they have been based around traditional photographic practices, and will help you form a more visually balanced piece from your original image.

As well as the View options, the Crop tool can be set up to keep cropped parts of an image, and Photoshop CS6 includes the Classic mode to revert back to the more familiar version of the tool, so you can still use it to simply crop your images.

ORIGINAL

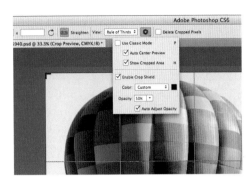

01 Auto Center

The Crop tool can be set so that it always stays central as you move its boundary. This option, called Auto Center Preview, is available by clicking on the cog symbol in the top Options bar, with Show Cropped Area underneath it in the list.

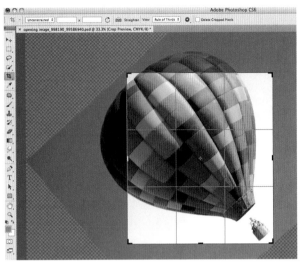

02 Rotate and resize

With Auto Center Preview on, you're actually rotating and resizing the image and not the cropping boundary. This allows for a better preview of the final positioning of the image before it's cropped, so you can see what's level and what's not.

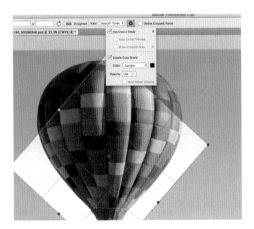

03 Classic mode

Classic mode takes you back to the style of Photoshop CS5 and earlier. This means that the cropping boundary is rotated and not the image. Pressing P will quickly switch the mode on and off, depending on your preference.

04 Delete pixels

In CS6 you have the option to keep areas that you have cropped away intact. By deselecting Delete Cropped Pixels, you're able to position the image using the Move tool after the image is cropped. This way, changes are never permanent.

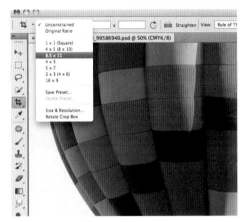

05 Crop ratios

The new Crop tool comes with different preset sizes that change the ratio of an image. They're found in the Options bar and include 1 x 1 (Square), 5 x 7 and 16 x 9. The Unconstrained option will let you reshape the boundary to any size.

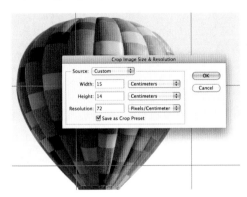

06 Know your shortcuts

There are a number of shortcut keys that can be used with the Crop tool. Press X to turn the cropping boundary 90 degrees, or press R to open up the Image Size & Resolution menu. Here you can manually choose the final width, height and resolution of the area being cropped.

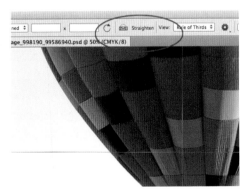

07 Straighten tool

The Crop tool comes with an additional option to level horizons or objects in an image that may be askew. Click on the Straighten symbol in the Options bar and then draw a line across the part of the image that's meant to be level. Photoshop will adjust the angle of the cropping boundary.

QUICK TIP

Cycle the View modes

When using the Crop tool, the O key cycles through the different views quickly. By pressing this shortcut key multiple times, you can go from the Rule of Thirds to Triangle in an instant, or any other that suits your image. To use the tool's shortcuts, adjust the boundary of the cropping area first. Otherwise, other tools will be chosen in Photoshop and you'll have to go back to the Crop tool.

Basic corrections

ORIGINAL

Edit easily in Quick mode

Who says that image editing has to take time? Elements has a speedy solution

O f the three editing modes in Elements, Quick mode lives up to its promise. In Quick mode the panel to the right has a whole bunch of sliders that you can use to give fast and effective results.

These cover everything from Lighting and Color to Balance and Sharpness. There are a number of these controls that have an Auto button, which enables Elements to do the hard work. You can always tweak the sliders further to help get the exact results that you need.

You can just jump right in, however, and play around with the sliders. If you don't like the results then there is a Reset button at the moment that can be hit at any time to put the sliders back to the default. The smallest tweak of the slider can make a really big difference here, so make sure that you keep your images looking realistic.

The Quick Edit options can be accessed from the Elements Organizer as well as the Edit interface, so if you see a shot that needs a quick fix, you can click and retouch in just seconds.

If you see a little lightbulb next to the slider headers, this means that you can access the Help menu and read more about the control that you are trying to use. Give it a go and you can transform your photos easily.

"Of the three editing modes in Elements, Quick Edit really does live up to its promise"

Quick mode
If you are in the Edit interface, then you can click on the Quick option in the top-right. If you're in the Organizer, then go to the Edit tab, and from the drop-down menu choose Quick Edit.

Reset
As soon as you start playing with the sliders, the Reset button is activated. Hit this if you make an error and you want to start again from scratch.

Sliders
These sliders are pretty self-explanatory and you can make a very big difference to your shots just using these. Take it slow though; you can always add more if you think the image needs it.

Help
The little lightbulb symbol is a help button. Click this and you will be taken to information about the tool that you are wanting to use.

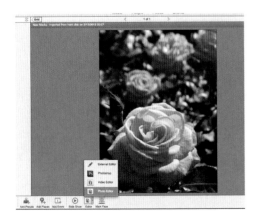

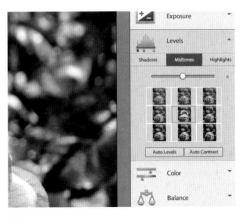

01 Take it to Elements
Click on the Edit tab from the Organizer and you get the choice of where you'd like to open your image. Once in Elements choose Quick Edit.

02 Auto options
We're going to use the Auto Levels option, which will help to balance the tones, followed by the Auto Contrast. This gives a good starting point.

03 Tweak the sliders
Now we work down the rest of the sliders making subtle tweaks until we're happy with the way that the image looks. Don't forget to press Save.

Work with guided edits in PS Elements

We explore three exciting guided edits in Elements that make life easy for those new to the photo editing game

Elements 11 came with three new guided edits, which include an effect called Orton, named after the photographer Michael Orton and his signature editing style. This effect changes your photo in several creative ways by saturating the colours and then blurring the focus to achieve an artistic-looking dream effect.

Then there is the new Depth of Field effect that enables you to apply a blur or fake bokeh by selecting and dragging with the Gradient tool and recovering the area you want to remain in focus.

Last but not least, the Picture Stack edit takes a single photo and breaks it up so that it resembles a collection of prints laid out in front of you. This one really is a lot of fun and works best with group shots. You can choose to divide your photo into four, eight or twelve prints, and pick the border size and background of your images. If you switch to Full Edit mode, you can resize and reposition the frames.

These new edit guides are a great way to easily add some professional effects without buying any of the special camera gear and require very little editing experience, so let's give them a try!

Use discretion
When doubling up on editing effects, it is a lot of fun to play around and see what you can come up with. However, use discretion and adjust the sliders under each effect with care. Sometimes all it takes is a slight adjustment to make your image shine, so don't overdo it.

Start with a great image
To get the best outcome with the new guided edits, be sure to start with a good image. These tools are meant to increase the quality and enhance your favourite shots, but do not expect too much. The Depth of Field will not bring a blurry image into focus.

ORIGINAL

ORIGINAL / CORRECTED

Orton effect
Add vibrance and fun

The Orton effect is named after Michael Orton, as he is the photographer who first made this style popular. It is an easy way to add a dreamy, watercolour look to your portraits or landscapes. Just open you image, click on Guided Edit to the right and there you will see the Add Orton Effect icon. After you choose the effect you can alter the blur, noise and brightness of the image by adjusting the sliders. Here you see a before and after of a portrait shot with the Blur and Brightness at the halfway settings and the Noise at 0.

ORIGINAL / CORRECTED

Magical depth of field
Beautiful bokeh at your fingertips

Have you ever wished you could have the beautiful background blur that you see in professional images, but can't afford to spend a fortune on the right camera lens for the job? Well now you can have the ability to apply beautiful bokeh to your background while keeping your model in perfect focus. Just open your image and find the Depth of Field option in the new Guided Edit menu. Click on Add Blur, then choose the Gradient tool and select the focal point of your image with one click of the mouse. Magic!

CORRECTED

Where to focus
When using Depth of Field, be sure to study the image and choose the most important area to add sharpness to. This will usually be the face of the model. You will want to blur the background quite a lot to really add focus to the face.

Which effect first?
Sometimes it is important to add effects in the proper order. With this image, we used the Depth of Field effect first because the Orton image adds more blur.

The subject matters
Both of these effects together create a dreamy and soft look, so be sure your subject matter is appropriate. For instance, this application looks great on our model and would also look pleasing on an autumnal landscape, but would not suit a male model very well.

The Depth of Field edit

The new Depth of Field effect is wonderful, but there are a few things you need to know before just punching it in. We want you to get the best bokeh while recovering the important aspects of your image and maintaining sharpness in the right places, so follow these simple tips.

01 Create bokeh
Open your image. Select Depth of Field guided edit and click Add Blur. Move the Blur slider to the right to increase the effect.

02 Define the area of focus
Click on the Gradient tool. Once selected you will be able to click your mouse or stylus directly on the part you want to bring back in focus.

03 More focus selection
Use the selection Gradient tool to drag and choose other important elements of your image. When finished, click Done to save your effect.

ORIGINAL

CORRECTED

Picture Stack effect
Separate the group with one click
This new effect is great for group pictures such as sports or family shots. Just open your image in the Guided Edits mode and you will see the new Picture Stack effect in the list. Select it and then click on the number of prints you want to appear (we chose eight). You then have a choice of border and background styles. This effect is sure to be a great scrapbooking or poster choice, so have fun and experiment.

Mix it up
Let's try a few new edits together
Here we played around a little and tried two of the new guided edits on one image. First we applied the Depth of Field effect, focusing on the model's face, making it nice and sharp and blurring the background. We then added the Orton effect and really made this model shine. You don't have to stop with one effect, though. You can add as many as you want to one image, just remember to click Done before moving on to the next one.

Basic corrections

ORIGINAL

Fix images the Smart way

We take a look inside Photoshop Elements' Smart Fix option for perfect pics

hotoshop Elements prides itself on making good images great with the minimum of effort. The Smart Fix control is definitely a tool that we promise you will be using time and again.

It is a simple command that can be found in both the Edit and Organizer interfaces. If you are already in the Edit window, then you can go to the Quick Edit interface, which we have already covered in more detail on page 64.

Right at the top is the Smart Fix slider, which can be moved to the right to set the level of 'fixing' needed. Try taking it one notch at a time until you are happy with the result as a little can make a huge difference to the tonal range of your photos. Of course you could just hit the Auto key and the program will analyse your image and decide what tonal and colour edits are needed. You can also find the Auto Smart Fix option by going to the Enhance menu in the top toolbar. And if you want to get your fingers in a twist, then you can use the Auto Smart Fix shortcut, which is Opt/Alt+Shift+M.

If you are in the Photoshop Elements Organizer section of the program, then you can use the Auto Smart Fix button in the right-hand panel when you select the Fix tab, so that you do not have to even go into Elements to make quick changes.

> "The Smart Fix control is definitely a tool that we promise you will be using time and again"

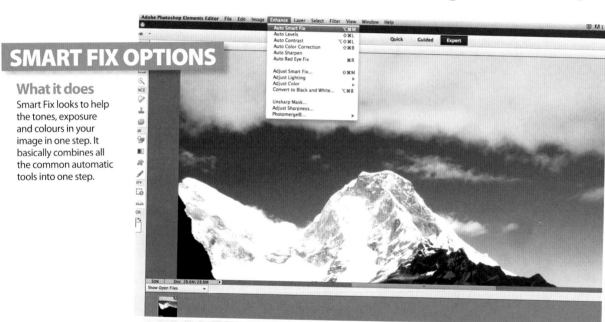

SMART FIX OPTIONS

What it does
Smart Fix looks to help the tones, exposure and colours in your image in one step. It basically combines all the common automatic tools into one step.

Smart Fix slider
This is the slider that controls your Smart Fix strength. You can do this one notch at a time to get the right result.

Menu options
Use this menu to access the Auto Smart Fix controls, or use the three-key shortcut that is denoted here.

01 Auto Smart Fix
Directly from the interface within the Elements Organizer you can hit the Fix tab and then select the Auto Smart Fix from the menu here.

02 Photoshop does its bit
A dialog box will pop up to show you that Photoshop is thinking and analysing, which usually only takes a number of seconds.

03 Control it
If you prefer to have a bit more control over the way that the image is fixed, then use the slider under Smart Fix in the Quick option.

Introducing the Transform tool

Rotate, skew, warp or flip your images in Photoshop with the amazing transformation tools

Hiding under Edit>Transform you will find a menu with a whole host of useful tools which will literally transform the way you use Photoshop. The Transform tools allow you to alter the entire shape of an object, group, vector, smart object, path or selection, but they can do a lot more than this too.

Showing you how to use these tools is our objective, so the first thing to learn when using any of them is that a bounding box will appear around the object. On each of the corners sits a square, and hovering your mouse over one brings up the rotate icon but to shift the item's shape you will need to click onto and move these squares.

In this two-page guide we will cover which tools suit your needs best and suggest how to use them effectively. All of the essentials will be explained, and we will present to you some clever uses of the tools that you may not have even considered before.

You might have noticed another transform option under the Edit menu, that is Free Transform. Using this means you can use more than one of the transform options at one time, saving you having to hit Enter and selecting another option if needs be. Once you have learnt how to use all of the options, this tool will be all you need. So let's start working our way through the menu and see what you can do with these great options.

> "Alter the entire shape of an object, group, vector, smart object, path or selection"

Rotate

A slightly wonky angle is easy to correct with the Rotate tool in Photoshop. Double-click on your background layer to make it editable. Make sure rulers are showing (Cmd/Ctrl+R) and drag a line from the top ruler so you know where your horizon line should sit. Go to Edit>Transform>Rotate and a bounding box will appear with four corner squares. Hover over one square and you will see a rotate icon appear. Now move the image round until lined up with the guide line. Hit Enter when you're happy and then select the Crop tool. Get rid of any excess chequered background and hit Enter.

This tool allows you to amalgamate many of the transform features. Use it to rotate, scale and add perspective all in one neat package.

Flip direction

To begin, we drag the cutout car image into our street image so we can create a convincing scene. Go to Edit>Transform>Flip Horizontal so the car is facing the right way. Go back to Edit and select Free Transform.

Scale the car

We need to resize the car so, holding down Shift, increase the size of the car slightly to sit more naturally within the image. When you're happy with the size, do not hit Enter yet because we are now going to alter its perspective.

Add perspective

To add perspective hold down Cmd/Ctrl+Alt+Shift or Cmd/Ctrl+Option+Shift and drag the top left corner downwards. The bottom left corner will lift up, creating a vanishing point. Then hit Enter.

Work to scale

When you need to combine several images together, chances are you will need to resize elements within a canvas. To do this we will use the Scale tool. Open up two images and drag and drop one onto the other (with some images you will need to cut it out first and get rid of it's original background). Go to Edit>Transform>Scale and a bounding box will appear again. We want to scale and keep the image proportions correct so hold down Shift and drag one of the top corner squares inwards. The whole image will resize evenly, then hit OK when done with your perfectly proportioned image.

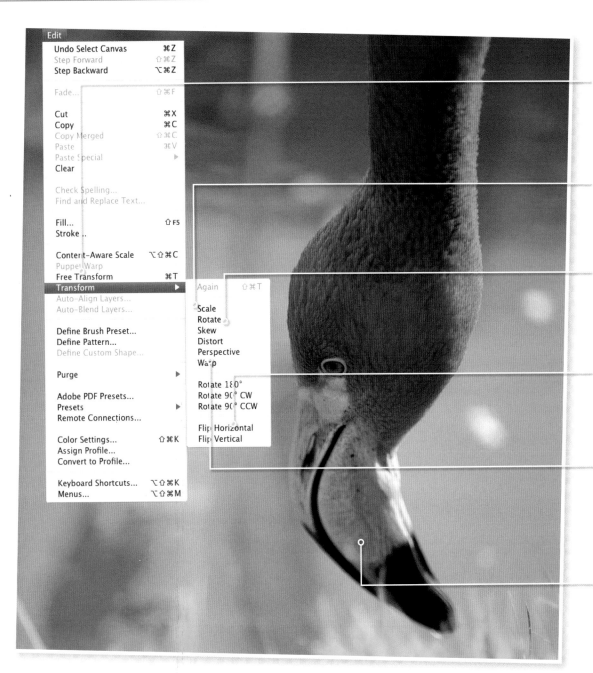

Edit

Undo Select Canvas	⌘Z
Step Forward	⇧⌘Z
Step Backward	⌥⌘Z
Fade...	⇧⌘F
Cut	⌘X
Copy	⌘C
Copy Merged	⇧⌘C
Paste	⌘V
Paste Special	▶
Clear	
Check Spelling...	
Find and Replace Text...	
Fill...	⇧F5
Stroke...	
Content-Aware Scale	⌥⇧⌘C
Puppet Warp	
Free Transform	⌘T
Transform	▶
Auto-Align Layers...	
Auto-Blend Layers...	
Define Brush Preset...	
Define Pattern...	
Define Custom Shape...	
Purge	▶
Adobe PDF Presets...	
Presets	▶
Remote Connections...	
Color Settings...	⇧⌘K
Assign Profile...	
Convert to Profile...	
Keyboard Shortcuts...	⌥⇧⌘K
Menus...	⌥⇧⌘M

Again	⇧⌘T
Scale	
Rotate	
Skew	
Distort	
Perspective	
Warp	
Rotate 180°	
Rotate 90° CW	
Rotate 90° CCW	
Flip Horizontal	
Flip Vertical	

Free Transform
If you want to make general transformations to an object just press Cmd/Ctrl+T to activate the Free Transform tool. Using keyboard shortcuts like this saves precious time.

Scale it up
Use the Scale tool to increase or decrease the size of elements within the image. Make sure that objects are in proportion to one another though.

Rotate
Select Rotate from the Transform menu or use the Free Transform tool. When the bounding box appears, hover over a corner to make the Rotate symbol appear and move. Hit Enter to finish the transformation.

To flip or not to flip
Remember you can flip images horizontally or vertically in the Transform menu so you don't need images to be facing the right way before using them.

Perspective
Use the Perspective transform option to make adjustments to your subjects, making them sit within the image a bit better. Using this tool makes items seem less plonked in place.

Finish it off
Make the scene look natural when compositing images together. Use the Levels tool to even out colour tones and blend bits in. For example, use the Smudge tool to add the effect of grass.

Get some perspective
Sometimes adding a vanishing point to an image makes for a more convincing effect; even a small amount of perspective can make a big difference. Make sure your layer is editable (double-click on the Background

layer before starting) and go to Edit>Transform>Perspective. The usual bounding box with four squares will appear. Move one of the top corner boxes downwards and the bottom corner on the same side will move upwards. This works if you move a top corner side to side too. Remember to crop away any excess background afterwards.

Warp
Go to Edit>Transform>Warp and a bounding box with a mesh will appear on your image. Move any of the control pointers on the mesh to move parts of your image. Start with the corner pointers then move any internal pointers if needed. Directional lines will appear on the corner squares when moved. Move these and lengthen or shorten them to alter image areas. This tool will require some practise but you can fix camera lens flaws with it as well as adding pages to a book convincingly, for example.

Use the Gradient tool
Turn a daytime image into a dramatic sunset shot

The setting sun
Position the sun near the horizon line on the right side of your image for the best composition. Mixing white and yellow help create its glow.

Orange sky
Carry the orange tint from the sky over background elements such as hills or cliffs. This is controlled using Scale in the Gradient Fill options.

Tint foreground
The foreground part of your image will also need a slight orange tint. Use a separate gradient (shown in the steps opposite) to do just this.

Color Picker (Foreground Color)

new

current

⦿ H:	35	°	◯ L:	75
◯ S:	87	%	◯ a:	28
◯ B:	100	%	◯ b:	74
◯ R:	255		C:	0	%
◯ G:	164		M:	41	%
◯ B:	34		Y:	96	%
			K:	0	%

☐ Only Web Colors

ffa422

OK
Cancel
Add To Swatches
Color Libraries

There's nothing quite like gazing into the distant glow of a sunset, and with just a few quick layers and some careful tweaks you can create this effect using any daytime image. The sun doesn't even need to be present in your shot, as we will show you how to brush it on afterwards. Trying not to overdo the effect requires a balance of opacities for each layer. Too bright and the image will look unrealistic, too faint and you'll instantly know that the picture was manipulated.

By the time you're done you should have a firm grasp of the Layers palette. Using a fill and an adjustment layer together means that you can control brightness and ...... of the overall image for a believable landscape.

Choose a colour
Whenever you see a # symbol in the steps, apply this number inside the relevant box in the Color Picker menu

Transform a landscape Tint, darken and apply glow

ORIGINAL

"Incorporate subtle pink tones if you want to evoke a sunrise rather than a sunset"

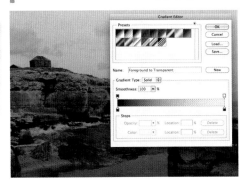

01 Gradient fill
Open up the landscape image that you want to apply a sunset to and add a Gradient fill layer (found by navigating to the circular icon at the bottom of the Layers palette). In the fly-out menu click on the Gradient option and choose the Foreground to Transparent thumbnail in the Presets.

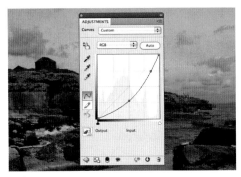

03 Lower brightness
Now you want to merge the coloured layer with your photograph, so set the gradient layer's blend mode to Color and add the Curves adjustment from the same icon. Pull the curve's line downwards to lower the brightness. This will depend on how bright your image is to begin with.

05 Paint on yellow
To create a bright glow around where the sun is actually rising in your sky, select the Brush tool (B) and, in the Options bar under Brush, set Hardness to 0%. Set Opacity to 30% and paint over the sky starting from your sun. Keep this effect subtle by not concentrating too much on a small area but diffusing it out.

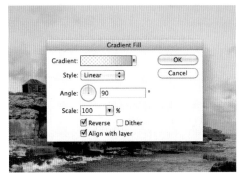

02 Colourise the sky
Now you can set the orange colour for your gradient and the tone of your image. Click on the bottom two of the four colour boxes, setting the left swatch to orange (#ffa422) and the right to white. Hit OK in this window and then tick Reverse in the Gradient Fill menu followed by OK.

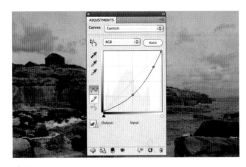

04 Set Foreground colour
To add realism to the effect you need to incorporate more colours, in our case a yellow to go with the warm orange. Create a new layer between the Curves adjustment and the Gradient fill layer, changing its blend mode to Overlay. Click on your Foreground swatch in the Toolbar and set its colour to a bright yellow (#ffdf4b).

06 Glowing sunlight
Change the Foreground colour to white and paint over the patch of sky where you want the sun to be placed. At 30% Opacity, this will take a couple of stamps of the Brush to reveal a bright white glow, but you need to keep this setting low or you'll end up with an unrealistic white blot and no cloud texture will show through.

07 Final colour
To finish off the effect, add a blank layer to the top of the stack. Set your Foreground colour to a light orange (#ffae00) and press Alt/Opt+Backspace to fill this layer. Change its blend mode to Soft Light and lower the Opacity to 20%. This unifies the effect by giving the rocks and sky a slight tint of the same tone.

Gradient text effects
Customise text in your artwork by adding a gradient

You can transform text in Photoshop using the Gradient tool and clipping masks. Discover how to apply unique colour effects to your font using clipping masks in the Layers palette. Here we outline all the essential steps you'll need to know.

ORIGINAL

ENHANCED

01 Initial settings
Open the image you want to add text to in Photoshop and select the Text tool. Place the cursor on the background and drag out a suitably sized box for text. Now type out your text.

02 Add text
Highlight the text and select a font style from the font dropdown at the top of the screen. Select a font that offers a good width and size, so that you can see more of the gradient effect.

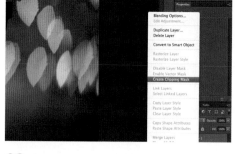

03 Create a new layer
In the Layers palette select the icon to create a new layer and rename this 'gradient effect'. Now Ctrl/right-click on the layer and select Create Clipping Mask to connect the layer to the text layer below.

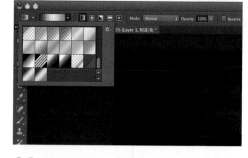

04 Select the effect
Select the Gradient tool and choose a suitable preset from the Gradient Picker menu. If you want to include colour from the background, use the Eyedropper tool to select a specific hue.

05 Apply the gradient
You can now choose which type of gradient you want, to determine whether it will fade downwards with linear or spiral out with radial. Now click on the image and apply the gradient to the layer.

06 Make some adjustments
You may need to make adjustments to the clipping mask to get the right result. Hit Cmd/Ctrl+T to transform the layer and enable you to adjust its size and fit more of the gradient effect in the font.

07 Complete final tweaks
You can also adjust the opacity of the clipping mask layer to control the strength of the gradient within the text. When you're pleased, flatten files via Layer>Flatten Image and then save your shot.

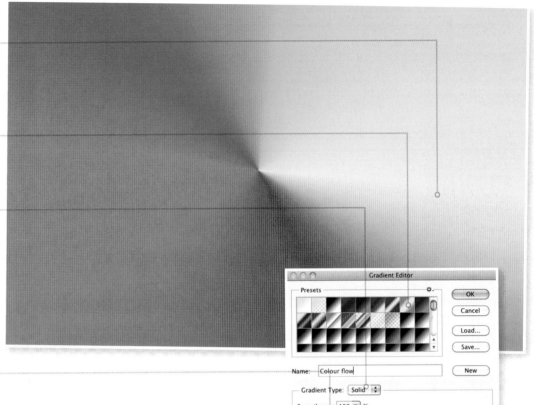

Unique effect

Once you've created your own custom gradient, save it to the preset folder and use it again on your images and/or artwork.

Customise presets

Load up the Gradient Editor dialog box and select an existing preset to customise with colour.

Gradient type

Choose how smooth you would like your gradient to be by selecting between Solid or Noise gradient types. Solid offers smoother transitions in tone, whereas Noise has a broken appearance.

Colour control

Change the colour hues in your gradient by adjusting the colour tabs. Double click to bring up the colour picker dialog box and make a selection.

Custom gradients

Make your own gradients for greater creative control

You are able to take direct control over the gradient that you are using by customising existing gradient presets or even by creating your own unique ones from scratch. Have a go at experimenting with some different colour hues and see what kind of results you can achieve. Follow along with us below and we'll show you how it's done.

01 Start a new document

Start by opening a blank document in Photoshop (File>New). Hit Cmd/Ctrl+Shift+N to get a new layer, which you can apply your custom gradient to later on. Now select the Gradient tool.

"Experiment with different colour hues and see what kind of results you can get"

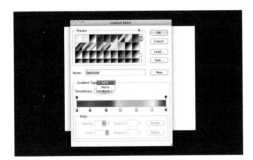

02 Customise preset

Click on the gradient picker box at the top of the screen to open the gradient editor dialog box. Select an existing preset to customise with colour. Select between solid or noise gradient types.

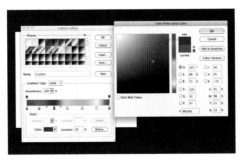

03 Select colour

Adjust the smoothness of the gradient to control how the colours blend. Now adjust colours to get a unique gradient. Double click on the colour tabs and select a hue from the colour picker dialog box.

04 Apply the custom gradient

You can add fade-outs to the end of your gradient by adjusting the opacity tabs along the top. Once you're pleased with your gradient, rename it and select New to save the preset.

Colour & tone

"Now you can go back and change the amount of light in a scene"

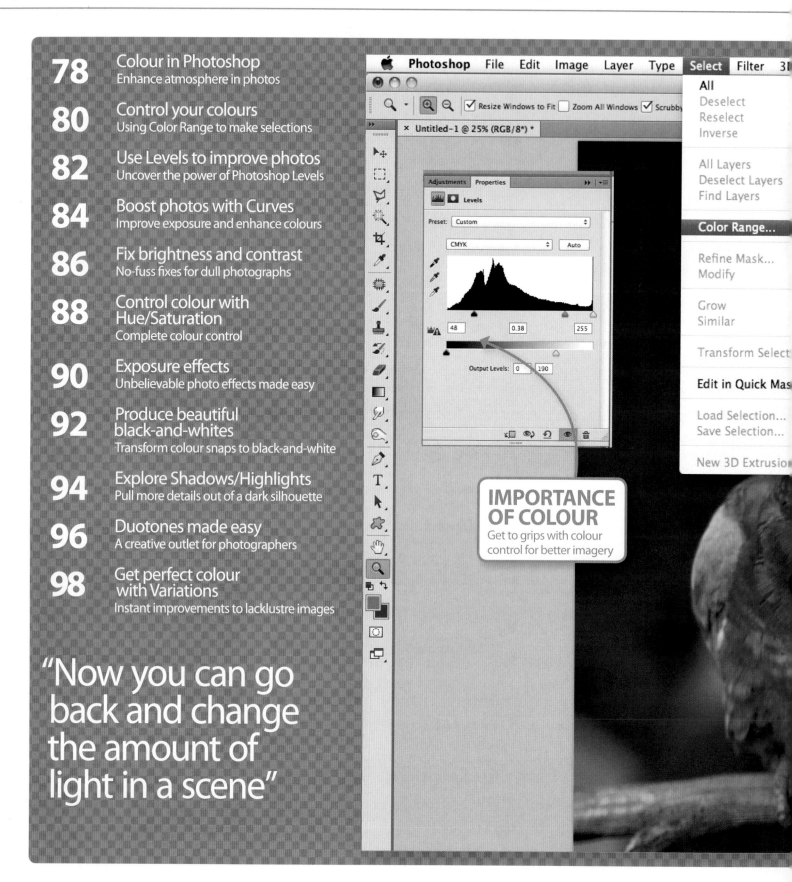

IMPORTANCE OF COLOUR
Get to grips with colour control for better imagery

COLOR RANGE
Get complete control over colours and watch as your image transforms from boring to vibrant in seconds

BRIGHTNESS AND CONTRAST
Two important photographic edits and how to do them correctly

Colour in Photoshop

Offset colour casts and enhance atmosphere in your artwork

Colour is an inevitable part of photo editing and as a result, seeps into all parts of Photoshop in some form or another.

Controlling it is usually done with the Color Balance adjustment, which is best for offsetting colour casts, but it can also be used for changing colour to more abstract hues for artistic effects.

The Color Balance adjustment is only a small part of Photoshop. The best thing about using Color Balance is it's non-destructive. Here we show you how to intensify the yellow and green hues in this image of an insect in flowers.

You'll also find two swatches, Foreground and Background, at the base of the Toolbar for picking out colour and using with tools and adjustments.

> "The best thing about using Color Balance is it's non-destructive"

Adjust colour

Color Balance as an adjustment layer

ORIGINAL

01 Load adjustment
To load the adjustment go to Layer> New Adjustment Layer and select Color Balance. In the name dialog box, hit OK and there should now be a Color Balance 1 layer in your Layers palette.

02 Set tone
For basic alterations, set the Tone option in the Color Balance adjustment to Midtones. Start with the Cyan/Red slider. Slide it left to cool down the image, or push it right to warm it up.

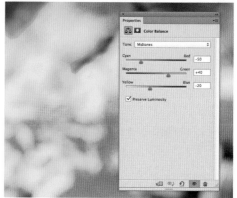

03 Alter colour
Tweak the other two sliders depending on how far your colours in your image are off. As an adjustment layer, the colours can be re-edited later on by double-clicking on the layer's thumbnail.

COLOR BALANCE ADJUSTMENT

The Color Balance adjustment presents a set of sliders that work by adding and subtracting amounts of colour. This is helpful when the tone of an image isn't quite right, such as when there's too much orange in an image that was taken indoors. Here's what the adjustment looks like and how it can be used.

Colour sliders

There are six colours inside the adjustment. They work in pairs, and when one colour is reduced the opposing one is increased.

Tone Balance

The Tone Balance section of the adjustment is split into Shadows, Midtones and Highlights. This is where colour in all three regions of your image can be tweaked to perfection.

Adjustment location

The Color Balance adjustment can be found inside Image>Adjustments, as well as Layer>New Adjustment Layer. The latter option comes with a mask on its own layer.

Color Levels

If you know the exact amount of colour to adjust in your image, enter the values under Color Levels.

Add a swatch

When you've found a colour you like, click the Add to Swatches button to send the colour to the Swatches palette. This palette is found inside the Window menu.

FOREGROUND & BACKGROUND SWATCHES

The Color Picker menu is where colour for your Foreground and Background swatches are set in place. From saturation to brightness, it's all done here.

Change saturation

The strength, or saturation, of colour is adjusted by sliding the picker left or right. The far right contains the colour in its strongest form, whereas the far-left side contains less.

New and current

The current colour is shown just underneath the new colour being chosen, so you can see just how they differ.

Choosing brightness

The brightness of a colour is changed when the picker is moved up and down the colour chart, with complete black at the bottom and the brightest tone at the top.

Hue

The hue of the colour is selected by sliding the arrows up and down the vertical spectrum.

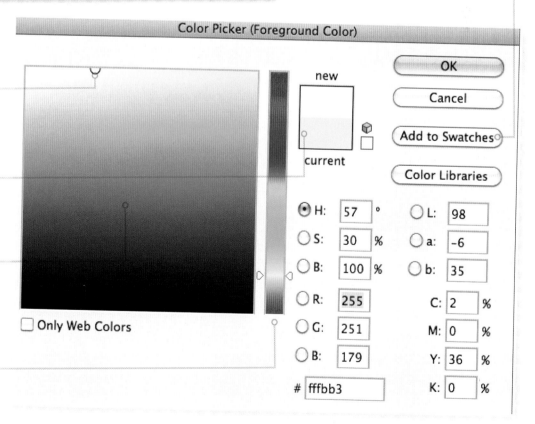

Control your colours

How to use the Color Range method for forming selections

ORIGINAL

Photoshop's Color Range feature is designed to isolate a colour. In a similar way to the Magic Wand tool (W), it uses areas of colour to form selections, but the advantage of using Color Range is that you can control the size of the selection area and can preview the results.

There are many more advantages too, such as the ability to select only skin tones if your image has people in it (available in Photoshop CS6). Follow our work on this feathered friend to find out just how to make selections and apply adjustments using this special Color Range technique.

Control colour

Change a hue using the Color Range selection method

01 Open Color Range

Find the Color Range option inside the Select menu at the top of Photoshop. If you have the Marquee (M), Magic Wand or Quick Selection tools (W) at hand, Ctrl/right-click over your image to see Color Range listed.

Detect Faces
If there are any people in your image, tick the Detect Faces box to make skin tones the active selection.

Localized Color Clusters
When this option's on, you control the spread of the Color Range selection. For an effect such as this parrot's feathers, Localized Color Clusters is a must.

Fuzziness
Increasing the Fuzziness slider softens the selected area, depending on how precise you need it to be.

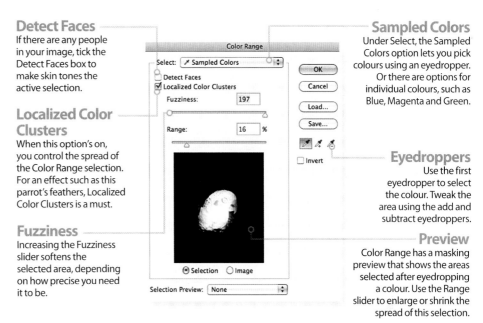

Sampled Colors
Under Select, the Sampled Colors option lets you pick colours using an eyedropper. Or there are options for individual colours, such as Blue, Magenta and Green.

Eyedroppers
Use the first eyedropper to select the colour. Tweak the area using the add and subtract eyedroppers.

Preview
Color Range has a masking preview that shows the areas selected after eyedropping a colour. Use the Range slider to enlarge or shrink the spread of this selection.

02 Sample method

Decide how you want to sample the colour you want to change. Click on the Select list and choose a colour option. White areas represent the selection, but if this is too faint, set Select to Sampled Colors to do things manually.

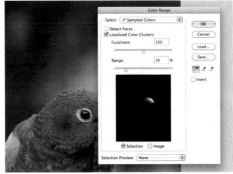

03 Localized Color Clusters

To select a colour in just one area without affecting the rest of the image, tick the Localized Color Clusters option. The Range slider should now be visible, as well as Fuzziness. Set Range to 20% and Fuzziness to 100 to begin with.

04 Eyedropper tool

To make a selection, click on the colour that you want to alter. All of the areas in your chosen colour should show up on the preview in white. Start from the edge of the colour and a small area of white should show inside Color Range.

05 Add selection

With the selection started, click on the eyedropper with the plus symbol and click and drag to continue to add colour. More white should appear inside the preview. Don't worry if the white area bleeds over to other parts of the image.

06 Remove selection

Now use the minus symbol and, with the preview as a guide, click over the extraneous white areas. This will tidy up the selection even more. You can alter the Fuzziness and Range sliders for further refinement. Hit OK to apply the selection.

07 Masked colour

With a selection of just the colour, adjustment layers such as Hue/Saturation can be added via the Layers palette. The adjustment layer uses the selection for its mask, so you can change the hue of only this colour for a creative effect.

Use Levels to improve photos

Photoshop's trusty Levels adjustment is a must-have for solving a range of photographic problems

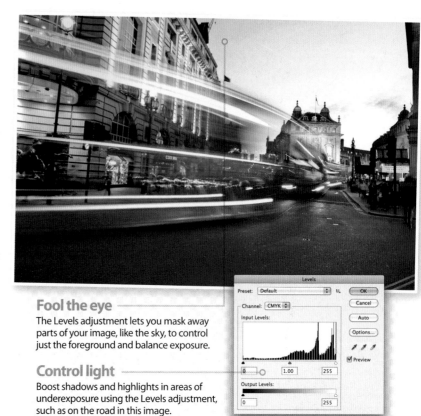

The Levels adjustment layer is a staple of Photoshop and should be one of the first places you go to tweak lighting and colour. In fact, it is so versatile that it can be used to perform multiple fixes in one go, which makes it purely indispensable for any budding Photoshop artist.

Here we'll guide you through the different uses of the Levels adjustment and demonstrate how even dull images can be completely turned on their heads with new life, colour and better overall lighting.

The Levels adjustment is commonly used to correct undesirable lighting, but due to its relationship with colour channels it's also helpful for correcting tinted images.

When applied as an adjustment layer, a mask enables you to selectively brush away areas on certain parts of the image. This is a great way to get creative with lighting, as well as add or even distort colour.

Fool the eye
The Levels adjustment lets you mask away parts of your image, like the sky, to control just the foreground and balance exposure.

Control light
Boost shadows and highlights in areas of underexposure using the Levels adjustment, such as on the road in this image.

01 Open Levels
Find the supplied 'Headlight trails.jpg' to replicate the results shown in this tutorial. Load your Levels adjustment by going to Layer>New Adjustment Layer>Levels. Hit OK in the pop-up box.

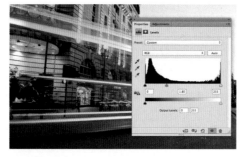

02 Middle of the road
We can brighten up this dim street by shifting the middle of the three sliders to the left. This lightens the dark road, but as a result of this the sky will lose its impact.

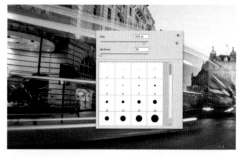

03 Adjust your brush settings
Grab the Brush tool (B) set to 100% Opacity and make your Foreground black. Ctrl/right-click over the image, set the brush Size to 1,000px and Hardness to 0%.

04 Improve the sky
Select the adjustment's layer mask from the Layers palette, paint over the sky in order to reveal the unedited version and then balance the exposure.

05 Focus on the red
Click on the adjustment's icon in the Layers palette and then change the Levels from RGB to Red using the list of options inside the graph. Also slide the Midtones marker to the right until it reads 0.84.

06 Boost the contrast
To give the image one last injection of contrast, switch the Levels adjustment back to RGB. Grab the white marker to control the highlights and slide it up to 200. This gives the light more vibrancy.

Take it to the next level

Combine Levels with blend modes for extra contrast

ORIGINAL

ENHANCED

Try using Levels with selections

The mask that comes with the Levels adjustment can be used creatively to stop changes being made to a particular colour. Apply the Magic Wand tool (W) to create a selection (uncheck Contiguous) around one colour. To finish, apply the Levels adjustment and invert its mask (Cmd/Ctrl+I).

01 Fix the flat contrast

Open the supplied 'Close up flower.jpg', which will currently lack a bit of contrast. Load up the Levels adjustment from the Layers palette by clicking on the Create New Fill or Adjustment Layer button.

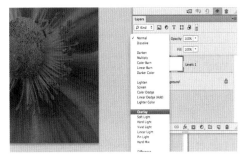

02 Use a blend mode

Before making any changes to the adjustment, change its blend mode from Normal to Overlay in the Layers palette. This improves things slightly, but we can tweak settings to suit the blend mode.

03 Control the highlights

Grab the Highlights marker inside the Levels adjustment and slide it to the left to boost contrast and brightness. Be wary of the brightest parts of the image, but these can also be fixed later.

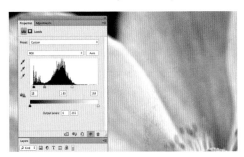

04 Alter the shadows

Pull the black marker to the right in the Levels adjustment until you find that the contrast is balanced. Slide the Midtones marker to the left to enhance this result.

05 Original detail

Use the Brush tool (B) set to 10% Opacity, 400px Size and paint over the highlights on the petals. This reduces any over-exposure in these areas by revealing the original Background layer.

> "The Levels adjustment layer is so versatile that it can perform multiple fixes in one go"

Boost photos with Curves
Improve exposure and enhance colours

The Curves adjustment is used to control the exposure in images. It can also be used to edit colour, as it's divided up into red, green and blue. When worked with individually, these separate colours can actually give you the chance to restore exposure and create more abstract effects.

Like many adjustments in Photoshop, Curves can be added to an image as a separate layer, which also means that it comes with a mask. In Photoshop Elements, however, Curves isn't available as a new layer. Instead, it comes in the form of an editing filter found under the Enhance menu.

If there's a distinct colour in your image, you can easily use Curves to increase or decrease its contrast by changing the adjustment from RGB to one of the three colours. We show you how across these pages.

ORIGINAL

No maths needed!
The Curves adjustment may look like a mathematical nightmare, but it simply shows how the highlights and shadows are distributed across your image.

Target colour
The colours were especially lacking in this image before the Curves adjustment was put to use.

Creating curves
Push the diagonal line upwards to brighten the image or downwards to darken the tone.

Colour curves
The curved lines indicate how the three primary colours (red, green and blue) have been manipulated in the image.

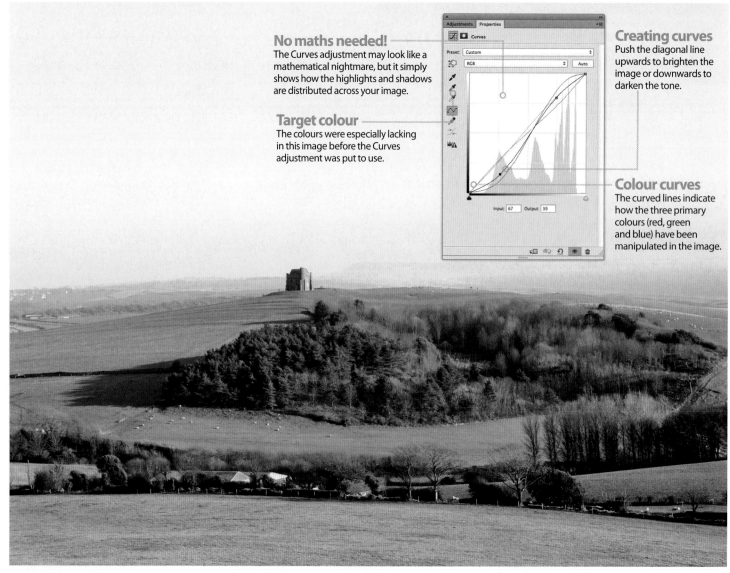

Better colour
Increase the contrast of colour using the Curves adjustment in Photoshop

01 Find the adjustment
Load up the Curves adjustment layer from the circular icon at the base of the Layers palette. It will appear as a new layer, with a white mask and a small thumbnail containing its settings.

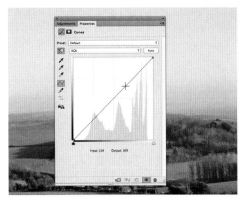

02 Curves structure
You'll see a straight diagonal line that cuts through a graph. The graph shows the shadows on the left and the highlights on the right. Hover over this diagonal line to see a pair of crosshairs.

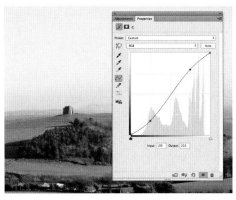

03 Increase contrast
Click and drag the diagonal line upwards on the right to boost highlights and downwards over the left to deepen shadows. Use the eye symbol in the adjustment to compare it before and after.

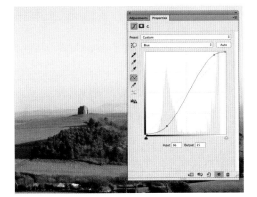

04 Improve colour
The letters RGB are selected. Change this to Blue to improve a blue sky or green for a grassy landscape. Adapt the diagonal line in the same way as before, until you see an improvement to the colour.

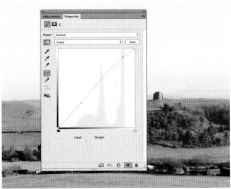

05 Colour correction
Go through Red, Green and Blue lifting the diagonal line upwards. Keeping the changes subtle, you should see an overall improvement to the image. Go back to RGB to adapt just the exposure.

> "The graph shows the shadows on the left and the highlights on the right"

ORIGINAL

CURVES IN PHOTOSHOP ELEMENTS

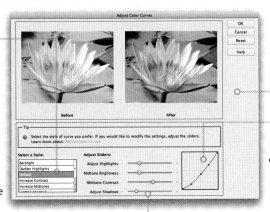

Choose Style
Under Style, there are several presets that can be used to increase contrast, darken highlights, or improve midtones.

Correct exposure
For this image, which was too bright, we lowered the sliders Adjust Highlights, Midtone Brightness and Adjust Shadows to bring the exposure down to a normal brightness level.

Where to go
The Adjust Color Curves menu in Photoshop Elements is found under Enhance and inside Adjust Color.

Perfect contrast
Adjust Color Curves lets you control the entire dynamic range of an image, to create perfect contrast and to give images that extra finishing touch.

Fix brightness and contrast

This quick 'no-fuss' option is a surprisingly capable feature for exposure corrections and very easy to get to grips with

This adjustment feature is one of the oldest and most intuitive available for altering the lighting of a photograph in Photoshop. While Curves and Levels have an interface that includes a graph to explore and learn, Brightness/Contrast has just two sliders: rather predictably, the Brightness slider and the Contrast slider. And they do exactly what you would expect them to do.

Brightness lightens or darkens an image and Contrast enhances or removes conflicting tones. The Brightness slider is much the same as the middle slider handle in the Levels control that adjusts the gamma of the midtones. In the same vein, the Contrast slider is similar to tweaking the two outer handles in Levels at the same time.

One of the dangers of this tool is the unwanted side effect of clipping the shadows and highlights. This means that dark pixels are turned completely black and pixels that are close to the white limit are turned completely white. This destroys details and is generally considered bad form.

Previous versions of Photoshop (ie pre-CS3) included a Brightness/Contrast adjustment that would easily clip the highlights and shadows. Now the feature is reworked to avoid this, but it can still happen if you're not careful. This is one of the rare tools that operates exactly the same in Photoshop as it does in its sibling Photoshop Elements. The Use Legacy option is missing in Elements, but other than that the tools are identical.

"While Curves and Levels have a graph to explore, Brightness/ Contrast has just two sliders"

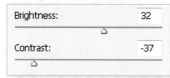

QUICK PHOTOSHOP TIPS

Simple sliders
Complete control with just two straightforward sliders. One for brightness, one for contrast. It really doesn't get much easier than that.

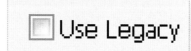

Brightness: 32

Contrast: -37

Use Legacy, or not
Prior to Photoshop CS3 the Brightness/ Contrast controls would harshly clip highlights and shadows without care. To revert to this behaviour for effect, simply check the Use Legacy box.

☐ Use Legacy

Shadow details
Look closely! The Brightness/Contrast adjustment has revealed details in shadow areas that were nearly imperceptible before it was applied.

01 Photoshop proper
Launch Photoshop and open a JPEG file of your choice. Find a shot that feels a bit dark and can use some work to pull details out of the shadows.

02 Adjust Brightness
In Image>Adjustments>Brightness/Contrast, uncheck the Use Legacy box. Up the Brightness to just before the highlights start to clip; we used 32.

03 Adjust Contrast
Next reduce the Contrast to e[...] midtones; we used -37. Toggle[...] see how much the image cha[...]

Beware of clipping
Watch the highlights carefully as you brighten the image. You want to avoid any clipping of the light areas, especially near a focal point.

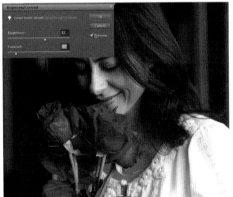

04 **Photoshop Elements**
Now let's try it in Photoshop Elements. Launch the app and open the provided image again. The Elements interface makes it look even darker!

05 **New program, same sliders**
Go to Enhance>Adjust Lighting>Brightness/ Contrast. A very familiar palette appears. Set the Brightness to 32, keeping an eye on highlights.

06 **Compare and contrast**
Pull the Contrast slider to around -37. Check the before and after via the Preview box. If you are satisfied with the adjustment, press OK.

Control colour with Hue/Saturation

Bring out the Hue/Saturation command and add some zing to your photos

Colour can mean the difference between a disappointing image and a triumphant one. But you never need to feel sad or disheartened if your image is looking a little dull, because it's really easy to improve this, especially with the Hue/Saturation command at your fingertips.

This little beauty lives in the Image>Adjustments menu in Photoshop, or the Image>Color Control menu in Elements. Despite its name, it consists of three parts. One changes the hue of an image, one changes the saturation and the other sees to the Lightness. Don't worry about that last one – when it comes to fixing colour, Hue and Saturation are all you need.

With Hue, you can alter the colour of an object. This can be something subtle like changing eye colour in a portrait to something really crazy like creating pink snow! Simply move the slider to swap between a range of different colours, almost like brushing a rainbow over an object. The saturation is what controls the intensity of these colours in an image – a jump to the left will reduce saturation, while a step to the right will increase it. You can control the effect by making a selection of the area you want to edit, or use the Master pull-down menu to target a specific shade. Don't believe how easy it is? Read on and see it in action.

Edit an image with Hue/Saturation Slide your way to perfection

01 Saturate it all
Our image is dull everywhere so demands a widespread blast of saturation. With the image open, it's just a case of bringing up the Hue/Saturation dialog and moving the Saturation slider to the right.

02 More control
It might be that you only want to increase the saturation of part of the image, like the sky. You don't have to make a selection, just click on the Master drop-down and pick the specific colour that you want to edit.

03 Even more control
The best way to constrain an edit, however, is to make a selection. Select the object to edit and then open the Hue/Saturation dialog. Any changes you make will only be made to the selection.

04 A different hue
If boosting a colour isn't enough, you can change its hue altogether. Pick out a part of your object and open up Hue/Saturation. Go to the Hue slider and move it left or right.

05 Strip colour
You can use the Saturation slider to strip all colour away, or maybe leave a small amount for an almost hand-tinted effect. This involves nothing more than moving the Saturation slider towards the left.

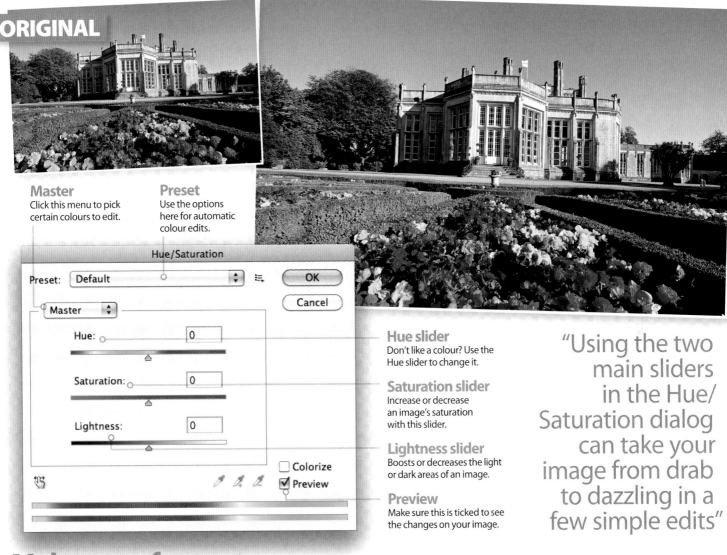

ORIGINAL

Master
Click this menu to pick certain colours to edit.

Preset
Use the options here for automatic colour edits.

Hue/Saturation

Preset: Default ▼ ⚏ (OK)
(Cancel)

Master ▼

Hue: 0

Saturation: 0

Lightness: 0

☐ Colorize
☑ Preview

Hue slider
Don't like a colour? Use the Hue slider to change it.

Saturation slider
Increase or decrease an image's saturation with this slider.

Lightness slider
Boosts or decreases the light or dark areas of an image.

Preview
Make sure this is ticked to see the changes on your image.

> "Using the two main sliders in the Hue/ Saturation dialog can take your image from drab to dazzling in a few simple edits"

Make use of presets
Apply some one-click effects

The Hue/Saturation command ships with some ready-made effects, which are found in the Preset drop-down menu where there are eight to choose from. Simply click on one for it to be applied. Here are three of the best.

01 Cyanotype
Using this technique will transform your image into just tones of the colour blue. If you find that it is a little bit flat, use the Saturation slider to add more pop to proceedings.

02 Old Style
As it's name suggests, using this method will give a vintage feel to any given image by stripping away some of the saturation and increasing the lightness of the whole shot.

03 Strong Saturation
This is a good place to start if you need to quickly boost the colour levels. If it causes any of your colours to go too far, just reduce the Saturation value a wee bit.

Colour & tone

Layers
Layers contain various effects that are stacked up, the order of which can be altered by dragging them up or down the panel.

Lighten   Opacity: 100%

Layer 2

Levels 1

Layer 1

Background

Photoshop Elements 11
This is how the Layers panel looks inside Photoshop Elements 11. Commands for adding new layers, masks and adjustments are featured at the top.

Extra style
To add distortion to the effect, the highlights were bleached out in this image using the Levels adjustment.

Levels
Channel: RGB   Auto

15   1.00   210

Output Levels:

0   255

Reset

Levels adjustment
The Levels adjustment layer only affects the layers underneath it. Pull the points under its graph to the left and right to adjust the contrast in the highlight and shadow regions.

Exposure effects
Add movement to subjects and double up on exposure with these techniques in Elements

Some artists refer to Photoshop Elements 11 as a condensed **Photoshop CS6.** To an extent this is true, but this shouldn't lower your expectations of what can be done. For effects such as these that involve exposure, Photoshop Elements performs just as well as its big brother. Masking, blurring and adjustment layers are all included in Elements, and in an interface that's much friendlier for beginners. Here, we show you three types of effects involving layering and blurring. The

double-exposure effect creates a two-in-one image, whereby details from one are overlapped onto another and then faded out. Any images can be used to create this, and the results can be quite abstract.

Blurring techniques are great for adding movement and rotation to objects such as water and an umbrella. By learning these nifty editing tricks you can replicate these great techniques using Photoshop Elements, which lets us skip this difficult camera work and get straight to it!

Create double-exposure
Photoshop Elements 11 for creating a layered composition

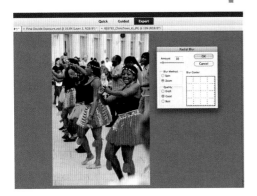

01 Radial Blur
Duplicate the Background layer (Cmd/Ctrl+J) straight after opening your image in Photoshop Elements. Head to the Filter menu and down to Blur>Radial Blur, then set Method to Zoom and Amount to 10.

ORIGINALS

02 Layer mask
Add a mask by clicking the Add Layer Mask button in the Layers panel. Select the Brush tool (B) and set the brush size to 700px. Set your Foreground colour to black and paint over the faces and central parts of your image to bring back the focus.

03 Boost contrast
Go to Layer>New Adjustment Layer and add the Levels adjustment. Increase contrast by sliding both the black and white markers on each end inwards. The adjustment layer comes with its own mask for customising with the Brush tool if needed.

04 Double up
Load up your second image by going to File>Open. When it's loaded, head to Select>All and then Edit>Copy. Turn to the first image by double-clicking on its picture in the Photo Bin (called Project Bin for Photoshop Elements versions 10 and earlier) and then head to Edit>Paste to insert the new image into the first.

05 Blend layers
Press Cmd/Ctrl+T to activate Free Transform. Use the corner boxes around the second image to resize it so it fits over the first. Change the blend mode of the second image's layer to Lighten from inside the Layers panel. This is set to Normal for every layer by default, but changing the blend mode creates different effects.

06 Customise effect
Details can be removed by adding a layer mask to this second image. As with the first image, use the Brush tool to hide areas of the second image that are covering up the subjects in the first image. This will depend on the types of images you choose to use for the double-exposure.

07 Save As
Since this is a multi-layered image, it needs to be stored as a PSD to retain all the layers. Go to File>Save As and change Format to Photoshop. Enter a name for the image and make sure Layers is ticked. Name the image and then hit Save to finish off.

Colour & tone

Produce beautiful black-and-whites

Photoshop gives you maximum creative control to transform colour snaps into stunning black-and-white imagery

Black-and-white photography is a study unto itself. By limiting colour range, the strength of a shot must be carried on tonal value and composition – a restriction which forces the photographer to focus on shapes, line and contrast. This can result in some wonderfully striking images that often seem to be even richer than their fully hued counterparts.

Black and white means more than just a lack of colour though. Photoshop provides several means of eliminating colour from an image, but simply desaturating a shot does not allow for the creative process required to produce a truly exceptional black-and-white image. The preferred method is to use the Black & White adjustment. This allows for fine control over the grey values of each colour family in the image. This can be remarkably useful if you are attempting to lighten a sky but darken skin tones, etc. By using Black & White,

this requires no masking or selections of any kind. It truly strikes a wondrous balance between ease of use, high level of control and effectiveness.

Not every image is appropriate for black-and-white conversion. When evaluating a photo, consider the tonal range and contrast. Also, monochrome can give a sense of formality, so if the topic is serious, it will probably work well. Rich details like rusted metals or rugged portraits are always favourites too.

In this series of steps we'll show you how to take a pleasant enough full-colour image and transform it into a truly striking black-and-white one.

"Black & White allows for fine control over the grey values"

ORIGINAL

Best of Black & White
Learn the ins and outs of this remarkable little adjustment tool

01 Select a photo
Black & White works best on shots with strong lines and contrast that don't rely on colour information. We invite you to use the source file provided.

02 Black & White adjustment
This particular conversion feature is found under Image>Adjustments>Black & White. Or use the keyboard shortcut: Cmd/Ctrl+Opt/Alt+Shift+B.

03 Browse the presets
Photoshop provides a host of preset conversions, worth browsing through to get a sense of what approach may or may not work for your image.

04 Auto button
Automatic PS functions are seldom reliable, but in this case, the Auto feature offers a solid starting point. The Auto button is on the right of the dialog.

05 Adjustable skies
Bring down the brightness of the sky by adjusting the Cyan levels. The goal is to darken the sky just enough so it doesn't distract from the bridge.

06 Water control
Next we'll brighten the water by tweaking the slider bar for the Blues. Pull the slider handle towards the right so the sea isn't quite so dark.

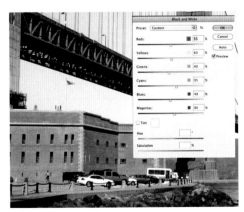

07 Lighter tones
Mouse over the image and the cursor becomes an eyedropper. Click and drag on the building to adjust its tones (watch the Yellows slider).

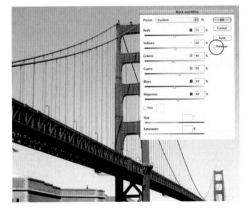

08 Check your work
Use the Preview checkbox to toggle the effect on and off. This provides great before and after visual feedback. Use it frequently to check your work.

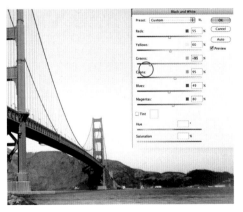

09 The grass is always greener…
To add more details to the grass, knock down the Greens slider substantially. Bringing out texture here helps visually balance details in the structure.

Colour & tone

ORIGINAL

Explore Shadows/Highlights

Use this sophisticated adjustment to pull more details out of a dark silhouette than you might have ever imagined

Backlit images can frequently pose quite a dilemma. How do you lighten the dark subject pixels while darkening the overblown background area? And how do you do this without spending endless hours creating a selection or mask? With Shadows/Highlights, that's how!

Even though it lives in the Adjustments menu, the Shadows/Highlights command is technically a filter. It cannot be applied through an adjustment layer. Therefore it's good practice to duplicate the Background layer before running this adjustment. That way, mistakes aren't permanent.

While this feature allows you to pull a remarkable amount of detail out of dark silhouettes, it will not create details out of total darkness. If the shadows are clipped, ie completely black, Photoshop can't create what is not there. So be aware that the subject must have some degree of detail left that hasn't been obliterated by the dark. In fact, while working to restore the details to the darkened areas, be on watch for introducing noise into the image.

Photoshop offers a plethora of controls in this feature, most of which you will probably never use, while PS Elements pares it down to just three sliders. Find them under Enhance>Adjust Lighting>Shadows/Highlights. Elements enables you to brighten Shadows, darken Highlights and make more subtle adjustments with the Midtone Contrast control. In this example we strive to illustrate just how much detail can be recovered from an image using this tool.

"Duplicate the Background layer before running this adjustment"

WHAT YOU'LL LEARN

More options
The default operation of Shadows/Highlights has only two simple sliders. Check Show More Options to reveal many more useful controls.

Watch out for haloes
One thing you need to watch for with this adjustment is haloes around subject edges. The Radius settings will help spread them out but won't eliminate them completely.

Tonal Width
It's recommended that these settings be left at their default 50%. However, if you change one, the other should be adjusted so that they equal 100% when combined.

Colour with caution
While this setting provides an easy way to boost colour values in the image, it's not always the best solution in that it can introduce undesired saturation values.

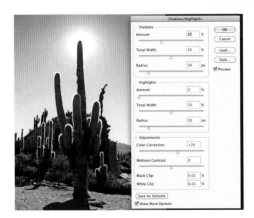

01 Into the swing of things…
Open the source file provided. While backlight is clear, the subject details are also still there. Now go to Image>Adjustments>Shadows/Highlights.

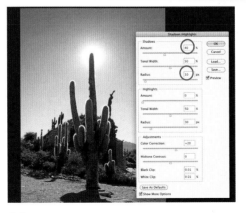

02 Open the shadows
Use the Shadows Amount slider to brighten the details in shade. We used a setting of 40%. Then, for the Radius, we applied a value of 10px.

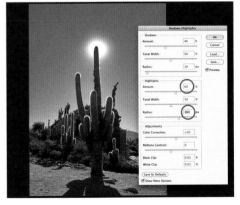

03 Pull in the highlights
To reveal details in the highlight areas, adjust the Amount slider to around 60%. If you get haloes, counter these with a high Radius setting of 160px.

Duotones made easy

What started out as a technical means of saving ink has turned into a creative outlet for photographers

Anybody who has ever had something printed will know all too well that ink isn't cheap. In fact the more types of ink you use in a single print, the more expensive the job is. To counter this, layout artists in the past have used a duotone process to help reduce costs. That means that every pixel in an image would be some combination of only two inks. Since most full-colour printing is done with at least four inks (cyan, magenta, yellow and black) plus any spot colours, working with only two inks can almost halve costs.

It didn't take photographers long to realise that this cost-saving measure could actually be used to create some very striking and creative imagery. Just adding that tint of colour can give life and interest to your images. Some photographers are so enamoured with the flavour of duotone imagery that they even use other techniques to mimic the appearance.

Here we explore the technical process for creating a true split-tone image. Photoshop's approach appears intimidatingly technical, but really is pretty easy. First, an image is converted to black and white (see page 96) and then split toning is applied. Photoshop provides fine control by allowing you to specify how much of each ink is given to each level of brightness. So you can easily assign one ink to the shadows and midtones and another to the highlights.

Traditionally, black is the first ink colour assigned. But we encourage you to experiment with different combinations to obtain more unusual results.

"This cost-saving measure can create some very striking imagery"

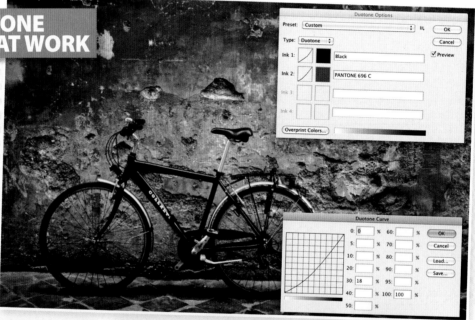

THE SPLIT-TONE INTERFACE AT WORK

Delicious duotones
By carefully using limited colours, duotones can add deep, rich flavour to photographs. This process infuses a certain character and mood in to an image.

Select a setting
Specify how many inks to use in the split-tone process. Choose from a single ink (ie monotone) to four (ie quadtone) and then assign the inks to be used.

Colour assignment
The control box allows you to assign specific colours to each ink. You may choose from a preset colour library or use the traditional picker.

Dangerous curves
Adjust points on the curve for each ink colour. This controls how much of the ink is given to each luminous value.

01 Majestic monotones
Usually monotone printing is straight black and white, which can look great. But the same process can be used for any ink colour, so experiment!

02 Dynamic duotones
Dual colouring is the main use for this tool. Two tones can add a subtle mood to a black-and-white photo. A common pairing is black and yellow.

03 Terrific tritones
Simply adding one more ink to the mix can open up many new possibilities. This combo of black, magenta and yellow creates a sepia-toned image.

Duotone in Photoshop Save on ink and add creativity to a photo with just one technique

01 Find a file
Let's begin with a full-colour image to work with. If you wish to follow along with our steps, open the accompanying file which we have provided.

02 Lose the colour
Select Image>Adjustments>Black & White. For our image, we set Reds to 9, Yellows to 103, Greens to 16, Cyans to 73, Blues to 10 and Magentas to 70.

03 True colour loss
Next go to Image>Mode>Grayscale to discard all colour information. Now go to Image>Mode>Duotone. In the control box, set Type to Duotone.

04 Ink 2 (PANTONE 696 c)
Click on the colour chip for Ink 2 to invoke another dialog. The default library is the PANTONE Solid Coated. Select the 'PANTONE 696 c' colour.

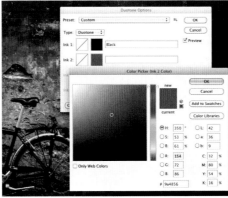

05 Color Picker
If you prefer the more traditional Color Picker over the library, click the Picker icon in the dialog. This method requires you to name the colour.

06 Curves ahead
With a colour picked, select the diagonal line icon for Ink 1. The new control box presents a graph that adjusts ink levels for each brightness level.

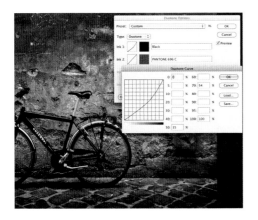

07 Small adjustments
Either by adding points to the curve or using the numerical boxes, set the 50 level to 35% and the 70 level to 54%. This will lighten midtones for starters.

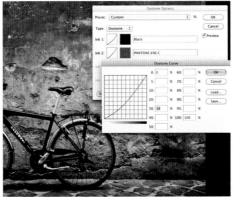

08 Further refinement
Now click on the curve icon for Ink 2. For this curve set the 30 level to 18%. This will help brighten the quarter tones and add more depth to the scene.

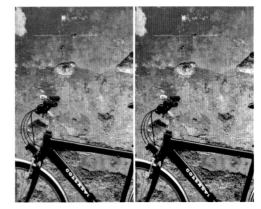

09 Before and after
Toggle the Preview box to see the results of your work contrasted with the greyscale version. You'll see the duotone has a much richer ambience.

ORIGINAL

Get perfect colour with Variations

In this quick tutorial will learn what Variations are, where to find and how to use them to make quick colour corrections in your image

The Variations command is a handy colour correction tool that uses visual colour presets and allows you to compare and preview the results in real-time. Variations combine several adjustment tools into a user-friendly environment that shows you thumbnails of your images that are variations of the original image, basically you just click the one that looks best for you or combine the colours until you get the colour variation of your choice. It is a helpful command to make quick adjustments in images that don't require precise colour adjustments. You can find the Variations command under the menu Images>Adjustments>Variations. If you are not able to see the Variations command in your Photoshop version, make sure you are using the 8-bit colour mode (go to Image>Mode and click 8-bit).

When you first open the Variations panel you see several image thumbnails which represent colour variations. On the top left you have your original image side by side with the current pick. The current pick works as your preview window. You have the choice to adjust the shadows, midtones, highlights and the saturation values. You can drag the Fine to Coarse slider to make the adjustment colour affect more or less the image you are working. You can also darken or lighten the image by clicking on the thumbnail windows on the right side. Each setting is independent of the others it means you can apply different colours settings for the shadows, midtones and highlights.

"Learning how the Variations works is an excellent way to understand colour correction"

01 Duplicate the image
The Variations make permanent changes on the image so the first thing we need to do is duplicate the layer to preserve the original image.

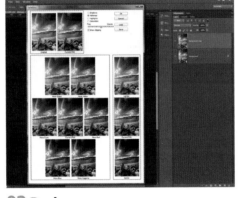

02 Darker
Click on the top layer and choose Image> Adjustments>Variations. On the variations dialog box, check the Midtones and click on the Darker thumbnail to make the midtones darker.

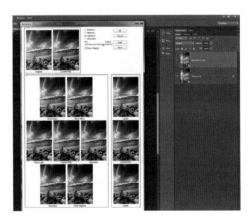

03 Improve highlights
Check the Highlights radio button and click to add More Blue colour variation. Remember to look at the Current Pick window to see the changes.

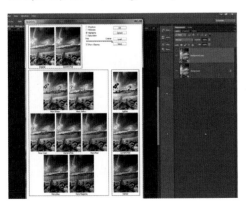

04 Fine/Coarse
The neon colours on the thumbnails windows shows how much of the image is affect by the variation, drag the Fine/Coarse slider to determine how much to apply.

05 Improve shadows
Check the Shadows radio box and drag the Fine/ Coarse slider to the centre. Click to add More Cyan colour variation and move the Fine/Coarse slider to control the variation.

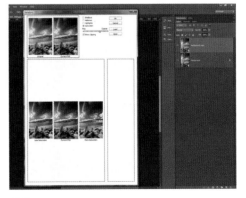

06 Saturation
Now check the Saturation radio box and drag the Fine/Coarse slider to the centre. Click to add More Saturation, and again control the amount by moving the Fine/Coarse slider.

Colour & tone

Undo Adjustments
To undo the adjustments made in the Variations Colour Panel, click on the Original Image window to reset the image and to start over all adjustments you've set previously.

Show Clipping
Clicking the Show Clipping box display a neon colour over the areas that has been affected by the adjustments. You aren't able to see the clipping when you adjust midtones.

All Variations
Here you can view how your final image would look with the different effects applied. Variations are shown in the menu, along with the original and current adjusted versions of your image.

07 Save image
Click the Save button, and name it 'House'. This will save you a lot of time and effort if you need to apply the same settings to another picture.

08 Load button
If you have other pictures that need the same kind of correction, you can use the Load button to locate the file you just saved and apply the same settings.

Sepia effect using variations
Combine variations to create a cool effect

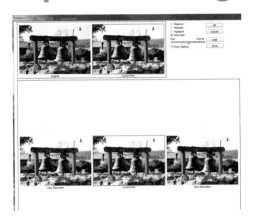

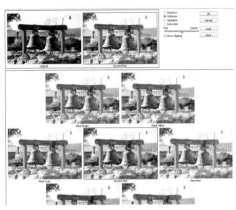

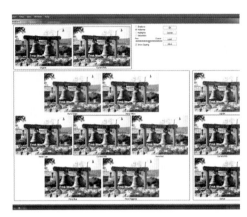

01 Less saturation
Duplicate the image and go to Image> Adjustments>Variations. Check the Saturation, and on the Saturation panel, click on Less Saturation; you can then click few more times until the image is almost desaturated.

02 Adjust Midtones
Now check the Midtones and click on More Yellow. You will then need to click few times to keep adding more yellow until you're happy with the midtone colours and drag the Fine/Coarse slider to the Fine position.

03 Darker
As a final touch to add a little impact to your image, you can click a couple times on the Darker thumbnail to add a little more contrast. Once you're finished you can then save your work and click OK.

Colour Variations examples
Apply different colour effects

More Yellow Variation

More Green Variation

More Cyan Variation

More Red Variation

More Blue Variation

More Magenta Variation

Layers

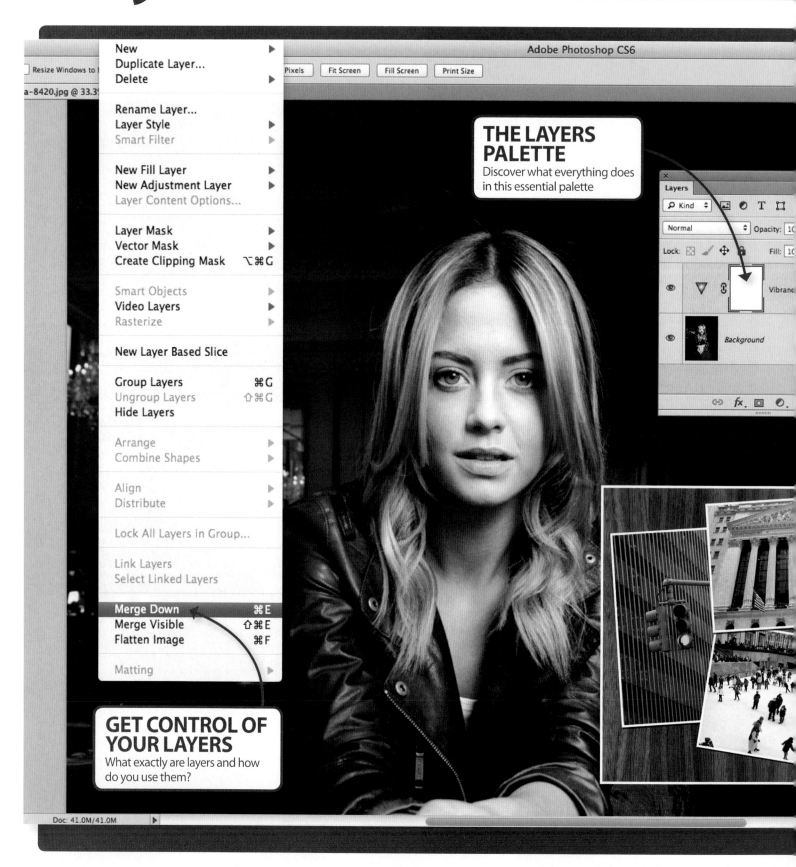

THE LAYERS PALETTE
Discover what everything does in this essential palette

GET CONTROL OF YOUR LAYERS
What exactly are layers and how do you use them?

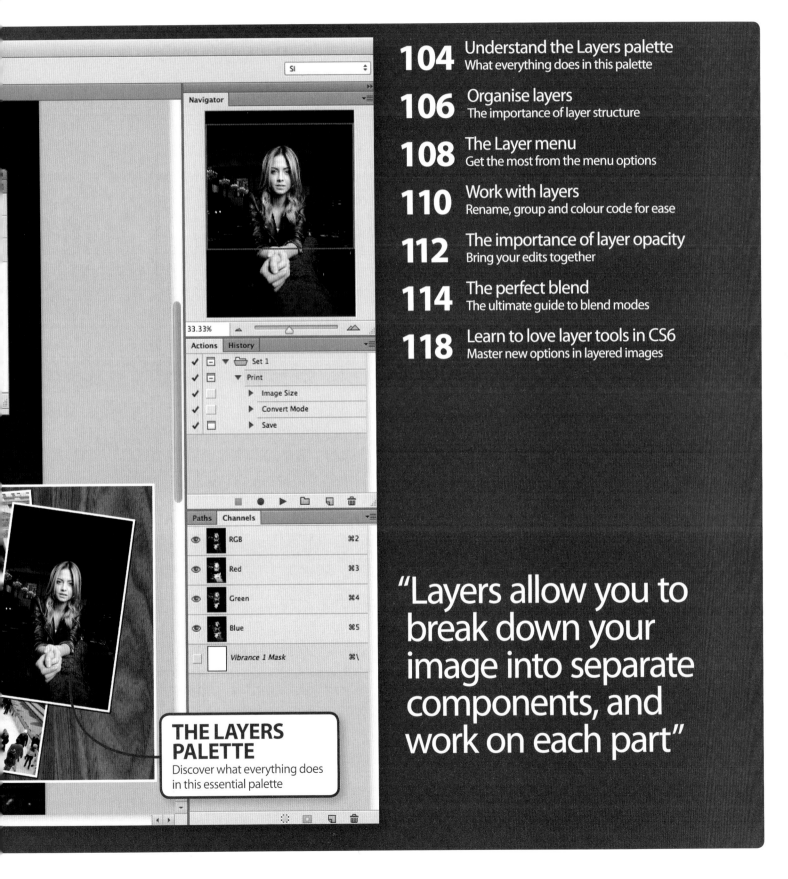

THE LAYERS PALETTE
Discover what everything does in this essential palette

"Layers allow you to break down your image into separate components, and work on each part"

Understand the Layers palette

Get to grips with this essential palette and learn how layers are arranged

Here's a palette that no Photoshop user should be without. Learning how layers are arranged inside this palette, and how to move them around, will open up many possible effects and ultimately improve your artwork. Layers come in many guises and can attach themselves to a composition in different ways. From blending together your photographs with seamless precision to using layer styles and adjustment in your work, they are the most adaptable aspect of Photoshop, and something we all should use. There are different levels of using layers, from the basics to the impressive. Read on through our guide to the Layers palette and find out how to do the bare essentials like adding new layers, organising them, blending them together and deleting them too. Whether you want to use just one layer or many, there are no limitations to how useful they can be in your edits.

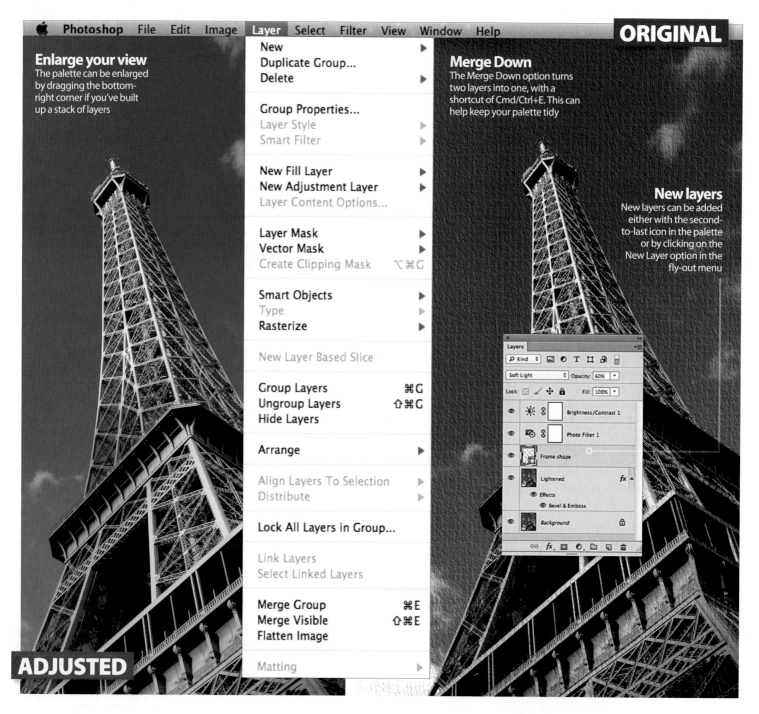

ORIGINAL

Enlarge your view
The palette can be enlarged by dragging the bottom-right corner if you've built up a stack of layers

Merge Down
The Merge Down option turns two layers into one, with a shortcut of Cmd/Ctrl+E. This can help keep your palette tidy

New layers
New layers can be added either with the second-to-last icon in the palette or by clicking on the New Layer option in the fly-out menu

ADJUSTED

Layers in Photoshop
What to expect when using layers in Photoshop

Blend modes
If you have more than one layer, select one of these blend modes to change the way they interact. From Multiply to Screen and Soft Light to Luminosity, they create slightly different effects.

Opacity
The opacity, or transparency, of each layer is adjustable and shown as a percentage. This lowers the visibility of the contents of a layer to help blend everything together. 0% Opacity completely hides the layer, whereas 100% shows it all.

Layer effect
Layer effects, also called styles, appear just below a layer with their own eye symbols. Bevel and Emboss, for example, is added by double-clicking on a layer. There are many styles available, opening up a whole different side to photo editing.

Layer stacks
New layers in an image are always added to the top of the stack. Drag layers around to reorder them and to change the appearance of the image. To unlock layers, simply double-click them.

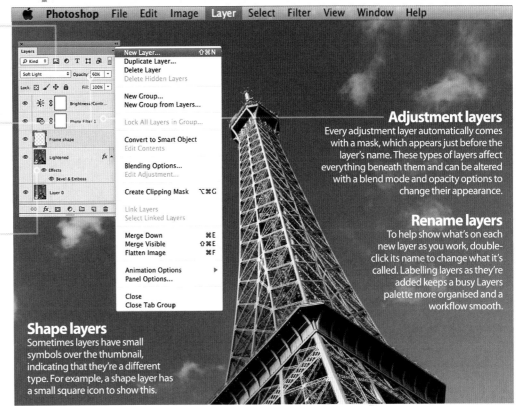

Adjustment layers
Every adjustment layer automatically comes with a mask, which appears just before the layer's name. These types of layers affect everything beneath them and can be altered with a blend mode and opacity options to change their appearance.

Rename layers
To help show what's on each new layer as you work, double-click its name to change what it's called. Labelling layers as they're added keeps a busy Layers palette more organised and a workflow smooth.

Shape layers
Sometimes layers have small symbols over the thumbnail, indicating that they're a different type. For example, a shape layer has a small square icon to show this.

Work in Photoshop Elements
How the palette works inside of Elements

Layer masks
Layer masks are shown either as solid black, solid white or a mix of both. Black parts of a mask show whatever's underneath while white keeps the current layer visible.

Empty pixels
Layers showing the chequerboard pattern are mostly empty layers. There may be a small object on it somewhere, such as a photo corner. Cmd/Ctrl-click over this thumbnail to convert it to a selection to reveal its location.

Switch layers on and off
Use the eye symbols next to each layer to turn them either on or off. Running your cursor across multiple eyes is a good way to turn more than one off quickly.

Deleting layers
If, for any reason, you no longer need to keep one or more layers, drag them onto the trash-can icon to remove them. If you change your mind, simply press Cmd/Ctrl+Z to undo and bring them back.

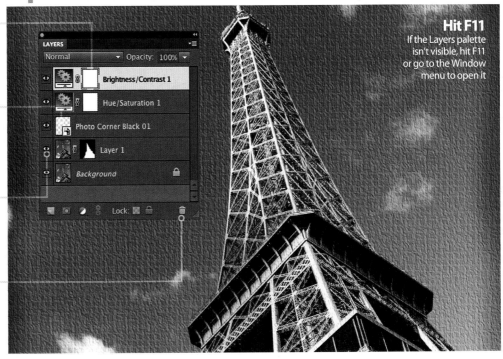

Hit F11
If the Layers palette isn't visible, hit F11 or go to the Window menu to open it

Organise layers

Photoshop wouldn't be Photoshop without layers

Layers form the basis for all editing, either from scratch or with a photo to start you off. Every layer contains new information that changes the way your image looks. Adding a new layer is easy enough, but keeping them organised is usually more difficult.

We take you through the various ways in which you can arrange a busy Layers palette. It could be a matter of merging or grouping a bunch of layers, so that you have a better sense of where everything is located inside the palette.

These techniques should help you become a more efficient Photoshop artist. Understanding the basics of using layers, and ordering them in the palette, is essential before jumping straight in the deep end. Try creating your own photo collage by following the steps opposite.

"Layers form the basis for all editing"

Controlling layers Different ways in which layers can be handled

Merge layers

Multiple layers in an image can be merged together for easier editing. This reduces the number of layers in your palette, and there are no limits on how many layers can be merged. To do this, select the layer you want to merge and go to the Layer menu and down to Merge Down (or press Cmd/Ctrl+E for its shortcut). When a layer is merged it joins with the one directly underneath it in the palette.

Making duplicates

If you ever want to make a direct copy of one layer during the editing stage, press Cmd/Ctrl+J, or drag a layer onto the Create a New Layer button in the palette. This makes an exact duplicate of whatever's on that layer and are usually called the same, except for having 'copy' after their name. Get into the habit of pressing this shortcut whenever you open an image, so that you always work non-destructively.

Create a Group
Keep a closer eye on your layers in a photo collage

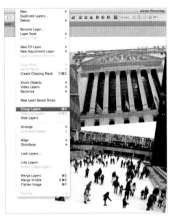

01 Create new document
In Photoshop, go to File> New. From the Preset drop-down list select International Paper, and then A4 for the Size. Give your file a name at the top of the Open dialog box, such as Photo Collage. Hit OK.

02 Place images
Go to Image>Image Rotation>90 CW. To open images one by one, head to File>Place and pick your first image. Hit Place and rotate and resize holding down Shift and using the corner points. Hit Enter to confirm its position.

03 Group up
When all of your photographs have been placed, click on the first image in the Layers palette and the last while holding Shift. Choose Layer>Group Layers. The layers should hide away inside a new Group folder.

04 Reorder layers
To change the order the layers overlap in the composition, click and drag a layer up or down the palette (Cmd/Ctrl and [/]). The current active layer is always highlighted blue, so you know at any stage which one you're working on.

Moving layers
The Move tool (V) set to Auto-Select: Layers at the top of Photoshop will instantly recognise the image's layer clicked on in your canvas.

Groups
Group folders can contain multiple photos, which will keep your palette looking tidy. Click on the drop-down arrow next to the folder's icon to hide or show the contents.

Rename layers
To rename a layer double-click on its name inside the palette. Doing this regularly will help you recognise what's on a layer, especially if its content is small.

Layer styles
Layer styles show up with the letters fx on the layer. The Stroke and Drop Shadow styles were added to these images (from Layer>Layer Style) to add extra elements to the design.

Locked layers
To lock a layer into position, click on the third button in the Layers palette under Lock. The wooden background in this image has been secured into place under the images.

The Layer menu

Learn how to get the most from the Layer menu

Layer menu
If your image has layers, you'll want to get familiar with this menu.

Start a new
New layers are added here and duplicates can be made.

Style it up
Layer Styles can be accessed through this menu to apply effects to a layer's contents.

Layers menu

New layers
Head into New at the top of the Layer menu and you have the option to perform a number of different tasks. Either add a layer or add a new group to contain layers in. Also, use Layer Via Copy to place the current selection onto a layer of its own.

Smart Objects
Convert a layer to a Smart Object to edit its contents on a separate document. They're especially useful if you have a part of your image with lots of detail, making it editable on its own. When Smart Objects have been edited, save the changes and your image will be updated.

This is the control centre for all things layered. From a layer mask to Smart Objects and adjustment layers to groups, there is a long and extensive list of handy options available to you.

Getting to know this menu will make your general Photoshop experience much easier. There are helpful options for applying photo edits, controlling the placement of layers, adding masks and merging layers

together all in the same handy place. In this feature we look at the most important options in the Layer menu, comparing it with what Elements has to offer in this department. The two versions have a similar array of options – but Elements is minus a few of the more advanced offerings that Photoshop CS users can revel in. The best place to start is at the top – so what are you waiting for?

WHAT'S IN ELEMENTS

How the Layer menu looks in Photoshop Elements

Duplicate and delete
The Duplicate and Delete Layer commands are in Elements. These will remove the layers completely from the document or create a direct copy in the palette for you to use.

Rename Layer
Use Rename Layer to stay organised when editing multiple elements. When a new layer is added you can give it a name in the pop-up box.

Simplify Layers
There's no Rasterize option in Elements, as the Simplify Layer command does the same job at turning vector layers into normal working ones. This means you'll be able to use the Eraser tool, among others, to edit it.

New Adjustment Layer
Elements has fewer adjustment layers than full Photoshop, but all the vital ones are there, enabling you to apply creative effects, which can be edited later on.

Layer Mask
Just like Photoshop, the layer mask options are the same in Elements. You'll add new masks to either show or hide parts of a layer. They can also be removed using this option in the Layer menu.

Create Clipping Mask
You can add a clipping mask through the Layer menu. This will place one layer into the contents of another, making it seem inside of it. Clipping masks can be released just as quickly as they can be added.

Which options to look out for…

Duplicate Layer
You can take the entire contents of a layer and place them onto a new one using the Duplicate Layer option. A new dialog box will pop up where you can set the Destination for the duplicate, whether that's a new document or the one you've got open.

Layer styles
The list of layer styles holds effects such as Drop Shadow and Inner Shadow, Bevel and Emboss, and Gradient Overlay too. These only change the layer you're working on and can be edited at any stage. A new layer style is attached in the Layers palette.

Create new adjustment layers
This is where the editing tools are kept. Adjustments – when applied as new layers – can be re-edited as many times as you need. Adjustments include Levels, Curves, Hue/Saturation and Photo Filter, for endless edits.

Layer masking
This provides a different route for adding and removing a layer mask. A Hide (black) or Reveal (white) layer mask can be applied through here, and if you have a selection you can use the additional options to apply a mask to that too. The best advice is to experiment with the tool.

Group layers
To help organise your Layers palette, select more than one layer and click on Group Layers. This will arrange all of the selected layers into one folder, so you can hide or show its contents and navigate to them easily. Use Ungroup Layers to remove the folder and release the layers.

Arrange layers
The menu has options to move layers around and rearrange them in the palette. Under Arrange you can use the Bring Forward and Send Backward commands to go one by one up or down the Layers palette. Invaluable when you're using blend mode effects.

Merge layers
Merge Down and Merge Visible at the bottom of the Layer menu will compress multiple layers into one. This not only keeps your Layers palette looking tidy, but also means you can edit the contents of both layers at once, rather than having to repeat the process multiple times.

Flatten Image
To merge all layers into one single one, select the Flatten Image option. The result is a locked Background layer that cannot be edited. Be sure to save a layered version of your image before flattening, just in case you change your mind and need to make edits later on.

Layers

Work with layers

Rename, group and colour code layers to keep your palette organised for later use

As you get a bit more proficient at using Photoshop, you'll find yourself using more and more layers. The numbers can quickly stack up and it can all become a little bit disorientating, making it vital that you keep your Layers palette nicely organised. The most important thing to do is to rename your layers, so that if you return to make edits a month or more down the line, you won't have to fiddle with each layer to work out just what it does. A name with a clear description like 'Eye colour change' saves you a lot of head scratching, so you can get right in and make the edits you need.

There are two other things that we can do to keep stuff organised. One is to place similar layers into a Group folder and the other is to make use of coloured labels. Normally one of these two options is enough to keep things ordered. There's one other advantage of using groups that goes beyond simple organisation, and that's that we can make sure adjustment layers apply only to those layers inside the group rather than everything below, kind of like a clipping mask but for more than one layer. A clipping mask you may recognise as a way of ensuring an adjustment layer only affects the pixel layer below it, and not everything else. You hold down Opt/Alt and click between the two layers to create one. To ensure that adjustment layers inside a group affect only that group, it's a matter instead of changing the default blending mode from Pass Through to Normal. It couldn't be easier.

> "A name with a clear description like 'Eye colour change' saves you a lot of head scratching, so you can get right in and make the edits you need"

01 Confusing layers
This image has had a lot of work and, as a result, layers have really stacked up. If we opened it later, it would be difficult to work out what does what.

02 Rename layers
The first thing we need to do is to rename each layer appropriately. Ctrl/right-click the text and select Rename or simply double-click the text.

03 Colour code
The other thing we can do is colour code our layers. In pre-CS6, Ctrl/right-click the 'layer' icon, select Layer Properties and pick a colour.

04 Select a colour in CS6
CS6 is slightly different, in that you just have to Ctrl/right-click on a layer to access the colours. Simply click one to apply it.

05 Devise a code
Use colours to highlight types of edits. Here we use Blue to describe global tonal changes, Red for local tonal changes and Green for detail work.

06 Search by kind
If you have CS6, use the Kind drop-down menu to locate layers according to type. You can search by name, group, colour or more.

QUICK PHOTOSHOP TIPS

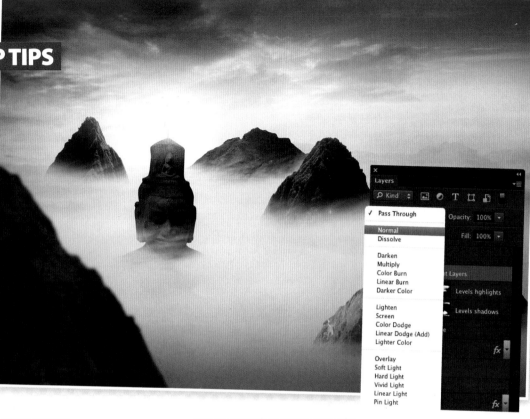

Mask a group

You can add a mask to a group to localise its effects, just as you can with a layer. Select the group and click the Add layer mask button located at the bottom of the Layers palette.

Save it right

Don't forget that to have the opportunity of accessing your layered file at a later date, you'll need to make sure that you save it in the Photoshop format (ie PSD) via File>Save As.

The right blend

You can ensure that an adjustment layer inside a group affects only the group layers by changing the group's blending mode from Pass Through to Normal.

Work smart

You can preserve the content of pixel-based layers by Ctrl/right-clicking and selecting Convert to Smart Object. Changes can then be reversed at any time.

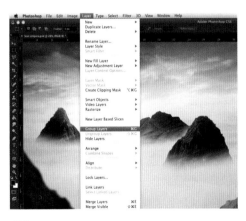

07 Group layers
We can also group our layers together. You can only Group adjacent layers so we'd need to change the layer order to group all of our colours together.

08 Select layers
Changing the layer order will alter the effects here, so we group adjacent colours only. Ctrl/right-click the first two layers and go to Layer>Group Layers.

09 Rename groups
We do this for all adjacent colours. We then double-click the name of each and rename it. Expand a group at any time by clicking its triangle.

Layers

The importance of layer opacity

Discover how to control the transparency of layers and added layer effects with the Opacity and Fill controls

Positioned at the top of the Layers palette, next to the blending mode dropdown menu, is a box called Opacity that contains a percentage figure. You can alter this value by clicking the triangle to the right and using the slider or alternatively you can click inside the figure box and enter a new amount manually. But just what does Opacity do?

Well, a layer's overall opacity determines to what degree it obscures or reveals the layer beneath it. A layer with 1% Opacity appears nearly transparent, whereas one with 100% Opacity appears completely opaque. If you think of these layers as sheets of acetate, you're essentially fading any work that you've applied onto that acetate as you drop the opacity.

There are a number of great uses for this; it can be helpful for temporarily lining up areas you've added to the image. Bring in eyes from another image, for example, and you've got to guess where they go unless you drop Opacity to something like 50%. Then you can easily see the detail behind, reposition with the Move tool before pushing Opacity back up to 100%. It can also be used to reduce the strength of an adjustment layer without having to go back into its settings. Just below the Opacity bar you'll notice a slider called Fill. This does the same thing as Opacity until you add a layer style such as Drop Shadow using the fx button at the base of the Layers palette. Dropping the Fill value reduces the opacity of pixels as per usual but doesn't touch the layer style – a great way of controlling one without touching the other.

> "A layer's opacity determines to what degree it obscures or reveals the layer beneath it"

UNDERSTANDING OPACITY AND FILL

Alter style settings
The added style is also listed underneath. You can turn visibility on and off using the 'eye' icon next to each layer and change settings by simply double-clicking the text.

ORIGINAL

01 Add text layer
Here's an image we've turned into an antique-looking photo to which we want to add some realistic text. Press 'T' to call up the Text tool.

02 The write stuff
Choose a suitable font (eg Cooper), colour and font size from the Options bar, click where you want the text and type. Simply click and drag to reposition.

03 Drop Shadow
We want to add a shadow effect to the text to help it stand out, so we hit Enter then click the fx menu in the Layers palette and select Drop Shadow.

The Opacity control

The Opacity slider adjusts the opacity of the whole layer, including any added layer styles, such as Drop Shadow in the case of our image.

The Fill control

The Fill slider controls opacity in the image too, however it only drops opacity of any pixel-based information on the layer, ignoring any added layer styles.

Adding layer styles

You can apply a layer style by clicking the fx button at the base of the Layers palette. An fx icon appears next to your layer to indicate a style has been added.

04 Shadow settings

In the Drop Shadow dialog, Angle is fine but we need to alter Distance to 20px. We use 15px Size to blur it a little and lower the Opacity to 50%.

05 Opacity slider

Next we need to fade the text to make it look realistic. Dropping Opacity to 20% doesn't look great, mainly because of Drop Shadow settings.

06 Fill slider

Time to try something different. With Opacity at 100%, we drop Fill to 0%, removing the text and just leaving the shadow. This does the trick nicely!

Layers

The perfect blend
Understand the blend modes in Photoshop

When people are new to Photoshop, they often tend to head to the Toolbar first. The Healing Brush, Dodge, Burn and Lasso tools can certainly help you to make powerful adjustments to your images, but to unlock the full potential of Photoshop you need to take a closer look at the Layers palette and the options it holds. It is in this palette that you will find the power to stack several elements and adjustments on top of each other, which can later be combined into one final image. In order to tell Photoshop how we want these individual layers to interact with the others, we can use blend modes and create exciting effects in no time.

Multiply
A useful blend mode that enables you to make the image significantly darker.

Screen
Screen is the exact opposite of Multiply and lightens the image up with ease.

Soft Light
Another handy blend mode for adding contrast to your images.

Two layers
Blend modes can only be applied when there are at least two layers, so you have to drag your background layer to the Create a New Layer button next to the trashcan at the base of the Layers palette.

The Blend Mode menu
The Blend Mode menu contains 27 different blend modes, some with very dramatic effects, some with effects that are very subtle and some producing effects that only work when some other aspect of the layer has been adjusted.

BOOST CONTRAST WITH SOFT LIGHT

A quick and easy way to improve overall image contrast

Soft Light is one of the most useful blend modes and useful for so many different effects and outcomes. It adds great contrast without being as drastic as some of its neighbours such as Overlay or Hard Light. One of the best uses for the blend mode is to ensure that your black and white shots don't look too flat.

Deeper shadows
When you use the Soft Light blend mode you will notice that the shadow areas become slightly deeper and richer.

ORIGINAL

Brighter highlights
Simultaneously, the highlight areas get brighter when using Soft Light. It's this combination of deeper shadows and brighter highlights that creates the high-contrast appearance.

Crispness
When you use Soft Light the image looks crisper and sharper, appearing to have gained clarity and definition.

Improve monochrome shots
Blend for a quick and easy way to add impact

01 Duplicate the background
The first step is always to make a duplicate of the Background layer (for safety) by dragging it to the Create a New Layer button at the very bottom of the Layers palette.

02 Select Soft Light
Now you should select Soft Light from the Blend Mode menu at the top of the Layers palette. You'll instantly see a big difference in your image, giving it a lot more impact.

03 Opacity
The Opacity slider enables you to reduce the effect of the blend mode if it looks slightly too strong for the image. Lowering the opacity can correct this quickly and easily.

BLEND MODES AT A GLANCE
A quick look at what each blend mode can do

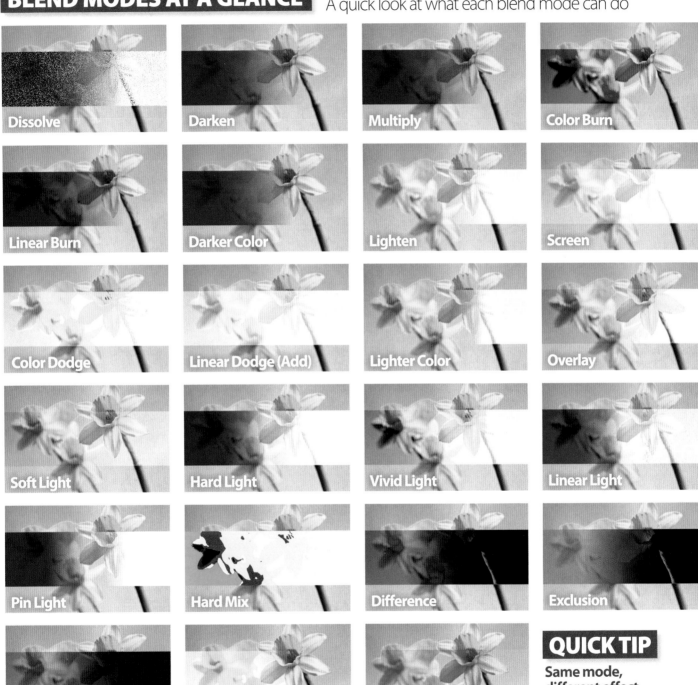

Dissolve | Darken | Multiply | Color Burn

Linear Burn | Darker Color | Lighten | Screen

Color Dodge | Linear Dodge (Add) | Lighter Color | Overlay

Soft Light | Hard Light | Vivid Light | Linear Light

Pin Light | Hard Mix | Difference | Exclusion

Subtract | Divide | Hue

Saturation | Color | Luminosity

QUICK TIP

Same mode, different effect

It's always worth remembering that while this guide is handy as a quick reference, the result is completely dependent on each individual image. Inevitable factors such as the colour and opacity of the layer beneath can massively alter the effect each mode has. When it comes to trying blend modes, the best advice is always to experiment!

Layers

ORIGINAL

Use Multiply for a subtle vignette
This mode can darken your images

Multiply is perfect for overexposed shots and works best when applied selectively to specific areas. One of the best applications for Multiply is for creating a subtle vignette around the corners of your shots.

01 Create a new layer
Again, begin by duplicating your Background layer. Drag the Background down onto the Create a New Layer button at the bottom of the palette.

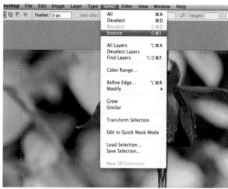

02 Create a selection
Now, using the Rectangular Marquee tool (M) start to drag a selection somewhere around the perimeter of your image.

03 Invert the selection
Press Cmd/Ctrl+Shift+I on your keyboard to invert the selection – this ensures that it's the perimeter of the image, rather than the centre that is selected. You can also do this via Select>Inverse.

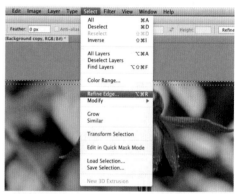

04 Refine the selection
Go to Select>Refine Edge. This will bring up a dialog box that enables you to feather the selection so that the transition to the darker edges from the lighter central area is smooth and subtle.

05 Adjust the Feather amount
Choose an appropriate value for the Feather. For high-resolution images, you should opt for a pixel value of around 204.

06 Multiply mode
Now select Multiply from the blend mode drop-down on the Layers palette. This will darken the whole image at this stage, but don't worry.

07 Add a layer mask
Now head to the bottom of the Layers palette and click the Add Layer Mask button, which is the third icon from the left.

Unchanged skin tone
We have left the model's skin and the rest of the image unchanged.

Use the Screen blend mode for a brighter view

Use this mode for beauty retouches

When you apply the Screen blend mode to a layer, the whole image gets much brighter. Much like the Multiply blend mode, this works far better when applied as a local adjustment rather than to the entire image. Once again, you can use layer masks to refine which areas of the image are adjusted.

ORIGINAL

Bright eyes
Using the Screen blend mode and a layer mask enables you to brighten the model's eyes.

01 Begin the adjustment
As before, you must begin by duplicating your Background layer. This enables you to begin the process of applying very selective, localised adjustments to the image.

02 Select Screen
Use the drop-down menu to select the Screen blend mode. You'll notice the whole image will look far brighter and overexposed, but you'll soon be able to easily fix this.

03 Behind the mask
03Be sure to hold down Opt/Alt on your keyboard and then click Add Layer Mask at the bottom of the Layers palette. This creates a black layer mask and makes the effect of the Screen mode invisible.

04 Brushstrokes
Press B on your keyboard to select the Brush tool. Set your Foreground colour to white at the bottom of the Toolbar. Paint over the eyes, ensuring that the layer mask is highlighted in the Layers palette.

05 Opacity matters
There's a fairly high chance that this effect will be too extreme, so go to the Opacity slider at the top of the Layers palette and simply drag it to the left to reduce the effect of your Screen layer.

Layers

Learn to love layer tools in CS6

Master new options in your layered images, with an improved palette that manages your projects better than ever before

The Layers palette has been part of Photoshop for a seriously long time. Without it, artists and designers – even enthusiasts – wouldn't be able to exact the creative freedom they do. The Layers palette is integral to every workflow for every creative user.

As this is used on a day-to-day basis, Adobe has applied numerous improvements to the way in which Photoshop layers work that will accelerate your own creative application and thus time management in this on-screen space. The Layers palette has never been so advantageous.

Here, we'll explore some of the new key enhancements that will make your layered design a whole lot easier and more efficient; for example, automatic interpolation, which afford intuitive pixel resizing of photo images – this means no more toing and froing from the Preferences options.

We'll also explore the new Layer Search menu, which lets you find exactly what you are looking for through key phrase and setting categories. A great addition to the software, the ability to search in this way means that working on files with a lot of layers a lot easier. Labelling your layers correctly is, as always, vital to the success of larger projects.

Version CS6 also opens up the ability to apply layer settings across multiple types, instead of singularly, which was ultimately counter productive.

Affecting multiple layers also extends to duplicating them, which can now be applied to a sequence of layers and even groups instantaneously, pressing Cmd/Ctrl+J. But it's not just individual layers that have been effected; groups have also been altered.

You can now pop layers into a group, applying a Layer Style or Clipping Mask, which affects the folder and subsequently its content – but not the actual layers directly within.

This means you can apply far more nondestructive effects, which is always a big plus. In a nutshell, Adobe has provided a Layers palette 2.0; now the best it's ever been at managing your projects.

DO MORE WITH YOUR LAYERS

Layer Style Group
The Layer Group can now also be applied to with Layer Styles. Couple these with your Clipping and Layer Mask application to create interesting effects.

New 'Blend If' icon
The Layer Style 'Blend If' option lets you blend lighting in two layers. Its application used to be easily forgotten, due to the absence of a Layers icon, but Adobe has now included this.

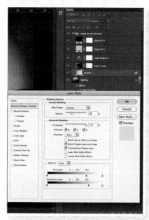

Interpolation options
When resizing, the Interpolation drop option appears in the Options menu. Set this to Bicubic Automatic for Photoshop to apply the correct smoothing to sharpening of pixels when resizing.

Colour tabs
Sorting layers through colour coding is much faster in CS6, by applying colour tabs to multiple layers. Ctrl/Cmd-click your sequence of layers, Ctrl-click the Visibility icon (eye) and select your preference.

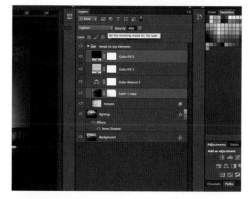

Multiple alterations
Blending Mode and Opacity/Flow settings can now be applied to multiple selected layers, saving time and effort. Again, Simply Ctrl/Cmd-click your sequence of layers then choose your settings.

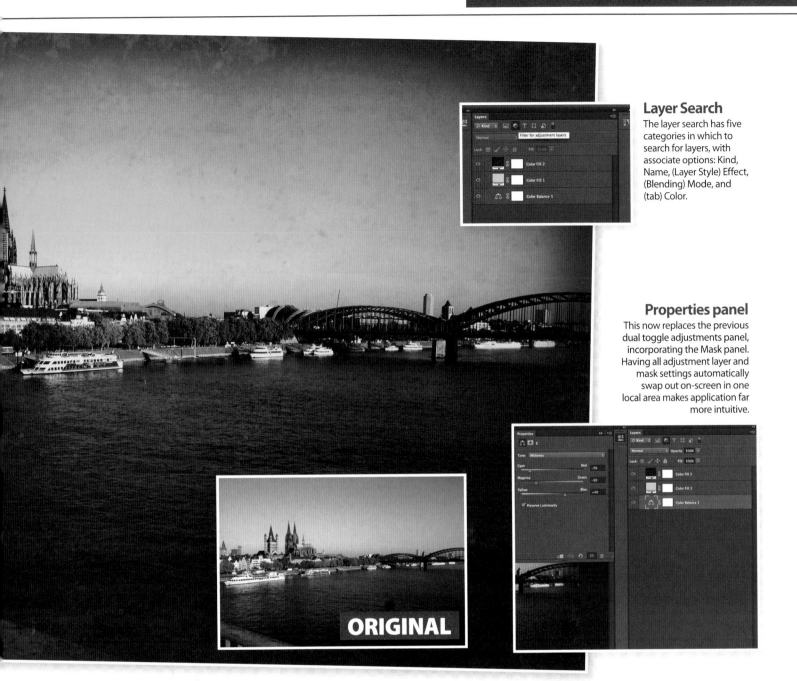

ORIGINAL

Layer Search

The layer search has five categories in which to search for layers, with associate options: Kind, Name, (Layer Style) Effect, (Blending) Mode, and (tab) Color.

Properties panel

This now replaces the previous dual toggle adjustments panel, incorporating the Mask panel. Having all adjustment layer and mask settings automatically swap out on-screen in one local area makes application far more intuitive.

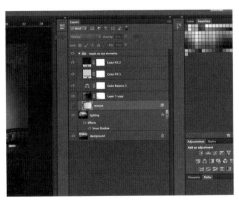

Edit Later Group

If you wanted to apply masking or clipping to grouped content you'd have to do it to every layer within. Now just apply your Clipping or Layer Mask to edit all, non destructively.

Rasterize Layer Style

Rasterizing was impossible in previous Photoshop versions; instead you had to separate layer from effect. Now you can merge the two, with the Rasterize Layer Style option (Ctrl-click layer).

Visual cues

Blending Mode and Opacity values used to disappear once you switched off a layer's visibility. This meant having to waste time reactivating, but now these values show, though greyed out.

Retouching

"Remove blemishes and correct problem areas in your pics"

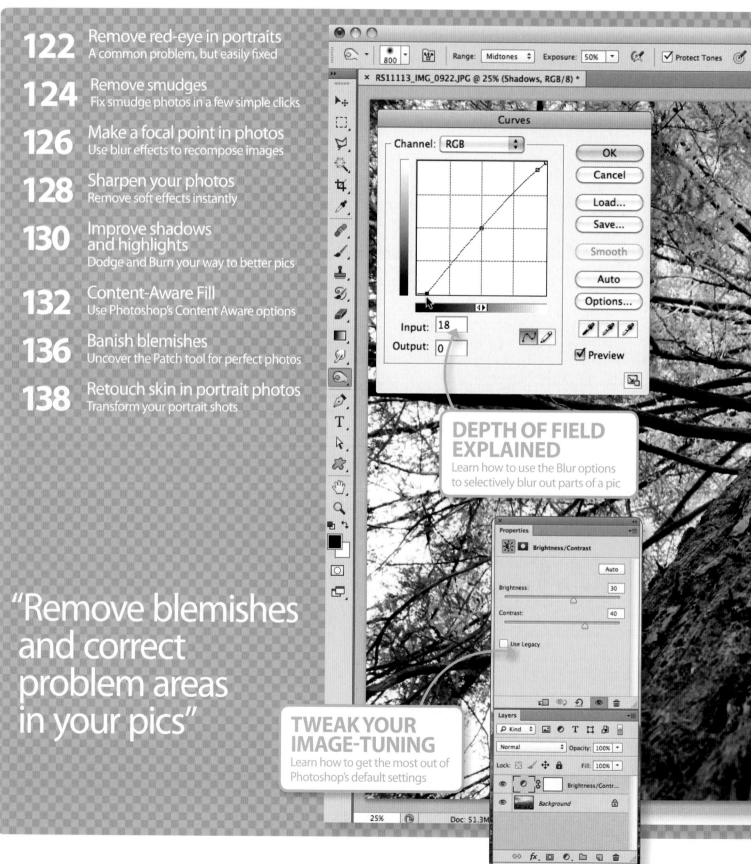

DEPTH OF FIELD EXPLAINED
Learn how to use the Blur options to selectively blur out parts of a pic

TWEAK YOUR IMAGE-TUNING
Learn how to get the most out of Photoshop's default settings

Adobe Photoshop CS6

Darken
Multiply
Color Burn
Linear Burn
Darker Color

Lighten
Screen
Color Dodge
Linear Dodge (Add)
Lighter Color

✓ Overlay
Soft Light
Hard Light
Vivid Light
Linear Light
Pin Light
Hard Mix

Difference
Exclusion
Subtract
Divide

Hue
Saturation
Color
Luminosity

Opacity: 70%

Fill: 100%

ows

ground

T

SI

Navigator

25%

Actions   History

RS11113_IMG_0922.JPG

Snapshot 1

Blending Change

Blending Change

Blending Change

Blending Change

Blending Change

Blending Change

Blending Change

Blending Change

Blending Change

Paths   Channels

RGB   ⌘2

Red   ⌘3

Green   ⌘4

Blue   ⌘5

EASY EDITING
Discover the best tools and tricks for the job

EDIT THROUGH CHANNELS
Discover what Channels are and why they're important

Retouching

Remove red-eye in portraits

Cure the curse of red-eye in your portrait photos with the dedicated Red Eye Removal tool in Photoshop

Red-eye is one of the most common flaws in portrait photos, caused by the use of flash in close-up situations and low light. If you're taking shots at a party or in a bar, you can almost guarantee that some of them will suffer. There are ways to prevent red-eye in-camera (see the side panel, right), but if the snap's already on your computer or memory card, then it's time to turn to your image-editing software for a quick fix.

All photo-editing software will have a quick fix for red eye, so it doesn't matter whether you have splashed the cash on Adobe Photoshop, or are using an older version, or even Elements – the basics are always the same. In most cases there will be a built-in one-click option for super-speedy results.

Red eye is caused by the flash from your camera. The flash light is too quick for the pupil to close, so the light passes through the eye, reflecting off the back of the eyeball and back out through the eyeball. The camera picks up this light and records it. It's red due to the amount of blood at the back of the eye, behind the retina. Red eye strength varies between people too; lighter coloured eyes show a stronger red eye effect than darker eyes. The effect is also seen in animal portraits.

Here we will show you, using the image provided, how you can use the simple controls in Photoshop to combat this natural effect.

> "All photo-editing software will have a quick fix for red eye, so it doesn't matter whether you have Photoshop or Elements"

THE ELEMENTS METHOD

Auto or manual – the choice is yours!

01 Elements offers three editing modes: Quick, Full and Guided. Both Quick and Full can be used to fix red-eye in slightly different ways. We'll start in the Quick mode.

02 In older versions of Elements, go to the General Fixes option in the right-hand panel, and click Auto next to Red Eye Fix. In newer versions, select Auto Red Eye Fix from the Enhance menu.

03 Should the Auto option not clear up red eye to your satisfaction, then try entering the Full edit option instead. Locate the Red Eye Removal Tool in the left-hand toolbar to begin.

04 In the top toolbar, there is an Auto option. However, you can do it manually too. There are two settings here you can tweak to suit, but the defaults are usually fine.

05 Click and drag the tool to create a box over your first problem pupil. Let go of the mouse button, and the red eye will be removed. Repeat for all pupils in a picture.

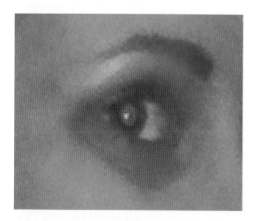

01 Load and zoom
Load the image with the problem and zoom in to the left eye. This may be around 300% depending on the file size.

02 Duplicate
Duplicate the Background layer in the Layers palette so it can be scrapped if you need to revert back to the original.

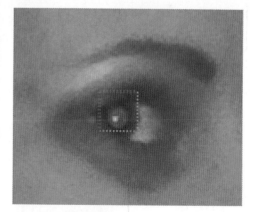

03 Use the tool
The Red Eye Removal tool is in the same group as the Healing Brush. Draw a large box covering the pupil and iris.

ORIGINAL

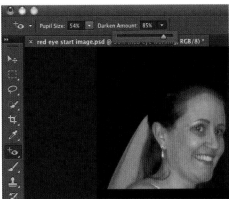

04 And repeat…

Repeat the process on the other eye and merge the layers when you're done so that you can keep the file size down.

05 The options

If the eye still looks slightly red, undo the action then increase the Darken Amount from 50% to 85% and try again.

06 Tweak the result

If the effect hasn't covered all the red area then increase the Pupil Size. If there's some black bleeding into the iris, reduce the Pupil Size.

Remove smudges

Remove lens smudges and banish blemishes in minutes

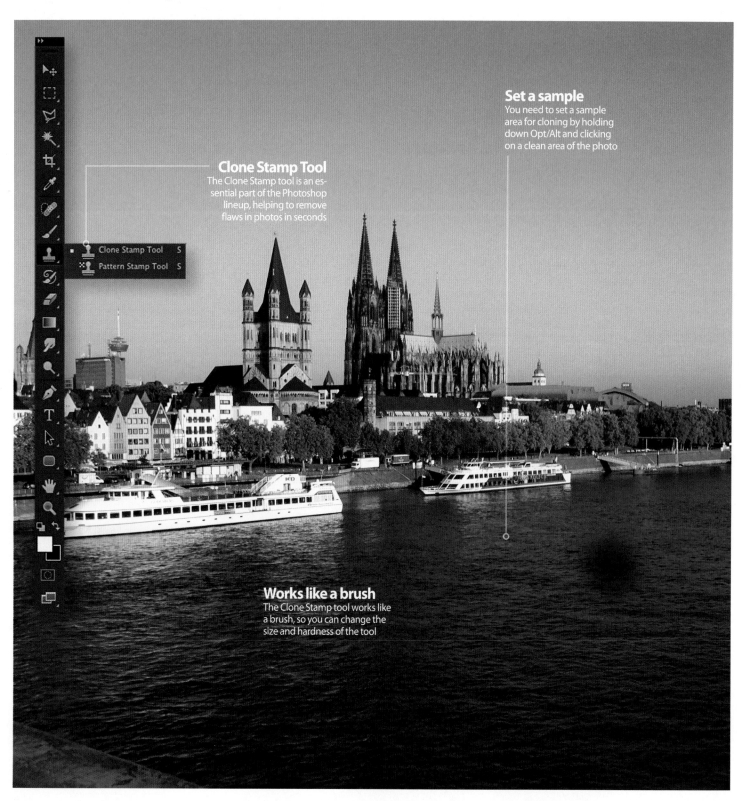

Set a sample
You need to set a sample area for cloning by holding down Opt/Alt and clicking on a clean area of the photo

Clone Stamp Tool
The Clone Stamp tool is an essential part of the Photoshop lineup, helping to remove flaws in photos in seconds

Clone Stamp Tool   S
Pattern Stamp Tool   S

Works like a brush
The Clone Stamp tool works like a brush, so you can change the size and hardness of the tool

The Clone Stamp tool is one of the most commonly used healing tools in Photoshop and Photoshop Elements. It can be tricky to get to grips with at first, but is a fantastic tool once you do. To use it, you pick a sample area within your image and paint it over a blemish or flaw to hide it from view. The trick to a good clone is to make sure that you sample a number of times so that your new areas blend perfectly. Sample from as close to the flaw as possible and keep your brush size small. The process takes time but it is worth it.

PHOTOSHOP OPTIONS

Airbrush
Click this airbrush icon if you want to be able to build up effects gradually as you apply them for a subtler effect.

Aligned
This enables you to use multiple strokes to paint on one copy of your sampled area.

Ignore
Click this little circular icon with a line through it and Photoshop will ignore any adjustment layers applied to the image when cloning.

PHOTOSHOP ELEMENTS OPTIONS

Brush setup
Here you can pick the type of brush tip that you want to use as well as the size, blend mode and opacity options.

Sample All Layers
It pays to do your cloning on a new, blank layer in case you make a mistake, and ticking this box means that you can pick the sample from the original layer and apply it to the new blank one.

Overlay
Click on this little icon made up of two squares and you can pick options for whether you want to see the overlay or not.

Do a basic clone   Remove a small lens mark in Photoshop

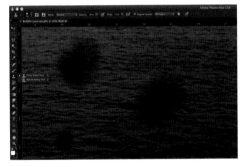

01 Find the flaw
This image is a great landscape that is ruined by the finger marks from the lens that appear over the water. This is the sort of task that the Clone Stamp excels at, as the blemish is surrounded by an uncluttered background. Zoom in to begin.

02 Set up the tool
Select the Clone Stamp tool from the side Toolbar. Now head up to the top Options bar and pick a Soft Round brush tip. Go ahead and set the size so it is about a quarter of the size of the flaw so that you get a decent sample.

03 Clone away
Now hold down Opt/Alt on your keyboard. Click on a clean area of the sea to sample it and then click again to brush over the flaw. You will need to keep resampling from an area of sea close to each bit of the smudge as you work for a realistic result.

Heal skin in Elements   Use the Clone Stamp on a blank layer to hide blemishes

01 Add a new layer
Open up your chosen image and add a new, blank layer at the top of the layer stack. Rename it something like Skin Heal. This means that whatever work you do will be non-destructive – you can hide the layer at any time during the process and see your original shot.

02 Sample All Layers
Pick the Clone Stamp tool and set the brush size so that it is slightly larger than the flaw that you want to heal, as the area we want to cover is so small. Make sure that the Sample All Layers checkbox is ticked, so you can work on the blank top layer but still sample from the original photo underneath.

03 Spot be gone!
Hold down Opt/Alt and sample a clean area of skin very close to the blemish. You can use the Overlay option here (click the icon of two overlapping squares) to see a preview of the sample as you hover over the blemish to ensure it will cover it evenly. Click to apply.

Retouching

Make a focal point in photos

Quickly fix distracting backgrounds with the Gaussian Blur filter, helping to bring the focus to the main subject

Getting close to a subject can make for a wonderful photo, and can make a real impact. The aim is to have one object nice and crisp, with a blurred background sitting quietly behind. Most digital cameras these days will have a dedicated Macro mode, which helps to achieve this effect, however these are not foolproof.

All too often, the background can end up distracting the eye so that what should be the centre of attention is lost. An easy way of sorting this is to blur the background even more, faking a new depth of field. This involves selecting the background and then setting a Gaussian Blur to work.

There are lots of blur options in Photoshop, but this one works perfectly when trying to create this kind of effect. Our butterfly image is lovely to start off with, but the leaves and flowers are rather distracting. Our aim is to softly blur these out, leaving the butterfly pin sharp and eye catching.

You can try this method out on any of your images to practise the effect, however each image will need slightly different settings. We give the values that we used in the step by step below, so you can use these as a starting point. If the effect looks too strong, then try lowering the Amount of the Radius, until you are happy with the result.

In order to perform the blur on just the background, we need to make a selection of the area that we want to blur – take a look at our dedicated Selections section, starting on page 164.

> "You can try this method out on any of your images in order to practise the effect"

HOW WE ACHIEVED THE EFFECT

Selections

We will go into selections in more detail later in the book, but it is essential to know how to only work on the background in this project. We use the Magnetic Lasso tool, which you can draw around an object and it will find the edges automatically.

ORIGINAL

01 Select the background

We are going to use the Magnetic Lasso Tool to select our background. Pick it from the toolbar and then go up to Feather in the top Options bar.

02 Set the Feather
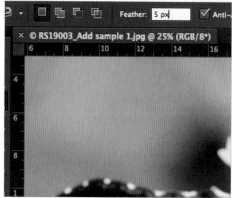
Enter a setting of 5 as this will soften the selection edge so there isn't a harsh line between the blurred area and the sharp part of your image.

03 Draw around the object

The Magnetic Lasso clings to the edges. Click once on the rim of a wing and drag the tool into the gaps and back out to cover each part.

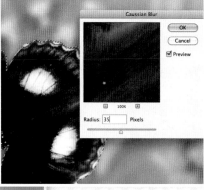

Blurred background

We have applied the Gaussian Blur to just the background of the image, which makes the butterfly really stand out, making for a better image.

Feathering

We have used the Feather control to help soften the line between the bit that we blurred and the bit that we didn't. If we didn't do that, then we would run the risk of making it look as though the butterfly was stuck on to the background – stopping it from looking photorealistic.

Sharp subjects

The aim of this project is to ensure that the main subject (in this case the butterfly) appears perfectly sharp, which it does as soon as the background has been blurred.

ENHANCED

04 Tweak away

You need to select the background. If your selection line goes astray, just hit the Backspace button on your keyboard to undo the last shape.

05 Final selection

Draw all around the background until you get to the first point you made. A little 'o' will appear next to the Magnetic Lasso icon.

06 Now blur

Go to the Filter menu and pick Blur>Gaussian Blur and enter a setting of 35. Press OK, then go to Select>Deselect to see the final result.

Retouching

ORIGINAL

Sharpen your photos

We show you how to fix camera blur using the Unsharp Mask filter

Camera blur is an extremely common problem and if you are like us, you will have your fair share of images that aren't as sharp as you'd like. Luckily, Photoshop and Photoshop Elements have a whole host of tools to help you to correct this flaw. You can use the Sharpen filters (see the Filters section of this book) or you could use the Sharpen tool to selectively sharpen certain areas of an image for effect, however there is a quick and easy method, which is what we are going to be looking at in this mini tutorial.

Whether you have Photoshop or Photoshop Elements you have at hand a nifty way of dealing with blurring problems in the shape of the Unsharp Mask filter. It seems strange that something called 'unsharp' actually does the opposite, but that's just one of Adobe's little quirks! It's easy to access the tool by going to either the Filter menu or the Enhance menu, depending on which version of Photoshop you are using.

You control the tool using a series of sliders in the dialog box that comes up and the Preview window means you can see exactly what effect the edit is having. It works by emphasising the object edges in an image, tricking the eye into thinking that the image is crisper than it is. This transforms soft, blurry images into crisper renditions of themselves.

We're going to show you quickly and easily how to use the Unsharp Mask for yourself using a typical image, which is blurred. We have provided this image for you to practise on, but you may want to use your own.

"Transforms soft, blurry images into crisper renditions"

THE UNSHARP MASK

Finding the tool
Click the Enhance or the Filter menu, depending on which version of Photoshop you are using, then select the Unsharp mask option from the drop-down list.

Dialog box
This is the Unsharp Mask box that pops up, which has all of the tools that you need to sharpen your image to perfection using a selection of sliders.

Preview
Make sure that Preview is ticked so that you can see the changes as you make them on your photo. The window in the dialog box lets you zoom in closer to see what's happening.

Amount
Experiment with the Amount control to change how strong the effect of the filter is. To keep it realistic try and use the lowest value possible for the effect that you want.

01 Open the command
In Photoshop, go to Filters>Sharpen>Unsharp Mask; in Elements go to Enhance>Unsharp Mask. Make sure the little Preview box is checked.

02 Set the Amount
This sets how intense the sharpening is – move to the right to increase the intensity. We have a bit of work to do here with this image, so move it to 179.

03 The Radius
The higher the setting, the more extreme the effect. We used 2.8. Threshold calms the edit down but a setting of 0 was all that was needed here.

Improve shadows and highlights

Image adjustments made easy with Dodge and Burn

The Dodge, Burn and Sponge tools are designed to edit exposure and colour in an image.

Being tools, rather than adjustment layers or filters, they give you a great deal of control and accuracy. They enable you to choose the exact position and strength of the effects by painting them onto the image. Adobting a brush as the main way in which you apply the treatments to your imagery, you use your mouse to add the effect wherever you need to.

Let's start with the Dodge and Burn tools, which are highly important when it comes to creating digital art and making subtle but effective photo edits. The two tools reflect the traditional photographic techniques used to enhance lighting, with Dodge brightening areas and Burn darkening them. You may have one subject in your image that has been under or overexposed, and that's where these two come into play. Lastly, the Sponge tool deals with colour, and can be set up to add or remove colour to a subject.

Big is better
Choose a large Size to cover more of your image at once, which helps to keep changes subtle.

A good range
Use the Range selection in the Options bar to change how each tool can perform.

Control
With edits made to a Background Copy layer, blend modes and Opacity can be adjusted to control the effect.

The three tools
The three tools are grouped together with the same shortcut key of O. Ctrl/right-click over the icon to reveal all three tools.

Dodge and Burn tools
Change how the light falls in your images

01 Burn tool
The Burn tool is used to darken parts of your image. Select the tool from the Toolbar or by pressing O on your keyboard. Check that you have the Burn tool selected, and not the Dodge tool, by clicking and holding over the icon to view all available options.

02 Range
In the Options bar, there are three Ranges to choose from: Shadows, Midtones and Highlights. We'll only need the first two for the Burn tool. Select Shadows and set the Exposure to 40%. Drag the Background layer onto the Create a New Layer button to duplicate it.

03 Darken
Set your brush size to a large, soft tip from within the Options at the top. Paint with the tool over the shadows in the background parts of your image. If the effect is too strong then lower the Opacity of tool. Use this sparingly over your image until the shadows darken.

04 Add contrast
Set the Range option to Midtones. Paint once more over the background elements to add further contrast. Try not to paint over one area too many times, as the effect will get increasingly stronger.

05 Dodge settings
Grab the Dodge tool, which is used to brighten up subjects. In the Options bar, set Range to Midtones and set Exposure to 40%. Paint over foreground parts of your image to brighten them up.

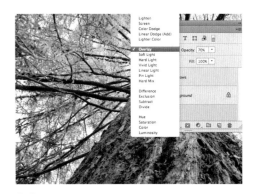

06 Overlay mode
See how much the lighting has changed by clicking on the eye symbol of the duplicate layer to turn it on and off. Alter the blend mode to Overlay and lower its Opacity to 70% for more contrast.

Make colours sing
Boost colours with the Sponge tool

01 Layers palette
Load your image into Photoshop or Elements. Duplicate the Background layer by dragging it from the Layers palette onto the Create a New Layer button. A Background Copy layer will appear.

02 Tool's Mode
Select the Sponge tool (O) and, in the Options bar, set Mode to Saturate and Flow to 30%. Tick the Vibrance box. Select an appropriate brush size for your image and then set it to 0% Hardness.

03 Paint saturation
Paint with the Sponge tool over the colour in your image and you'll see the saturation increase, adding more life. Don't overdo the effect, as noise will start to gather and degrade the quality.

Content-Aware Fill

The new Content-Aware toolset can seem more like magic than technology. Learn how to harness the power!

Arthur C. Clarke once wrote that "any sufficiently advanced technology is indistinguishable from magic." Photoshop's amazing Content-Aware technology fits rather well into that category, as you will soon see for yourself.

For many years, digital art teachers have been hammering home the point that objects in a photograph cannot merely be deleted – those pixels need to be replaced instead. At a first glance, the Content-Aware tools appear to prove that axiom completely and entirely wrong. Simply selecting a background element and pressing Backspace will remove those pixels and leave a gaping hole in your image. Add Shift to the mix, however, and that's when the magic really happens! That key combination triggers the Edit>Fill dialog that offers Content-Aware as a fill option. Photoshop then analyses the selected pixels and replaces them with an intelligent mash-up of the surrounding pixels. That same algorithm has now been applied to other tools, such as Patch, Spot Healing Brush and, more recently, Content-Aware Move.

Over the next few pages, we are going to show you some real-world applications for this technology so you will see how you can best use the various tools in order to speed up your retouching and improve the finished quality.

> "Photoshop analyses the selected pixels and replaces them with an intelligent mash-up of the surrounding pixels"

Speed up retouching

Improve the final quality of your shots with the Content-Aware tools

Background cleaner
With Content-Aware Fill you can seamlessly remove unwanted background elements without touching the Clone Stamp tool.

Don't crop, move!
Instead of trimming down the photo, the amazing new Content-Aware Move tool can reposition subjects for stronger compositions.

CORRECTED

01 Create a background copy
You should be aware that the Content-Aware tools will directly alter pixel information, so make sure that you work on a copy of the Background just in case you need to start over again or refer to the original. You'll be relieved you've done this.

02 Loose selection
Create a fairly loose selection around the little girl in the picture here. Make sure that you don't make it too tight, otherwise the tool will leave a halo. Also remember that you need to use the Lasso tool (L) there rather than the Quick Selection tool.

Light spill eraser
The Spot Healing Brush can use Content-Aware technology to make quick and light work of strange shadows from light spill.

Away, stray hairs
Content-Aware technology is ideal for easily removing those pesky flyaway strands of hair.

Content-Aware patch
The Patch tool has been retooled to be Content-Aware and it's now more useful than ever before!

03 Move it!
Grab the Content-Aware Move tool which is under the Spot Healing Brush (J) and set the Mode to Move. Slide the selection to the left to align with the rule of thirds. Upon release, Photoshop will calculate the move and edit the background accordingly.

04 Improve results
The move operation may leave some unwanted artifacts. Grab the Spot Healing Brush, set the type to Content-Aware and paint over the odd occurrences. The tool works best if the brush size is just slightly larger than the area you are painting.

Retouching

Enable the Patch tool's Content-Aware option

Use new tricks to breathe fresh life into your images

ORIGINAL

CORRECTED

> "The lighting won't match exactly, but Photoshop accounts for this as it calculates the resulting pixels"

01 Flyaway hairs

Use the Spot Healing Brush with a small tip size in order to gently remove the stray hairs along the little girl's cheek. Do not try to paint out the light spill – that's what we'll be using the Patch tool (J) for later!

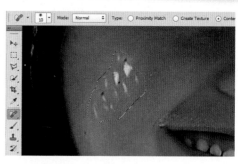

02 Patch things up

Grab the Patch tool and set the option to Content-Aware and Adaptation to Medium. Then lasso a loose selection around the sunny spots on her cheek. Keep the selection somewhat tight so there's room to move it about.

03 Drag and drop

Now drag the patch selection to a smoother area of the skin. The lighting won't match exactly, but Photoshop accounts for this as it calculates the resulting pixels. If there are any artifacts left over, use the Patch tool on those too!

04 Building removal

Use the same technique to select and remove the shed that's visible over the fence at the top left of the image. Select the rough outline and use the Patch tool to slide the selection along the top of the fence line to find a good sample area.

05 Board alignment

In the previous section, the Content-Aware Move left some irregularities in the fence boards. The Patch tool is ideal for helping to straighten those out. Select areas that don't match and slide the selection around until you find a good match.

Use a Content-Aware Fill

The tried-and-tested technique still has its place

ORIGINAL

CORRECTED

Adaptable adaptation

When using the Content-Aware Move tool, the Adaptation setting controls how closely the results match the original pixels. Just after using the Content-Aware Move tool you can change the adaptation setting and the selection will update with the new result.

01 Another selection

One last Content-Aware tool to go over, and it's the original! Make a loose selection around the ridiculous stump in the background. (You knew that thing was coming out, right?)

02 Stump removal

Go to Edit>Fill and set the Use to Content-Aware from the drop-down menu. This is where the feature lives, but it's easier to access it with the shortcut key Shift+Backspace.

03 Evaluate the results

Cancel the selection (Cmd/Ctrl+D) and evaluate the area for problems. If there seems to be a halo around the affected area, undo and try a larger selection instead.

04 Fine review

Go through the image looking for areas to clean up. Content-Aware Fill can be used to remove the rooftop in the upper right and the slice of empty area under the girl's right arm.

05 Final effect

Use a Curves adjustment to increase contrast by creating a soft, S-shaped curve, then finish with a lens vignette. Go to Filter>Render>Lens Correction, and slide the slider to the left.

Banish blemishes

Image repair has never been easier thanks to this great tool, which lets you clear up larger flaws in seconds

The Patch tool is incredibly easy to use, and is perfect for restoring and repairing any parts of your photographs that are damaged or blemished.

This tool is a Photoshop staple, and has been around since version 6.0 of our favourite app. It's the ideal option for quick image edits, as it enables you to replace large or small selections from your images with equally large or small portions of replacement image information.

The Patch tool is tucked away in the toolbar, sharing space with the Healing brush, and can be accessed by holding the cursor down on the small black arrow and activating the fly-out menu. Once the tool is selected, three options are added to the top menu bar: Source, Destination and Use Pattern – in this guide, we will be concentrating on the first two options, as they are the ones that you are most likely to use over and over again.

There are a few methods available to repair your images using the Patch tool. First, you can choose to select the 'bad' part of your image and move this selection around the photo to find an acceptable portion to put in its place. Alternatively, you can select a good part of your image first, and then move this to cover or 'patch' the unsightly part. Finally, if you don't have enough image to patch up the problem area, you can opt to patch the problem spot with a pattern fill, combining the texture of your pattern with the underlying colours present in your photograph.

> "This tool is a Photoshop staple, and has been around since version 6.0 of our favourite app"

QUICK PHOTOSHOP TIPS

Source or Destination?
When using the Patch tool, choose Source when selecting your problem areas and Destination when selecting a clean image to patch over the bad.

Smudge tool
For a quick touch-up to the seams of your patchwork, try opting for something like the Smudge tool to help soften the edges.

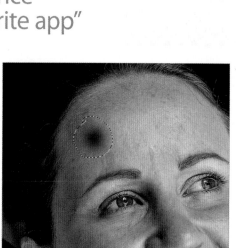
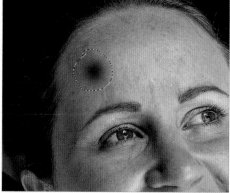

01 Get ready
Open your start image and activate the Patch tool (in the toolbar along with the Healing brush). Notice the options that appear in the top toolbar.

02 Select a source
Your source point is the area that needs fixing. Pick the Source option in the top toolbar and select the area just as you would when using the Lasso.

03 Drag 'n drop
Place the cursor in the centre of the selection. Now drag it to another area of your image that can be used to patch up the blemish, then release.

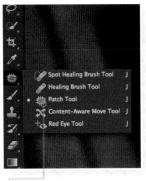

Transparent
For a very subtle bit of patchwork, try opting for the Transparent feature on the top toolbar. This gives a much less exaggerated effect – perfect for that barely there look.

Patch tool
This tool shares the same well as the Healing brush on the toolbar. To access the tool, just hold down the cursor over the small black arrow and the fly-out menu will appear.

01 Patch the bad bits
You can also do the opposite, and select a clean part of your image first, then drag this over the blemish. Simply hit 'Destination' instead of 'Source'.

02 Make selections
You can also make a selection with your favourite Selection tool first and activate the Patch tool next. This is a more controlled way of doing things.

03 Hide the patchwork
You can hide the fix using the Smudge tool. Turn the Strength down to 20%. Work at the edges of your new patch and watch it blend in.

Retouching

Retouch skin in portrait photos

Simple tools and edits can give stunning results

It's impossible to pick up a magazine these days without seeing an image that has been retouched. Any image can be subject to postproduction work as it can be useful for all sorts of things, but by far the most popular sort of image used is the portrait. For the Photoshop beginner, retouching is immensely useful for preparing shots of your friends and family for your stock library, to use in composites or just to show them at their absolute best for enlarging and printing to hang on the wall.

Photoshop enables you to tweak and preen an image for hours on end until you've got a picture of unattainable perfection, but that's not the effect that we are interested in here. What we are going to look at are the basic tools

and techniques you need to tidy up a portrait, get rid of anything that would distract from the subject and composition, and help your photo look the best it can. You'll end up with a better picture without falling into the land of soulless airbrushing.

"End up with a better picture without falling into the land of soulless airbrushing"

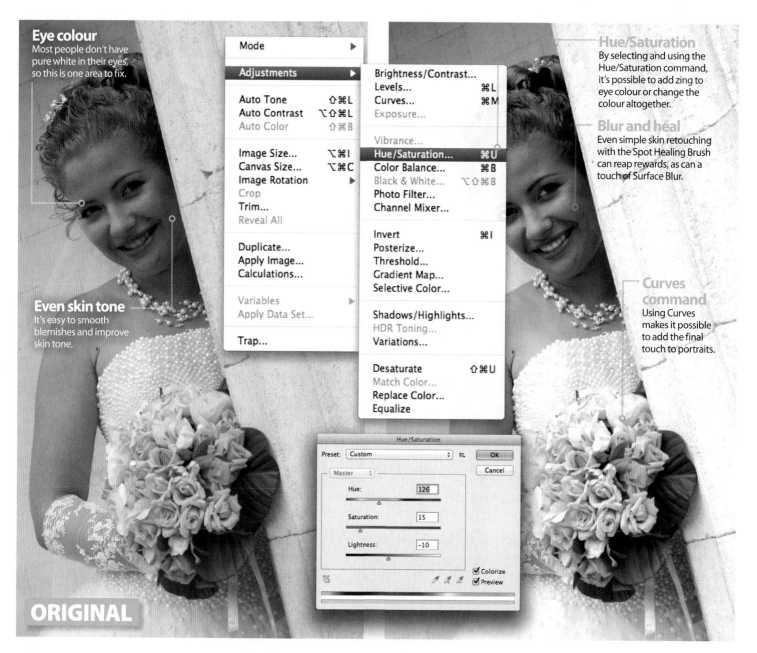

Eye colour
Most people don't have pure white in their eyes, so this is one area to fix.

Even skin tone
It's easy to smooth blemishes and improve skin tone.

Hue/Saturation
By selecting and using the Hue/Saturation command, it's possible to add zing to eye colour or change the colour altogether.

Blur and heal
Even simple skin retouching with the Spot Healing Brush can reap rewards, as can a touch of Surface Blur.

Curves command
Using Curves makes it possible to add the final touch to portraits.

ORIGINAL

Drag and dab

The Spot Healing Brush tool lets you dab on for correction. The Patch tool is for drawing around an area to replace and then dragging to the area to replace it with.

Make light work of small blemishes

Professional retouchers spend aeons on skin, painstakingly removing blemishes, wrinkles and pores, but there's no need to invest so much time. All you really need for a good (and natural) result is the Spot Healing Brush, the Patch tool and the Surface Blur filter.

Skin before
Our original image shows skin with a few blemishes and bumps.

Skin after
A quick retouch and they are all gone.

Smooth and improve skin It's easy once you know how

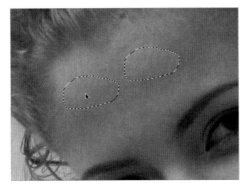

01 Spot Healing Brush tool

For small blemishes, pick the Spot Healing Brush. It can be found in the Toolbar, along with the other healing tools. Use the [and] keys to set the brush size slightly bigger than the area to fix and then click once on the offending part. It will disappear!

02 The Patch tool

A Toolbar bedfellow of the Spot Healing Brush is the Patch tool. Use this for larger areas of blemish, drawing around the area to fix then clicking and dragging this to a perfect area. Once you let go of the mouse, the bad area will turn into a good area.

03 Surface blur

This is a great way to smooth out skin. Go to Filter>Blur>Surface Blur and enter a Radius of 2 and a Threshold of 5. You don't want an obvious effect, just a little bit to smooth out pores. You can also select areas so the blur is only applied there.

Retouching

A vital technique to master

When it comes to portraits, any eye contact is instantly engaging and draws the viewer in. Because of this, it makes sense to spend a bit of time getting the eyes the best they can be. Concentrating on getting the whites clear is a start, as is intensifying the colour of the irises.

If your subject is smiling, you can also apply the same technique to the teeth for a dazzling effect.

A natural white Subtle is better than whitewash

01 Pick the Dodge tool

For a really straightforward method to whiten the eyes choose the Dodge tool. Open your photo, make a duplicate (Layer>Duplicate) and then go to the Toolbar and pick the Dodge tool.

02 Opacity setting

Go to the top Options bar, set Exposure to 50% and the Range to Midtones. This will keep things subtle and controllable. Use the [or] keys on the keyboard to set a good brush size and then paint over the eye whites. If the first wipe doesn't work, go over again and build it up gradually.

03 Same again

Apply the same method to the teeth, just brush over to whiten them up. If you find that the effect is too much, call upon the Ctrl/Cmd+Z command to Undo and then lower the Exposure setting.

04 More zing

To add intensity, start by picking the Lasso tool from the Toolbar and draw around the iris. Once you have finished one, hold down the Shift key to add to the selection and draw around the other.

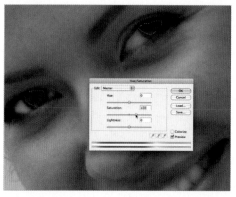

05 Saturate

Go to Image>Adjustments>Hue/Saturation and drag the Saturation slider to the right. As you do this, the eye colour will become more intense.

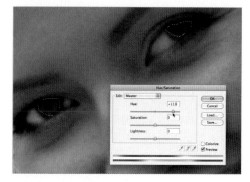

06 A different colour

Also use the Hue slider to change the eye colour altogether. Drag the slider left or right to get the hue you want and then use the Saturation slider if you need to reduce or increase the colour effect.

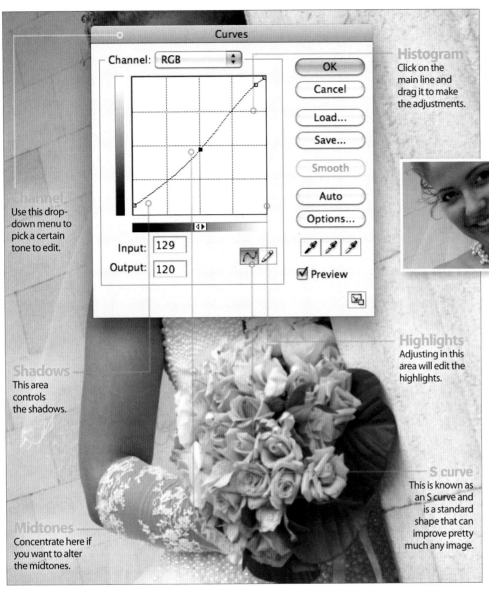

Channel
Use this drop-down menu to pick a certain tone to edit.

Shadows
This area controls the shadows.

Midtones
Concentrate here if you want to alter the midtones.

Curves

Channel: RGB

OK
Cancel
Load...
Save...
Smooth
Auto
Options...

Input: 129
Output: 120

Preview

Histogram
Click on the main line and drag it to make the adjustments.

Highlights
Adjusting in this area will edit the highlights.

S curve
This is known as an S curve and is a standard shape that can improve pretty much any image.

The final editing stage

After you have made all of the tweaks, it's always an idea to make tonal corrections across the whole image. The Curves adjustment is an excellent way of doing this and there is an S-curve rule that many image editors use as default. By spending some time finessing the tone, you can enjoy a truly remarkable makeover.

Tone in portraits
Reach retouching nirvana

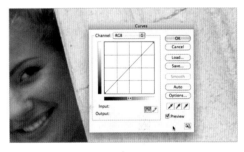

01 Open up Curves

To get started, go to Image>Adjustments>Curves or in Elements, Enhance>Adjust>Adjust Color Curves. Ignore most of the options and go with the default values in place. For now just concentrate on the diagonal line.

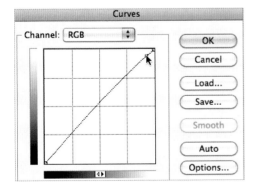

02 Alter the highlights

Move your mouse cursor over to the top-right corner. Click on the line, drag upwards and you should see that the highlights in the image have increased. You should also see a little point has appeared on the line to mark where you clicked.

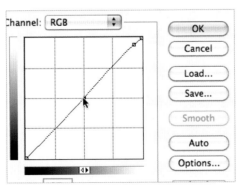

03 Midtones

Now it's time to see to the middle of the curve, which will take care of the midtones in your image. Click roughly on the middle of the line and drag down to the right slightly. This is the belly of the S and will darken the midtones.

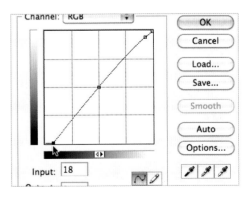

04 Shadows

This time we are clicking on the bottom left of the line and dragging upwards. Doing this makes the final loop of the S shape and works to boost the shadows. If you want to change any part of the edit, simply click and drag.

Adjustments

APPLYING ADJUSTMENT LAYERS
An introduction to these essential options and how to use them creatively

THE POWER OF MASKS
Learn why you need masks and how to make edits with them

CREATIVE EDITING
An introduction to these essential options and how to get creative with them

MAKE DRAMATIC CHANGES
Inject bolder colours and better contrast, resulting in creative effects, but without damaging your original

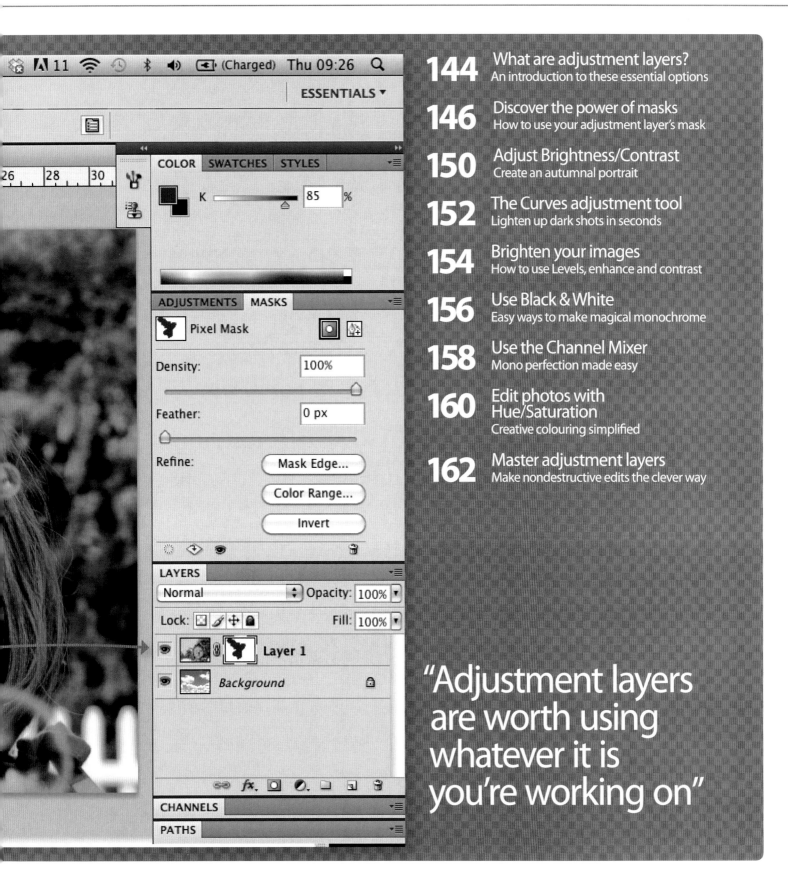

"Adjustment layers are worth using whatever it is you're working on"

Adjustments

What are adjustment layers?

Put adjustment layers into practice for edits that won't damage your original image

Adjustment layers are just like normal layers but apply a specific change to improve and alter an image in a range of different ways. Whether you're looking to change the lighting, colour or add a gradient to your image, adjustment layers will enable you to do all of these things and control the effect with sliders and options.

They sit in the Layers palette and, as with normal layers, they can be adapted to fit over your image. Adjustment layers have the ability to apply non-destructive changes because they are a separate layer from your image. Adjustments can therefore be deleted, edited and even masked away, so nothing is actually permanent.

ORIGINAL

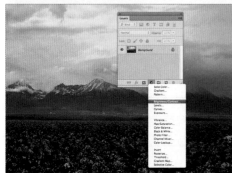

01 Choose adjustment
With an image open, head to the Layers palette and click on the black and white icon (in Photoshop CS4 or above, go to Window> Adjustments). For altering exposure, choose Brightness/Contrast.

02 Alter exposure
For dull lighting conditions, increase the Brightness amount to 30 and set Contrast to 40. The image will now brighten up. Some areas may lose detail and become overexposed, but that's okay.

03 Mask areas
We can edit the white mask that comes with the adjustment using the Brush tool (B). Make sure your Foreground colour is set to black and paint on the overexposed parts to remove the effect.

PROPERTIES PALETTE

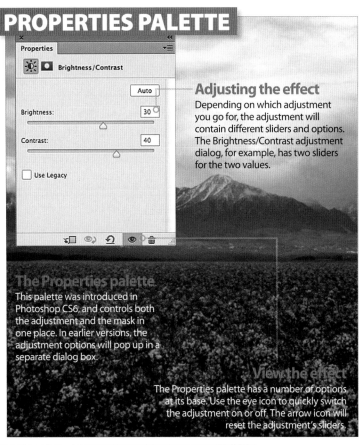

Adjusting the effect
Depending on which adjustment you go for, the adjustment will contain different sliders and options. The Brightness/Contrast adjustment dialog, for example, has two sliders for the two values.

The Properties palette
This palette was introduced in Photoshop CS6, and controls both the adjustment and the mask in one place. In earlier versions, the adjustment options will pop up in a separate dialog box.

View the effect
The Properties palette has a number of options at its base. Use the eye icon to quickly switch the adjustment on or off. The arrow icon will reset the adjustment's sliders.

LAYERS PALETTE

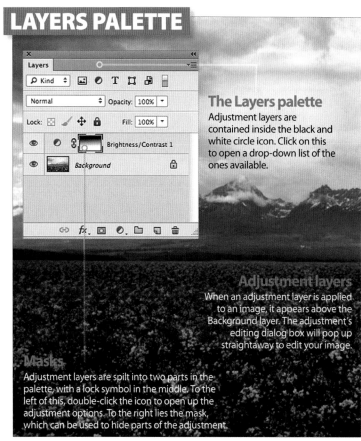

The Layers palette
Adjustment layers are contained inside the black and white circle icon. Click on this to open a drop-down list of the ones available.

Adjustment layers
When an adjustment layer is applied to an image, it appears above the Background layer. The adjustment's editing dialog box will pop up straightaway to edit your image.

Masks
Adjustment layers are spilt into two parts in the palette, with a lock symbol in the middle. To the left of this, double-click the icon to open up the adjustment options. To the right lies the mask, which can be used to hide parts of the adjustment.

ADJUSTMENT OPTIONS

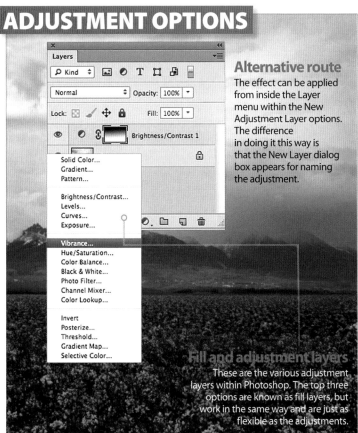

Alternative route
The effect can be applied from inside the Layer menu within the New Adjustment Layer options. The difference in doing it this way is that the New Layer dialog box appears for naming the adjustment.

Fill and adjustment layers
These are the various adjustment layers within Photoshop. The top three options are known as fill layers, but work in the same way and are just as flexible as the adjustments.

PHOTOSHOP ELEMENTS

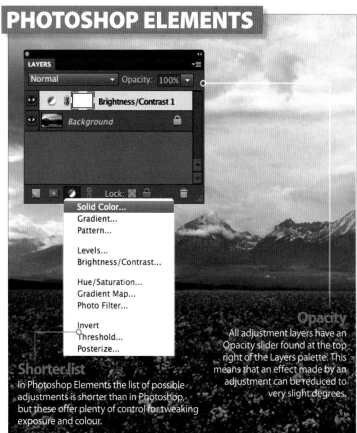

Shorter list
In Photoshop Elements the list of possible adjustments is shorter than in Photoshop, but these offer plenty of control for tweaking exposure and colour.

Opacity
All adjustment layers have an Opacity slider found at the top right of the Layers palette. This means that an effect made by an adjustment can be reduced to very slight degrees.

Discover the power of masks

A vital building block in Photoshop's structure, masks are a potent tool to harness

Layers form the basis of image creation in Photoshop and as layer masks work hand-in-hand with them, understanding what they do and how powerful they are is vital to mastering the program. To understand their functionality, it's good to start by thinking of layers as a stack of transparent pages that make up your image. Layer masks are like digital stencils that sit on top of each layer. When a stencil is placed over a picture you can only see what appears in the cut-out section, the rest is hidden from sight. Similarly, when you create a layer mask you effectively create a stencil that tells Photoshop what part of that layer to show and what part to hide.

The beauty of digital editing is that you're not confined to the two options of making a layer either completely visible or completely invisible. It may sound complicated now but rest assured, once you understand the basic commands behind these amazing tools you'll be able to play around with the attributes of your layers with very incredible results.

"Layer masks are like digital stencils that sit on top of each layer"

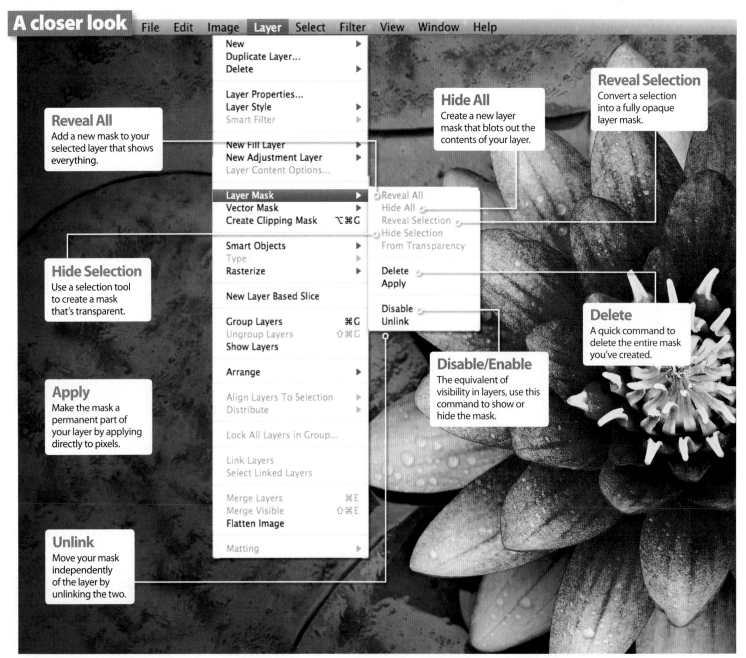

A closer look

File   Edit   Image   **Layer**   Select   Filter   View   Window   Help

Reveal All
Add a new mask to your selected layer that shows everything.

Hide Selection
Use a selection tool to create a mask that's transparent.

Apply
Make the mask a permanent part of your layer by applying directly to pixels.

Unlink
Move your mask independently of the layer by unlinking the two.

Hide All
Create a new layer mask that blots out the contents of your layer.

Reveal Selection
Convert a selection into a fully opaque layer mask.

Delete
A quick command to delete the entire mask you've created.

Disable/Enable
The equivalent of visibility in layers, use this command to show or hide the mask.

New
Duplicate Layer...
Delete

Layer Properties...
Layer Style
Smart Filter

New Fill Layer
New Adjustment Layer
Layer Content Options...

Layer Mask
Vector Mask
Create Clipping Mask   ⌥⌘G

Smart Objects
Type
Rasterize

New Layer Based Slice

Group Layers   ⌘G
Ungroup Layers   ⇧⌘G
Show Layers

Arrange

Align Layers To Selection
Distribute

Lock All Layers in Group...

Link Layers
Select Linked Layers

Merge Layers   ⌘E
Merge Visible   ⇧⌘E
Flatten Image

Matting

Reveal All
Hide All
Reveal Selection
Hide Selection
From Transparency

Delete
Apply

Disable
Unlink

LAYERS PALETTE

When added, layer masks appear as small boxes linked to a layer. This highlights the fact that they do not affect the layer directly but merely sit on top and affect how the layer behaves.

New Layer Mask
Add a new mask directly from the Layers palette. The mask will be white and show the entire layer.

Selection options
Use these options in order to apply your mask to a selection or to create one from a selection.

Disable, delete and apply
Like the options in the Layers menu, disable, delete or apply the mask permanently to your layer.

Mask palette
The Mask palette usually lives just above the Layers palette (CS4 and above) and gives you options to control your mask.

Density
Effectively controlling the shades of grey in your mask, use the slider to choose how much of the layer shows through.

Refine Mask
Control mask edges with the refine options and blend them into the background.

Feather
Soften the edges of your mask with the Feather slider.

Mask Options
Choose how your mask displays by setting the colour and opacity.

Pick your colour

Painting on a layer mask is different from painting on an image. Instead of adding colour, you're painting the areas that you want to reveal or hide. Photoshop communicates this in black, white and shades of grey. The colour you select tells the program whether the section you are painting should be hidden or revealed.

It's a fairly unusual concept to get around at first, but in this instance, the colour you choose doesn't signify a colour at all, rather the function of the tool.

> "Painting on a layer mask is different from painting on an image"

01 Mask in black
Painting with black tells Photoshop to hide everything you are painting over – this is the cut out part of your stencil. As you're hiding all the pixels the brush touches, the layer below will show through completely. You can see where you have painted over by looking at the black shape on the layer mask thumbnail as well.

02 White mask paint
White, as you would expect, has the opposite effect of black, commanding Photoshop to reveal the pixels. A completely white layer has no effect. Use this to fix mistakes made with the black brush.

03 Dark grey
Layer masks aren't limited to only Reveal All and Hide All; grey shades covers the bases in between, enabling you to choose how much you want to reveal. The darker the grey, the higher the opacity.

04 Light grey
The lighter the shade of grey the lower the opacity. Use a range of lighter greys when you want your background to show through a little bit, while still keeping the contents of your dominant layer visible over the top.

Adjustments

Create a composite

Compositing two images is easier than it looks if you make use of the actions and options that layer masks give you. Two layers are at play here; a landscape and a new sky layer. By creating a mask we can hide a section of our dominant layer and let the other show through without damaging or erasing any of our original pixels.

01 Two images, one layer

Open two images in Photoshop. Using a Marquee tool, go ahead and select the entire contents of the landscape shot and make a copy. Paste the image on top of the sky so it shows up on a new layer. Be sure the landscape sits on top as the dominant layer.

02 Add layer mask

With the landscape image selected, add a layer mask by clicking the new mask button at the bottom of the palette. The mask shows as a small white square linked. The white indicates that the entire contents of the layer is visible.

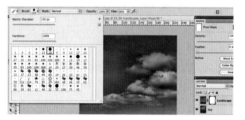

03 Choose a brush

Make sure that the layer mask is selected. First choose the Brush tool from the Toolbar and then, in the Brush options at the top, select a Hard Round tip and set the size to 150px. We'll use a large brush to mask over the sky area.

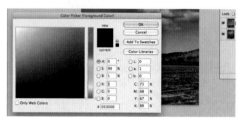

04 Pick a colour

When working in layer masks the only colour options are black, white and the range of grey, representing functions rather than colours. When white, all pixels in the layer are showing. Use black to be able to hide pixels as we paint.

05 Paint it black

Begin painting over the sky area and as you go the background will begin to show through. If you look at the layer mask icon you'll see black appears in the same shape you've painted, indicating that the section you've painted has been hidden.

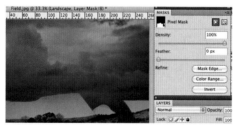

06 Fix with white

Paint out as much of the sky as possible without going over the edges of the horizon. If you accidentally paint over a part of the landscape, switch the colour of your brush to white and paint back over the mistake to rectify it.

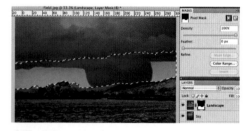

07 Make a selection

Use the Magic Wand tool to make a selection of the edge of the horizon, as this enables you to get between the trees and small details. Switch back to your black brush and paint over the selection. Nothing outside of this area will be affected.

08 Add a gradient

The contrast between the sky is stark and unnatural. One way to soften the image is to add a gradient to the layer mask. Select the Gradient tool and choose a black to white gradient. Draw a line down the centre of the layer mask to apply.

09 Feather

To further soften the edge, change the Feather setting on the layer mask. With the thumbnail selected open the Mask palette. Move the slider to a setting of 25px to lift the edge of the area and restore the details in the trees on the horizon.

10 Density

Decrease the Density of the mask by pulling the slider down to 85%. Some of the layer below will show through and you'll notice the colour on your layer mask has turned to a dark grey to indicate that the layer is not solid.

VIEW YOUR MASK

You can see what's painted on your layer mask rather than just viewing the effect it has on your image. To view your mask hold Alt/Opt and click on your mask icon in the Layers palette. It will appear in your main work area and you'll see which parts are black, white and grey.

"To view your mask hold Alt/Opt and click on your mask icon in the Layers palette"

Pick a brush

When merging images, the constant challenge is to make them seem like they were meant to fit together. One way to overcome this is to switch between brushes and choose one that gives your mask a finish that blends effortlessly with the other layers. Photoshop offers a host of brushes to choose from.

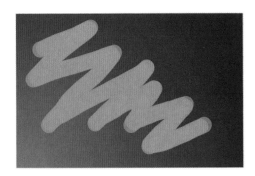

01 Hard Round

Use a Hard Round tip when working on edges where you need to be precise but still keep a natural feel. Keeping the brush size small and zooming in to the area you're working on gives you greater control. Switch between sizes as you paint to get around tricky areas of your image.

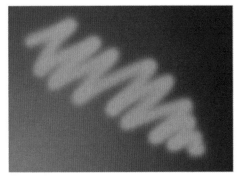

02 Soft Mechanical

Give a dreamy, soft and blended feel to your layer mask area by selecting a soft brush. The default Hardness is 0%. If that's a little too soft for you, take it up a notch by clicking into the Brush menu and moving the slider up to a value that suits.

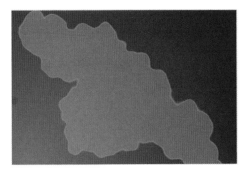

03 Drippy Water

Photoshop has a bag of creative brushes installed for fun and interesting effects. The Drippy Water brush (in the Wet Media set) is useful to create a solid splash. It can be tricky to control at first so be prepared to have a few goes until you create the exact shape you want on your layer mask.

Adjustments

SOURCE FILE AVAILABLE

Adjust Brightness/Contrast

Breathe some life back into your images with this
super-simple and effective adjustment

Some of the adjustment layers do what they say on the tin, but that doesn't make them any less effective or essential. We have covered the Brightness/Contrast controls briefly in the Basic Corrections section of this book, but here we are going to look at how they can be applied as an adjustment layer.

Getting the Brightness and Contrast values spot on can mean a lot of trial and error. If you get it wrong as a normal adjustment you have to hope that a quick Cmd/Ctrl+Z will undo the change so you can start again.

But what if you come back to an image and want to do more lightening on it? With adjustment layers, as long as you save a layered version of your work, then you can do just that. This is great if you are printing images, as sometimes you might find that your printer darkens or lightens prints and you will need to play with the controls over and again to get perfect prints. Adding an adjustment layer is so simple, that it really is the best solution when editing the fundamentals of your photos.

As you can see from our sample images below, there is a significant amount of lightening that has been carried out, and yet the final image looks natural. Use the sliders subtly and you can emulate this result. You may need to do further post-processing after this command has been applied, depending on the final result.

> "What if you come back to an image and want to do more to it?"

ORIGINAL

QUICK PHOTOSHOP TIPS

Using Eyedroppers

There are three Eyedroppers in this dialog box, for selecting the White Point, Black Point and Mid Point. To use, click the one that you want and then click on your image in the area you need. For the White Point, click the area that should be the most white in your image, for example, and the image is adjusted around this.

Presets

There are a couple of Presets built in to this adjustment layer. These allow you to quickly push the exposure up or down, and they work just like the exposure controls on cameras. Try a couple of these out before you start as they give you a good base to work from.

Color Balance

After finishing our image we found that there was a slight magenta hue, which we decided to correct using Image>Adjustments>Color Balance and push the Magenta-Green Slider toward Green.

Merge layers

When we are happy with the effects of our adjustment layer, we choose to merge the adjustment with the original layer – only do this if you don't need to re-edit at any point in the future.

01 Add the adjustment

We are selecting the adjustment directly from the Adjustments palette, but in older versions use the icon at the bottom of the Layers palette.

02 Start tweaking

You can use the sliders to help boost the Brightness and the Contrast of your image easily with the effect shown immediately.

03 Eyedroppers

The Eyedroppers allow you to set the black and white points in the image, which give you an automatic correction.

Adjustments

The Curves adjustment tool

The Curves tool is a powerful Photoshop feature that when properly applied can transform contrast, colour and tonal range

The Curves tool in Photoshop is deceptive. To the Photoshop beginner its graph-like appearance can be intimidating, bringing back memories of early maths lessons. However, it's a powerful tool that can be used to adjust tonal ranges, change colour levels, alter exposure, boost contrast and even create some less conventional photo effects.

Although the Curves tool is not as intuitive as some of the other features in Photoshop, the basic functions are simple, and dramatic results can be easily achieved. We have had a look at it in the Color & Tone section, but this tool really comes into its own when applied as an adjustment layer. In the Layers palette, hit Create New Fill Or Adjustment Layer and select Curves. Adjustment layers let you make changes without degrading the original. It also means you can continue to edit a Curves adjustments by double-clicking the adjustment layer. If the changes aren't wanted, you can revert to the original by deleting the layer.

In this tutorial we will demystify the Curves graph, and in doing so show how you can make practical improvements to your images. We'll look at understanding the graph and at exactly what happens as the line changes shape. We'll reveal tips and tricks to make editing your image quick and easy. We will also look at editing the colour channels to recover and boost lost colour. The Curves tool has many more facets than might at first be obvious, and we'll introduce you to as many as we can on these pages.

"The Curves tool has many more facets than might at first be obvious"

Curves window
This is where the action happens. This window graphically represents the pixel information in your image. The curve runs from the bottom left, which is where the dark pixels occur in the image, through the midtones up to the top right, which represents the highlights, the light pixels. Moving the curve upwards makes the image lighter; moving it downwards makes it darker.

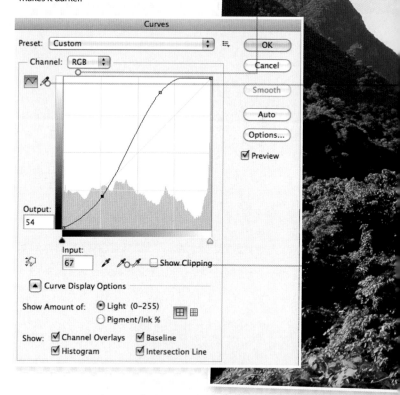

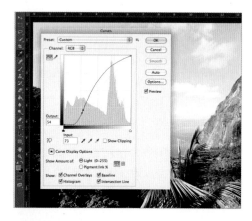

Try in mono
Try using Curves on black-and-white images, as the final image corresponds to the info that Curves use: shadows (black), midtones (grey) and highlights (white).

Colour channels
Curves allows you to edit separate channels. When a channel is selected, the curve affects the density of the colour, eg red and its opposite, cyan.

Using channels
Moving the curve upwards increases the red in the image; moving it down increases the cyan. The Color Balance tool uses the same principle too.

Channel

This drop-down menu allows you to select which channels to edit. You can edit the master (labelled RGB or CMYK etc) or individual colour channels. When editing individual colours, the curve affects the selected colour and its opposite colour.

Bezier/Pencil tool

There are two ways of changing the path of the curve. The common way is to use anchor points to create a smooth Bezier curve; this makes it easy to get consistent realistic results. The Pencil tool allows you to be more creative and get some interesting effects, but the results are hard to reproduce accurately.

Eyedropper tool

Use the left-hand Eyedropper tool to set the dark pixel limit, and the far right Eyedropper tool to set the highlight limit. The middle Eyedropper tool can be used to alter the colour balance. Experiment with these to find your optimal settings. The beginner however, may wish to leave these and adjust the curve manually.

Crazy results

To avoid the crazy effects make sure there are no flat spots. These occur when the curve follows a horizontal line across the graph.

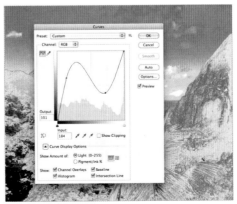

Rule number 2

The second way to keep images natural, is to make sure that the curve doesn't go beyond the horizontal to create a downward curve.

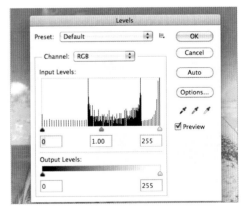

Quick reset

Hold Opt/Alt and the Cancel button will change to Reset. Hit this and the curve reverts to its original settings. This works in most PS dialog boxes.

Adjustments

Brighten your images

Use these tools to lighten your images intelligently for spot-on exposure levels

One of the main problems with portrait images, whether of people or animals, is that you want to lighten and brighten them but still want them to look realistic. Luckily, adjustment effects are perfect for this. For our image here, we are going to use a combination of adjustment effects. The first we are going to add is a level adjustment, which is designed to alter exposure problems. We want to boost the shadows in this image, so we are using the level slider and moving it to the right to darken areas of the image. As with any image-editing project, subtlety is usually the key, so push the slider just a little at a time. You can try playing with the other sliders too, to get exactly the effect you want.

Next, we want to boost the colours. We will use the Hue/Saturation command to enhance the image and bring out the warm glows and colouring. This will bring the portrait to life with vibrant tones. Again, use the slider in small increments to ensure that the result remains realistic. Lastly, we adjust the brightness and contrast to sharpen up those final tones and shadows, leaving the image full of life with realistic colouring.

> "You can find the need to lighten and brighten portrait images, but you still want them to look realistic"

WHAT YOU'LL LEARN

Levels
Our start image is on the dull side and the tones are not pronounced enough. We will use the level adjustment tool to correct this and add depth to the image.

Enhance
Use hue and saturation in your image to gain warmth and a realistic glow. Finish off with adjusting the contrast to bring out finer areas.

Skin
We need to lighten and brighten the fur, but we don't want a shiny, orange result. This is why it pays to be subtle with enhancements – start small and you can always add more.

01 Work the levels
On the Edit section, click the Guided tab and Adjust Levels. Slide the darker input level to the right to increase the darker tones.

02 Enhance the colours
Under the Color and Lighting header, select Enhance Colors. Adjust hue and saturation sliders to create a warmer glow, still keeping a realistic feel.

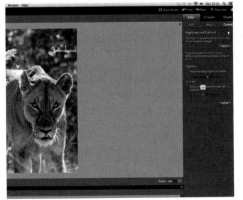

03 Brightness/contrast
Adjust the brightness and contrast sliders in the Color and Lighting section. This will bring out fine detail in the portrait and create a sharp effect.

Adjustments

Use Black & White

Get creative with your colour photos by adding a little monochrome magic – we show you how!

Black-and-white photography has always been popular. Perhaps this is due to the fact that it works with almost any kind of image. Portraits, landscapes and abstracts in particular, take on a whole new feeling when they are turned into a monochrome representation.

Of course, there are always exceptions. Images need to have a good contrast between the light and dark tones, as you would otherwise have a great expanse of grey that's just not overly appealing.

Using the Black & White adjustment as an adjustment layer gives you endless control over the conversion of your photos. As well as a whole host of Presets that give you instant results, you can target each channel that makes up the image independently. It takes a bit of getting used to when you're playing with the Reds in a black-and-white image, but each colour looks different in mono, so it is worth playing with your images to see how they can be adapted.

As well as using the sliders, there is a little hand icon with a double-ended arrow underneath. Click on this icon, then click and hold on an area in your image that you want to adjust. Photoshop will determine which channel is most prominent in that specific area and as you slide your mouse back and forth, the relevant slider will go up and down too. A really convenient and easy way to ensure that the tonal range of your black-and-white images is as close to perfect as possible.

"Images need to have a good contrast between the light and dark tones"

QUICK PHOTOSHOP TIPS

Using Presets
There is a list of Presets for every adjustment layer available. You can simply click on any of these to instantly apply them to your photos. You can also see the Presets as a drop-down menu at the top of each adjustment's individual dialog boxes.

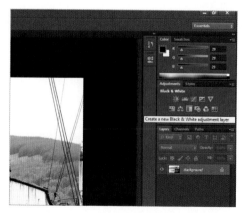

01 Option 1
You can click on the black and white circle icon in the Layers palette to quickly apply the Black & White adjustment layer.

02 Option 2
If you have CS4, CS5 or CS6, then you can use the Adjustments palette instead. The Black & White adjustment is the half-black, half-white square.

03 Presets
The Presets are a good place to start, so go through all of them and then find the one that best suits your image.

Perfect mono
There are so many methods that you can use to turn an image from colour to mono. But for the best results, this adjustment layer gives really good control.

The right kind of image
Not all images will look good in black and white and that is why it is so good when using adjustment layers. You can see in a second whether or not the adjustment looks right, then you can tweak or delete as you need, without harming the original colour photograph.

04 Customise
Now you can start tweaking the sliders to get the right balance of 'colours' in your image. Trial and error works best here.

05 Precise control
There is a little hand icon here, which you can use to click on a part of the image you want to edit and then slide along your image to adjust.

06 Check the edit
Using the little icon shown in the screenshot, you can click to see the image before its conversion to compare the result with the original.

Adjustments

Use the Channel Mixer

Bring colour to your night photos for instantly dramatic effects

A shot taken at night is often problematic when printed. However, as long as there's some sort of light source in the original scene, you can dramatically improve the photo by using a few creative editing techniques. By re-creating the look of infrared photography, we'll use filters and colour channels to turn an everyday image into something eye-catching.

We'll be using adjustment layers for non-destructive edits, specifically the Channel Mixer, to adjust how much impact each individual tone has on the image. We'll also be including a few different layer blend modes to experiment with interesting effects. However, the results you'll get with this effect depend a lot on which type of photo you're using.

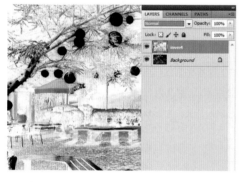

01 Duplicate and invert colours
Download the image being used here straight from the website: **www.photoshopcreative.co.uk** or choose one of your own to practise on. Hit Cmd/Ctrl+J to duplicate the main image.

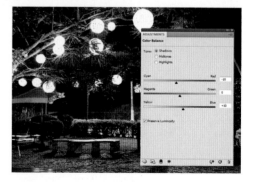

02 Apply blend modes
Invert the colours of the duplicate layer by hitting Cmd/Ctrl+I and set the blend mode to Color. You can preview the complete effect of this inversion by activating and deactivating the eye icon.

03 Move to the Channel Mixer
Create a New Adjustment Layer and choose the Channel Mixer. In the dialog box, configure the Red Output Channel to: Blue: +100; the Blue Channel to Red: +100 and the Green Channel to Green: +90.

04 Balance the colours
Apply Color Balance (Cmd/Ctrl+B) and for Shadows use Red: -10, Blue: +10 and Green: 0. For Highlights set Red: -10, Green: +10 and Blue: +10. For Midtones set Red: +10, Green: -10 and Blue: +10.

"As long as there's a light source in the original scene, you can dramatically improve the photo by using creative editing techniques"

05 Apply Hue/Saturation
Insert a Hue/Saturation layer (Cmd/Ctrl+U). Under the Red channel set Hue: +0, Saturation: +14 and Lightness: +40. Under Magenta, set Hue: +20, Saturation: +30 and Lightness: +20.

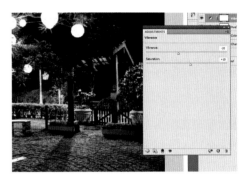

06 Boost the vibrancy
Now in order to boost the vibrancy, you need to add a Vibrance layer to the image, adjusting the Vibrance slider to -20 and the Saturation slider below it to +10.

07 Duplicate and merge layers
Select all your adjustment layers, as well as the inverted colour layers, and duplicate them. Now select all these duplicated layers and merge them (Cmd/Ctrl+E).

08 Tweak shadows and highlights
For Shadows set Amount: 30%, Tonal Width: 60%, Radius: 80px. For Highlights set Amount: 20%, Tonal Width: 30%, Radius: 30px. For Adjustments, adjust Color Correction: +20 and Midtone Contrast: -10.

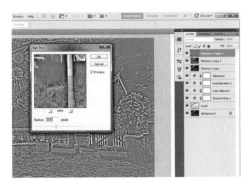

09 Add some drama
Duplicate the merged layer, but lock the original layer. Apply a High Pass filter with a 10-pixel Radius, then change the layer to Overlay blend mode with 100% Opacity. Now merge these two layers.

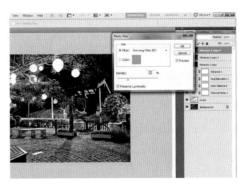

10 Use the Photo Filter
Go to Adjustment>Photo Filter, then in the dialog select Warming Filter (85) and keep the Density by default at 25%. Select Preserve Luminosity and click OK.

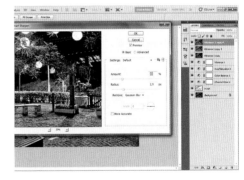

11 Vector shapes
Now select the Custom Shape tool. With white and #57b711, create various shapes using the presets Circle Frame, Circle Thin Frame and Boom 1 & 2. Feel free to add other shapes as you see fit.

Adjustments

Edit photos with Hue/Saturation

Do more with this dialog box by using it as an adjustment layer when editing image colours

Photoshop offers many different ways to control colour and tone in your images, but one of the absolute best is the Hue/Saturation command. Found under the Image>Adjustments menu or applied as an adjustment layer, the Hue/Saturation command allows you to alter the hue, saturation and brightness.

You can apply the changes over an entire image or target specific colours. It is this level of control that makes the command so powerful – if you have an image that's basically okay but one shade is letting it down, you can target the colour and improve it.

You control the edits by either moving sliders or entering numbers. There are three bars that control the hue, saturation or lightness, and these are in place whether you alter an entire image or just specific colours. You can also use the command to create monochrome and duotone effects, opening up

the creative possibilities even more. We're going to look at all the controls in these pages and show you how they can be used to create perfectly coloured images.

As we're looking at adjustment layers, make sure that you use this method to apply your Hue/Saturation command, as you can make as many changes as you like without harming the original photo at all. You can try this out with any image to get used to the controls.

"You can apply the changes over an entire image or target specific colours"

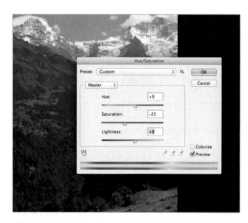

01 Assess the problem
Have a look at the image and work out what needs doing. It might be that using the sliders on the Master setting will work.

02 Blue sky
By selecting Blues and moving the Hue slider, you can improve the colour of the sky. Moving the Saturation slider right also brightens things up.

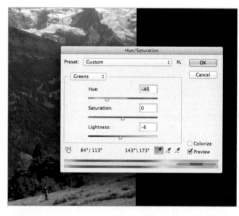

03 Not so mellow yellow
We want striking yellow flowers. This calls for Yellows to be set as the colour range. Moving the Hue slider left brightens things considerably.

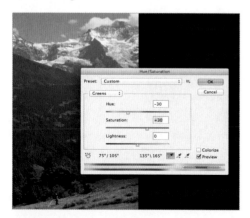

04 Boost some more
It's time to boost the effect even more. This involves moving the Saturation slider to the right. We also moved the Lightness slider to the right.

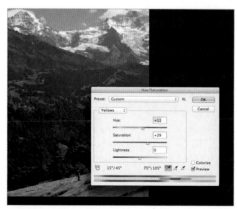

05 The final touch
The other colour that needs attention is green. It just needs the Hue and Saturation sliders to be moved to the right for the effect to improve.

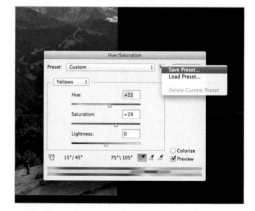

06 Save for a rainy day
If you have a collection of similar-coloured images, it's worth saving your settings. Click Save, name your settings and then save. Use Load to retrieve.

QUICK PHOTOSHOP TIPS

Preserve the original

It's a good idea to use a Hue/Saturation adjustment layer because then you know the original is safe and you can go back and edit it at any time.

Control the parameters

When you target a specific colour, you are given the option to set how far you can tweak it. By moving these parameters, you can incorporate more hues than set by default.

Preset tones

In addition to editing the entire image, you can select preset tones from this menu and concentrate just on one colour. This makes image editing far easier.

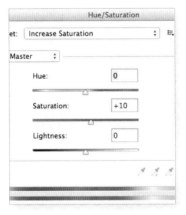

ORIGINAL

Slide edits

Control how the Hue/Saturation dialog works by using these three fields. You can enter values to make edits, but the best way is to move the sliders.

01 Colour grayscale

If you have a grayscale image, begin by going to Image>Mode and pick RGB. Open up the Hue/Saturation dialog box and tick the Colorize box.

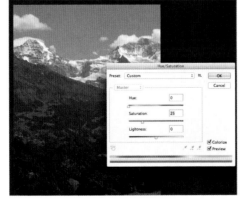

02 Colorize

If your foreground and background colours are black and white, the image will tint red. If not, it'll have the hue of your foreground colour.

03 Colour images

With a colour image open, hit Colorize. Your image will take on a duotone look, which can be altered by moving the Hue slider.

Adjustments

Layers

Kind

Normal   Opacity: 100%

Lock: Fill: 100%

Exposure 1

Curves 1

Background

Master adjustment layers

Find out how you can make major edits to your photographs that don't ruin the original image, and can be re-edited at any time

Adjustment layers are worth using whatever it is you are working on, but they are especially useful for retouching tasks. Because so much depends upon you creating a natural effect, being able to refer back to the original photo is extremely useful, especially if you need it to bring back information that has been lost through editing.

In case you aren't familiar with them, adjustment layers make edits on a layer above your original image. If something goes horrendously wrong, you can simply delete the adjustment layer and return to the original. Adjustment layers can also be edited at any stage, so if you decide part way through an edit that you need to alter the adjustment, it's easy to do so without affecting your later tweaks.

Adjustment layers also preserve image quality, as each time you edit a pixel value directly, you lose a bit of information. This doesn't happen with adjustment layers. There are various types of adjustment layers but the most useful ones for retouching are the Levels one and the Curves one, which are among the first that we will be looking at in this section.

Here we take a look at the Adjustment Layer menu options, which are accessed from the Layer menu. However, as you get used to using them, it is much easier to click the little button at the bottom of the Layers palette, which looks like a half-black, half-white circle. When you click on this, the same list of options will pop up and you just click on the one that you want.

If you have CS4, CS5 or CS6, there is a dedicated Adjustments panel too, which has icons for all of the adjustment layers available and you can simply click on those instead to add them to your project. You can also directly edit the settings for the adjustment layer at the same time. Let's have a look closer at adjustment layers.

"If you decide part way through an edit that you need to alter the adjustment, it's easy to do"

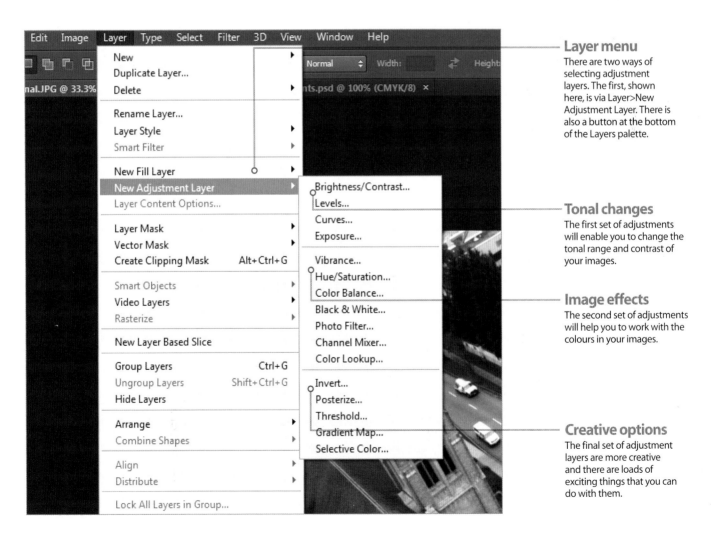

Layer menu
There are two ways of selecting adjustment layers. The first, shown here, is via Layer>New Adjustment Layer. There is also a button at the bottom of the Layers palette.

Tonal changes
The first set of adjustments will enable you to change the tonal range and contrast of your images.

Image effects
The second set of adjustments will help you to work with the colours in your images.

Creative options
The final set of adjustment layers are more creative and there are loads of exciting things that you can do with them.

Selections

MAKE A SPEEDY SELECTION
Discover shortcut ways to improve your workflow

FLYAWAY HAIRS MADE EASY
Discover the right selection tool for different outlines

"Selections enable you to isolate parts of an image if you only want to edit that layer"

REFINE EDGE
Get smoother selections with a time-saving trick you won't ever be able to live without

QUICK MASK
Discover why it's important to use masks and how easy they are to create

Refine Edge

View Mode

View: ☐ Show Radius (J)
      ☐ Show Original (P)

Edge Detection
☑ Smart Radius
Radius: 14.2 px

Adjust Edge
Smooth: 0
Feather: 0.0 px
Contrast: 0 %
Shift Edge: 0 %

Output
☐ Decontaminate Colors
Amount: %

Output To ✓ Selection
         Layer Mask
         New Layer
         New Layer with Layer Mask
         New Document
         New Document with Layer Mask

☐ Remem

Cancel   OK

Make perfect selections

Master various selection tools, and tackle intricate extraction tasks with confidence

Selecting complex objects can be one of most challenging and time-consuming aspects of image editing.
 With the right tool, this difficult process becomes easy! In this tutorial we'll use Color Range to make the initial colour-based selection. We'll then adopt the Quick Selection Tool, which acts like an improved Magic Wand in brush form. We'll also take a look at Refine Edge, a spectacular feature which helps us perfect selections around complex objects like furry animals and people with flowing hair. Using Refine Edge can make the difference between good selections and great ones. When extracting the tree, we won't actually delete any pixels. Instead, we'll be using a Layer mask, a non-destructive method to hide parts of an image. That way we can always go back and fine-tune our selection/extraction.

"With the right tool this difficult process becomes easy"

ORIGINAL

Make a complex selection

01 Crop
Open up your tree image. We don't need all that sky at the top, so let's use the Crop tool to get rid of everything above the tree. Now we can fully focus on the task at hand.

02 Colour Range
Go to Select>Color Range and click on the sky. Max out the fuzziness slider to increase the selection then, once happy, click OK.

03 Quick Selection tool
Click and drag with the Quick Selection tool to add to the selection. The left and right brackets size the brush. Alt-click and drag to remove areas.

04 Invert Selection
When you are finished selecting everything but the tree, invert the selection so that the tree itself will be selected. Go to Select>Inverse, or use the keyboard shortcut, Cmd/Ctrl+Shift+I.

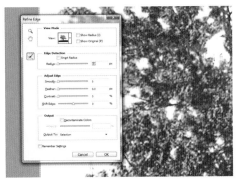

05 Refine Edge
We have just a rough selection at this point. To make it accurate, let's go to Select>Refine Edge. This dialog box contains lots of useful ways to perfect our selection. Use the Zoom and Hand tools to zoom and pan your image.

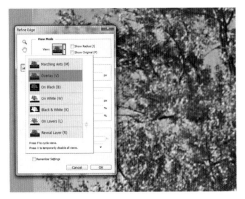

06 View Mode – Overlay
The View Mode option allows us to change the way the selection preview is displayed. You can use Overlay initially, which allows you to view the selection like a Quick Mask.

07 Refine Radius Tool
The Refine Radius tool improves selections by adding fine detail that would be hard to capture manually. Paint around the edges of the tree and in between gaps. Photoshop will think for a second, then magically refine the selection!

08 View Mode – On Black
Change the View Mode to On Black in order to check for any bits of sky you may have missed. Keep working with the Refine Radius tool to improve the selection.

QUICK TIP

Selecting with Channels

In the Channels panel, determine which channel best represents your target area. Click and drag it to the New Channel button. Pure black won't be selected, and you can use the Brush tool to refine the lighter areas that will be selected. Try adjusting with Levels to improve contrast. When done, click on the composite channel at the top, then Cmd/Ctrl-click your new channel and the selection will be loaded.

Selections

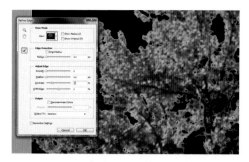

09 Contrast

While zoomed in, increase the Contrast to harden some of the soft-edged transitions in the selection. These can give the final extracted object a glow if not taken care of.

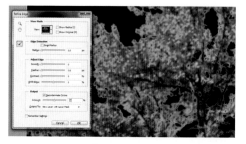

10 Decontaminate Colors

Check the Decontaminate Colors option to remove stubborn colour fringes. These are replaced with the colour of selected neighbouring pixels. Use the Amount slider to adjust the amount of colour fringe to remove.

11 Output

Choose New Layer with Layer Mask from the Output To drop-down at the bottom. The tree will appear on a new layer complete with its very own layer mask. You can now place the tree atop a new background with ease.

Selection tools
The many ways to extract objects in Photoshop

Layer Masks

Layer masks provide a non-destructive way to extract an object from its surroundings. Add a Layer mask to a layer by going to Layer>Layer Mask> Reveal All. By introducing black to the mask, you can hide parts of a layer, revealing only what you need. Use white to reveal hidden areas.

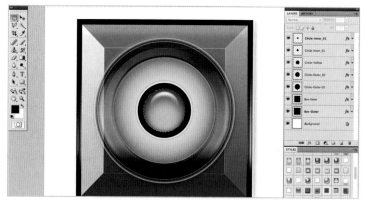

Marquee Tools

Great for creating selections around rectangular or elliptical objects. Hold Shift while dragging to create a square or circle. If there is an existing selection, you can hold Shift while dragging to add to it, Alt to subtract from it, or Shift+Alt to create an intersection between existing and new.

Quick Selection Tool

Make rapid colour and texture-based selections by clicking and dragging across the desired areas in your image. Doing this acts like a hybrid between the Magic Wand and Brush tools. To continue adding more areas to the selection, click or click and drag. To remove parts, hold Alt while clicking through those areas.

Pen Tool

The Pen Tool can be hard to get accustomed to at first. Keep practising, however, and you'll find this tool to be invaluable. You can create vector paths to outline complex objects, and refine these paths with the Direct Selection tool. Being vector-based, these paths ensure sharp outlines.

How to Cut out hair and other difficult objects

Flyaway hairs
Four simple steps to select flyaway hairs.

01 The Quick Selection Tool

Create the preliminary selection with the Quick Selection tool. Click and drag to add to the selection. Alt-click and drag to remove areas. If the layer is the Background, rename it so we can apply a mask

02 Refine Edge

To improve the selection, go to Select>Refine Edge. Use Refine Radius to paint around the edges. When you release the mouse, Photoshop will add details that would be hard to capture manually. Use F to cycle through views.

03 Further refinements

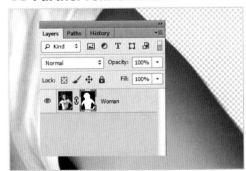

The image may still need some work. Perform some touch-ups on the mask by painting black to hide or white to reveal parts of the layer. For fine details, you can even use the Pen tool to help section off areas for editing.

04 Blend with new background

Now transport your image atop its new background. To prevent a cut-and-paste look, apply selective blurring. You can paint in ambient colouring from the background. Blend colours with the Soft Light Blend mode.

Awkward outlines
Bypass fancy features and get down and dirty with the trusty Pen tool

01 Rough outline

Using the Pen tool, create a vector path outlining the object. It doesn't need to be perfect, but try not to be sloppy either. It's easier to make these quick outlines and then refine them versus striving to make a perfect path from the get-go.

02 Save and refine

In the Paths panel, rename Work Path to save. To refine it, use the Direct Selection tool to adjust anchor points and move path segments. With the Pen tool, click a segment to add a point, or click on an existing point to delete it.

03 Layer Mask

Once your path is refined, convert it to a selection by pressing Cmd/Ctrl+Enter. At this point, you might feel the need to soften the edges by going to Select>Refine Edge and adding feathering. Click OK. Go to Layer>Layer Mask>Reveal Selection.

04 Blend with new background

Move the lizard to the background. A little blurring can alleviate any edges that haven't been smoothed out enough. Light painting with some of the background colour on the object can help blend it in its new environment. Work patiently and precisely.

Selections

ORIGINAL

Get more from Smart Brushes

Afraid of image editing? Get a stress-free jumpstart by tapping into the power of Smart Brushes, a unique and easy-to-use fusion of selections, adjustments, and masks

Selections and adjustments form a core workflow of Photoshop editing. You select what's going to be edited, and after doing so, you specify what adjustments will be made to the selected areas. Sounds straightforward, but with so many ways to make selections and a large assortment of adjustments to choose from, it can be hard for newcomers to know where to begin.

Enter the Smart Brushes, an ingenious set of tools in Photoshop Elements that combines several crucial concepts into one beginner-friendly feature. Selections and adjustments are made at the same time, shortening the learning curve and also boosting productivity.

It's very easy to start using Smart Brushes. Select one of the two brushes, then select from the ample library of effects. Elements 11 brings 15 new presets, including a satin effect and a flowery pattern.

The Smart Brush tool automatically applies adjustments to similar areas around where you click. It acts like a combination of the Quick Selection tool

and Adjustment Layers. Also on offer is the Detail Smart Brush tool, which allows you to simply 'paint on' adjustments. There is no automatic selection with this option, so you are free to apply your adjustments wherever and whenever you want.

The adjustments applied are non-destructive, meaning no pixels are permanently altered. Feel free to modify adjustments by double-clicking on the adjustment's icon in the Layers palette. The masks can also be refined until perfected. Paint on them with black to conceal and white to reveal. Practice with the examples here, then have fun with your own photos!

> ## "The adjustments applied are non-destructive, meaning no pixels are permanently altered."

01 Blue Skies
Select the Smart Brush and use the Blue Skies preset in the upper area. Use the 'Add to' and 'Subtract from' selection icons to help perfect the selection. Press Cmd/Ctrl+D to deselect.

02 Greenery
Use the Greenery preset on the middle line of tress. Again, use the Add and Subtract icons to help with the selection, and adjust brush size as needed, then deselect.

03 Details
Use the Details preset on the grassy lower portion. This will increase contrast in that area. By now you should be getting the hang of fine-tuning selection areas.

04 Going Green
Use the Going Green preset on the brown tree on the left. Lower the adjustment's opacity to 40% in the top of the Layers palette, then deselect.

05 Brighter
Let's brighten the whole image. Use the Brighten preset and cover the image with the adjustment. The adjustment's mask should be solid white.

06 Edit mask
Set the foreground colour to black, select the Brush tool and use a soft, round brush at 60% opacity. Paint the lower clouds to restore detail.

Selections

Smart Brush tool
The Smart Brush tool lives up to its name. Selectively apply special effects or adjustments to a section of your image. Effects are automatically applied to an adjustment layer so any edit can be instantly removed.

Detail Brush Tool
Use this clever tool to simply "paint on" adjustments without the automatic selection function the Smart Brush tool comes with, leaving you to brush where you want to.

Refine Edge
Use the Refine Edge setting to get a smoother outline to your Smart Brush selection. This is particularly handy when it comes to more intricate outlines like pet fur, grass or hair.

07 Vignette
Select the Detail Smart Brush tool, ensure New Selection is pressed, and choose Reverse - Night. Continually paint back and forth in the central area to get darkened edges.

08 Hue/ Saturation
To finalise, click the Adjustment Layer icon at the top of the Layers Palette and choose Hue/Saturation. Increase Saturation to +20 to make the colour more vivid.

No clouds? No problem! Fill up the empty blue with interest

01 Brighten subject
Use the Smart Brush with the Brighter preset on the statue. Use the 'Add to' and' Subtract from' selection icons to aid you in perfecting the selection.

02 Improve sky
Press Cmd/Ctrl+D to deselect so we can apply a new adjustment. Again use the Smart Brush, this time with the Blue Skies preset on the dull blue. Deselect again.

03 Add clouds
You can then go ahead and use the Smart Brush with the Clouds preset to fill in the blue. Now feel free to edit any of the adjustments you've made by double-clicking on the icon.

Other enhancement options Swap out those clouds with other effects

Brick Wall

Flowery

Honeycomb

Random

Satin

Wallpaper

Selections

Rectangular Marquee Tool   M

Elliptical Marquee Tool   M

Single Row Marquee Tool

Single Column Marquee Tool

The Marquee tools

Learn the basics of these straightforward selection tools

The Marquee selection tools have been around since the beginning of time (well, the beginning of Photoshop time, that is), and remain in place because of their versatility. Essentially a simple boundary acting as a selection, a Marquee tool has many uses. They enable you to make selections within your work based on a specific shape, so can help with creating fun graphical elements or manipulating things with a clear form in

photographs such as rectangular buildings. Read on to find out how to make the most of the Marquee tools using the given options and how they can interact with each other to break the normal boundaries.

If you're using Photoshop, you have the options of single pixel marquees, but for Elements users, the Elliptical and Rectangular tools are the only ones at your disposal. Read on and learn to feather, anti-alias and join marquees together for your artwork.

APPLY FEATHERING

01 Choose size
Set the amount of Feather before making a selection for it to work. The number must be between 0 and 250px, and will depend on the size of your image. This can help select things that have a less defined edge.

02 Make selection
With the Feather value set, make a selection using one of the tools. To see how the feathering looks, hit Q to turn Quick Mask mode on/off. Hit Ctrl/Cmd+D to remove the marquee if it needs doing again.

Cut or reposition
After making the selection

Cut and move
When a marquee has been laid over a subject, you can cut and move it with the Move tool. Hit V for a shortcut and, when you hover over the selection, you should see a pair of scissors appear enabling you to move it.

Reposition
To move a marquee selection without cutting out that part of your image, simply make sure the tool is still selected. You can then hover over the marquee to reposition it or nudge it using the arrow keys.

ADD AND SUBTRACT SELECTIONS

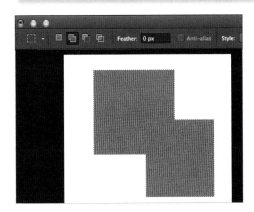

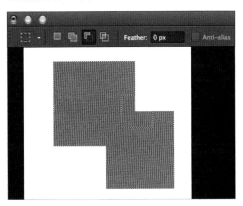

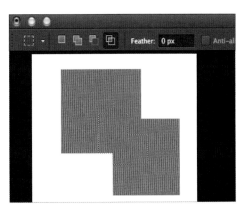

Add
After using one of the Marquee tools, hold Shift and draw another over the edge of the existing one. You'll notice that the two areas are added together for a more dynamic selection.

Subtract
The third box along in the Options bar is the Subtract command. For its shortcut, hold Alt/Opt and draw another marquee over the existing one. This will cut a hole in your selection in that shape.

Intersect
The last choice in the Options bar is for intersecting two marquee selections. You can instantly activate this with Shift+Alt/Opt. Any selections made over the existing one will cut from the touching lines.

SOURCE FILE AVAILABLE

Understand Quick Mask

Discover this versatile tool, which is great for making selections easily and quickly – hence the name!

The Quick Mask mode is one of the most versatile tools you are likely to find within Photoshop's expansive toolbox. Its primary use is for isolating areas that you want left untouched by any adjustments or tweaks, and it is easy to get to grips with.

Quick Mask mode has been around since Photoshop 6.0 and offers a fantastic alternative to the traditional Selection tools. If you find yourself more partial to using the Paintbrush rather than the fiddly Pen tool, then this could well become your ideal selection method.

The Quick Mask mode is activated by clicking on the square icon that contains a white circle. This is situated at the bottom of the Toolbar alongside the Standard mode (a white box with a white circle). For instant access, you can simply hit the letter 'Q' on your keyboard and Quick Mask mode activates or deactivates.

This is a fantastic feature to help in the creation of a whole host of effects. Use it to create quick and easy vignettes for your portraits, paint a Quick Mask on specific colours to achieve amazing selective colouring results, or simply use it to protect an area from an image adjustment you're about to perform.

If you've never used this feature before, we're certain it will be in constant use from this day forward!

"Use it to create quick and easy vignettes for your portraits or achieve amazing selective colouring results"

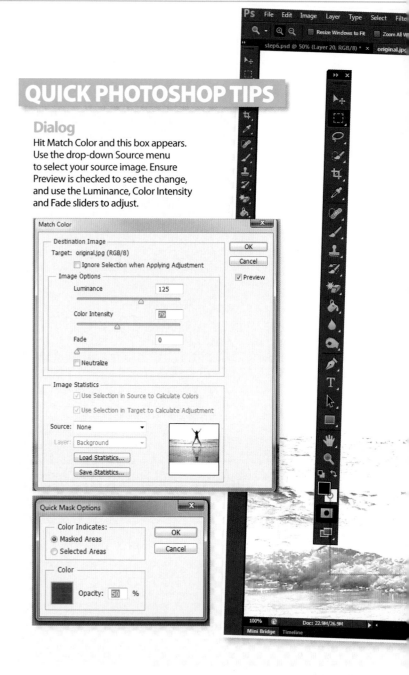

QUICK PHOTOSHOP TIPS

Dialog
Hit Match Color and this box appears. Use the drop-down Source menu to select your source image. Ensure Preview is checked to see the change, and use the Luminance, Color Intensity and Fade sliders to adjust.

01 Quick Mask
The Quick Mask mode is a fantastic way to select objects or people within a scene. It's not as fiddly as the Pen tool and is easily erased.

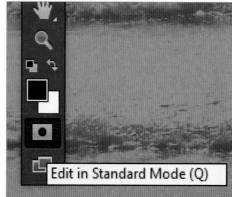

02 Activate
Open up an image in Photoshop and hit 'Q' to select the Quick Mask mode. You can also activate it by choosing the grey box with a circle.

03 Brush it on
Select the Brush tool and choose a suitable size. Paint over everything you don't need, using the Eraser if you make any mistakes.

Colour your mask
If the colour of your mask is too similar to the colours within your image, double-click on the Quick Mask icon. Now click on the Color swatch and select a colour. You can adjust the opacity here as well.

Get control with brushes
You can use any brush to apply a Quick Mask. We recommend you use a soft brush for details such as hair and fur – this will give you a softer, more subtle selection.

Settings
To reverse the way the mask operates, just double-click on the Quick Mask icon and select Masked Areas (masked areas are black) or Selected Areas (masked areas are white).

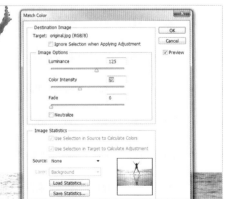

04 Enjoy
Deactivate the Quick Mask by hitting 'Q'. You'll have an isolated selection highlighted by marching ants. You are now free to do anything you like with this!

05 Colour change
The colour of the mask can often be hard to see. Double-click on the Quick Mask icon and a dialog box will appear. Choose a mask colour here.

06 Match Color
The Match Color tool is found in Image>Adjustments>Match Color. Ensure that both your images are open in Photoshop first.

Refine Edge in Photoshop CS6

A process that makes a difficult task that little bit easier, Refine Edge is a digital blessing in disguise

Refine Edge is a fantastic little tool to play with in Photoshop. It means that even complete beginners can cut out complex objects, like hair and trees perfectly, with little hassle.

You can easily create a simple, rough selection around the subject that you want to cut out, and then use Refine Edge to perfect it. There are loads of options to play with, but controls like Smart Radius and Decontaminate Colors mean that Photoshop can do most of the hard work for you.

As well as being far more intelligent than previous versions, Refine Edge now gives you a choice of output destinations once you've perfected the selection. One of the most useful is New Layer With Layer Mask, because this gives you a super-accurate layer mask based on your selection that you can continue to work with manually as needed. You can also choose to output to a new layer with transparency, or even a completely new document.

Another way you can use the Refine Edge command is directly on an existing mask via the Masks panel. In this form you'll find the Refine Edge technology labelled as Mask Edge, and you'll find all the same powerful controls at your fingertips. Our short tutorial will get you started.

"Refine Edge is a fantastic little tool… even complete beginners can cut out complex objects like hair and trees perfectly"

USING REFINE EDGE

ORIGINAL

IN PROGRESS

01 Make a quick selection
First make a rough selection of the subject. Thanks to the new technology, this selection doesn't have to be that accurate.

02 Invoke Refine Edge
Hit the Refine Edge button if your Selection tool is still active, or otherwise go to Select>Refine Edge. The Refine Edge dialog appears.

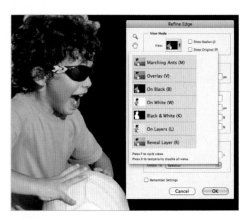

03 View modes
In the Refine Edge dialog you can pick one of many View modes. These help you to judge the quality of your hair mask.

FINAL

Smarter edges

The results of this new Edge Detection technology are truly remarkable, but to realise just how much difference it makes it's useful to see a direct comparison between the mask generated by the initial rough selection we made (left), and the mask itself after applying the new features of the Refine Edge command (right). You can see the before and after masks below, and easily see the level of hair detail you can achieve with just a couple of clicks.

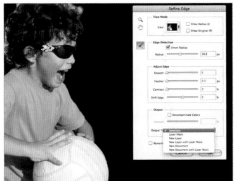

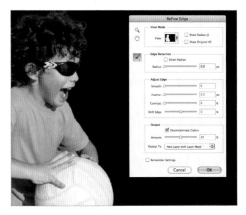

04 Smart Radius

Adjust the selection for the other edges (not the hair). Check Smart Radius and adjust the Radius slider. Choose Output To Selection and click OK.

05 Hair magic

Go to Select>Refine Edge again. Choose your View mode and click on the Refine Radius tool. Use this tool to simply brush over wispy strands of hair.

06 Decontaminate

Any remaining colour fringes around the edges of the extracted subject can be removed using the Decontaminate option.

Replace dull skies with selections

Don't let your skies be a washout – simply add a better one from another image

Even with an amazing camera and a masterful handling of its controls, there's little that can be done about bleak skies.

You know the ones we mean – those pale grey expanses typical of drizzly days. Because the skies are so bleak, there is nothing for Photoshop to hang onto in order to make a fix. So the best option in this case is to just replace the sky with a better one. It sounds a tad drastic but is actually very easy to do. Once you try it, you'll find yourself doing it again and again, meaning you won't lose an otherwise decent photo to bleak horizons.

It is always worth having a handy supply of sky photos on your computer for such occasions, so if it's a nice day and you are out and about with your camera, then consider taking a few shots of just the sky so that you can slot them into duller snaps and give them a new lease of life.

In order to make the selecting on the sky easiest, try to only snap the sky, otherwise you will have to cut out any distracting elements like birds, planes and the tops of buildings, adding to your workload.

What we are going to do in this project involves the use of layers. We have a whole section on layers in this book, which starts on page 106. We only use two layers here: one for our original image and one for our new sky. By showing just the sky in one layer, and just the house and gardens in the other, we can blend the two together easily.

"You won't lose an otherwise decent photo to bleak horizons"

ORIGINAL

New sky in minutes
Master the following steps to improve your shots

01 The problem
Here we have an image that was taken on a rather miserable day. The overall colours are good, but the sky is a bit dull and could look better.

02 Get a new sky
Find a new sky image with better colours. Open this up by going to the File>Open. Go to the Select menu and then scroll down to All. Click to accept.

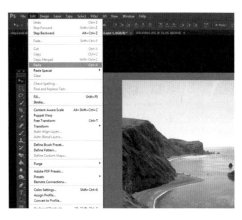

03 Paste
You will see some shimmery lines appear around the edges of the sky. Go to Edit>Copy. Now go back to the original image and go to Edit>Paste.

04 Line up
Your new sky will appear over the original image. Select the Move tool and move the sky up and into position. Now look at the Layers palette.

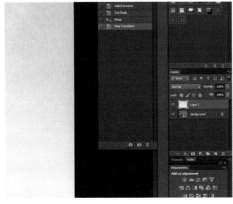

05 Some layer work
The sky is sitting above the original photo. Click the eye icon next to the sky layer to make it invisible and then click on the Background layer.

06 Magic selection
Pick the Magic Wand tool and set the Tolerance to 52%. Click on the sky area. Go to the Layers palette, click on the new sky layer and click the eye icon.

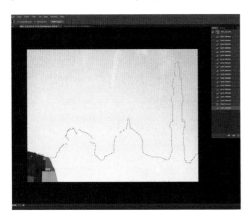

07 Inverse selection
Go to the Select menu and click on Inverse. This selects everything except the sky (ie the structure and the tree).

08 Tie it together
Press the Backspace or Delete key. The structure will magically reappear and you can see the new sky in its new setting.

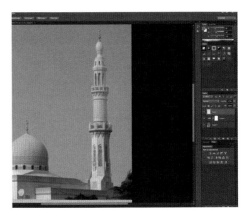

09 Finish it up
At the moment it looks a little too bright, so go back to the Layers palette, make sure you are on the sky layer and drag the Opacity slider.

Brushes

"The Brush tool allows you to paint in Photoshop. Brushes are divided into categories which you can swap between"

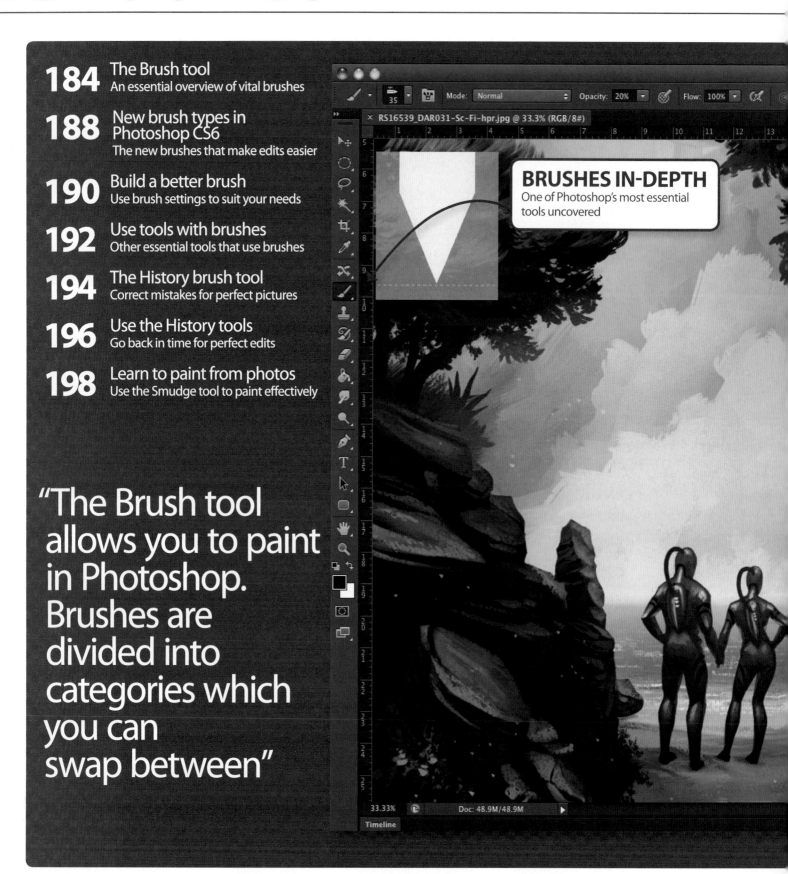

BRUSHES IN-DEPTH
One of Photoshop's most essential tools uncovered

MAKE YOUR OWN BRUSHES
When Photoshop's preset brushes just aren't what you're looking for - create your own to suit your style!

BRUSH EFFECTS
Navigate your way around the Brushes palette with ease

Brushes

Brush Tool | B
Pencil Tool | B
Color Replacement Tool | B
Mixer Brush Tool | B

Additional settings
Some special brushes in Photoshop CS5 and CS6 will have additional settings in the main Options bar to play with

Choose from a variety
There are lots of different categories of brushes to choose from, such as Calligraphic, Dry Media and Natural

The Brush tool

Add brushstrokes to your artworks with this handy tool

Photoshop and Photoshop Elements boast the Brush tool, which lets you apply digital paint strokes, just as if you were using the real thing. You can do just about everything with your Brush tool that you can with a real paint brush. Choose from a range of different brush types, change the size of the brush tip and decide how thick you want your paint to be (think of the Opacity as being how watered down your paint is so that you can see more or less through the paint to the canvas underneath).

While there are lots of different settings and you can get quite technical, it is easy to pick the Brush tool, set a colour and simply start painting. We'll be running through the key options that you need to know on these pages. While most Photoshop beginners will use a mouse, once you get a bit more comfortable with digital painting, you may want to try out a tablet!

"You can do just about everything with your Brush tool that you can with a real paint brush"

THE BRUSH TOOL OPTIONS Find your way around the palettes

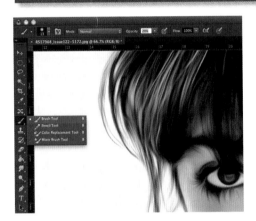

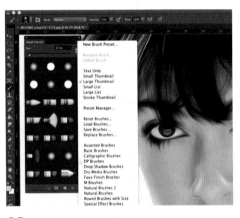

01 The Brush tool
The Brush tool can be chosen from the main Toolbar in both Photoshop and Elements. There are settings along the top of the interface.

02 The Brush Presets
The Brush Presets palette shows you all available tips to select and use (in versions CS2 and below these presets are within one Brushes palette).

03 The Brush palette
The Brush palette is where you can alter and customise the look of brushes. Have a play with the sliders and see how they affect your strokes.

SET UP A BRUSH IN ELEMENTS Pick the right brush for your work

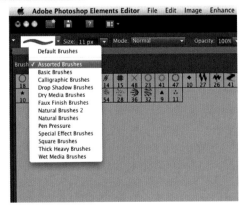

01 Select the Brush tool
Choosing the Brush tool (B) will open up the Brush options, which are shown at the top of the interface in the Options bar ready for you to tweak.

02 Choose a brush
The first palette in the Options bar shows you all brushes. You can choose different categories of from the drop-down menu to suit your needs.

03 Size matters
Alter the size of your brush by clicking the Size option and dragging the slider. Alter the blend mode of the brushstrokes in this Options bar too.

Brushes

Best brushes Get the most out of Photoshop's brushes

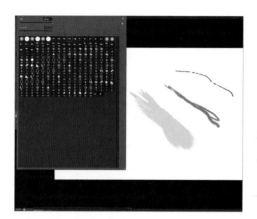

Calligraphic Brushes
The Calligraphic Brushes set contains a number of brushes tailored to emulate calligraphic nib shapes. Set the Angle Jitter to 'Tilt' for maximum effect.

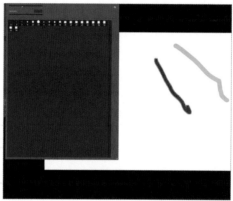

Drop Shadow Brushes
Drop Shadow Brushes provide brushes of both round and square varieties with feathered edges to render shadows with a soft edge to them.

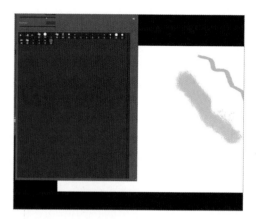

Dry Media Brushes
A great set of brushes that emulate traditional media such as pastels and charcoals. A great place to start if you want to create custom brushes.

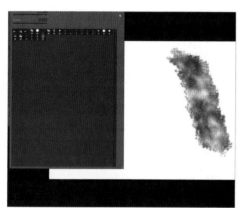

Dry Media Brushes
Most of the brushes here make use of many of the attributes you can alter in the Brushes Palette, such as adding Texture and Dual Brush functionality.

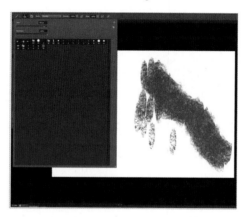

Dry Media Brushes 2
By looking through the Brushes Palette settings you'll get an idea of why these brushes behave the way they do, which will help you make your own.

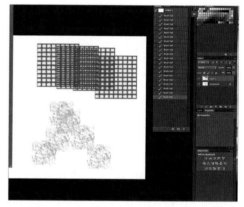

Faux Finish Brushes
With brushes like Plastic Wrap and Sea Sponge this set appears quite limited, but playing around with the settings makes them a lot more versatile.

Faux Finish Brushes 2
Toy with the settings of the Texture Comb brushes; with a little experimentation you can create some very expressive brushwork.

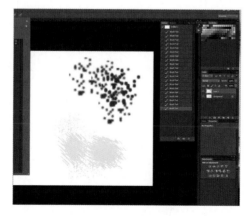

Natural Brushes
Natural Brushes includes Stipple and Spray brushes. The Stipple brush works well with Angle Jitter set to Pen Tilt and Opacity set to Pen Pressure.

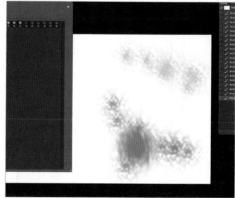

Natural Brushes
The Spray brush works like the Airbrush but has a faint stippling effect so the result is more textured. Set the Opacity to Pen Pressure for best results.

Natural Brushes 2

Natural Brushes 2 collects brushes that have textures built into them. Chalk and Pastel effect brushes are well represented here.

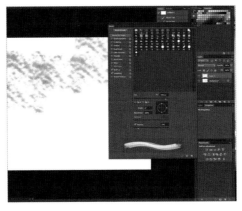

Natural Brushes 2

To get a natural build-up effect set Opacity and Flow to Pen Pressure. Set the Blending Mode to Multiply in the Toolbar to enhance it even further.

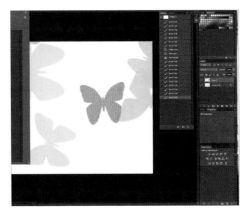

Special Effect Brushes

Other than Drippy Watercolor, which has some painting application, the brushes here are fun but slightly gimmicky.

Special Effect Brushes

The Azalea brush switches Foreground/Background colours, while the Butterfly brush's high Hue Jitter randomises them.

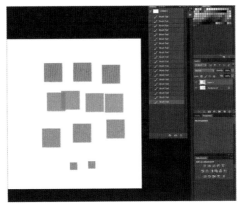

Square Brushes

Square Brushes is misleading; there is really just one brush here supplied at a number of different sizes. Its brush work is surprisingly pleasing, though.

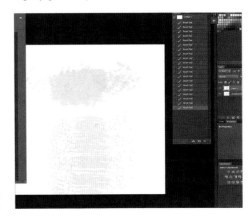

Thick Heavy Brushes

The Thick Heavy Brushes set features five bristle effect brushes that will add a little texture to your brush work.

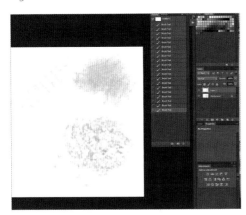

Wet Media Brushes

Wet Media Brushes includes a superb selection of assorted brushes. As well as watercolour brushes there are also ink, oil and dry brushes.

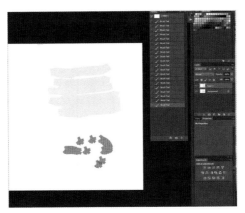

Wet Media Brushes

There are a number of Brush Tip Shapes employed in the Wet Media Brushes section, which makes the effects of each one noticeably different to the last.

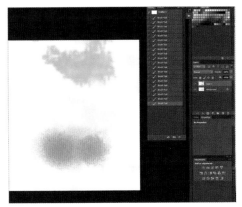

Wet Media Brushes

The variety of styles in this category is impressive; most use Textures and at least one other feature. The watercolour brushes use the Wet Edges option.

Brushes

New brush types in Photoshop CS6

The latest version of Photoshop offers two completely new brush types to play with

If you're into painting digitally, Photoshop CS6 has introduced two new types of brushes for you to achieve an even more authentic painting experience.

Adobe started to take digital painting very seriously in Photoshop CS5, with the introduction of Bristle brushes and Mixer brushes. The Bristle brushes are particularly useful because they have virtual bristles that react to tilt and pressure sensitivity in a much more advanced way than you'll be used to. With standard brushes, when you pushed down hard on your stylus you just got the biggest possible stamp of your brush; when you push down with a Bristle brush, the bristles actually splay out on the virtual canvas just like an actual paint brush, giving you more expressive brush strokes and a more realistic appearance.

The Mixer brush uses the Bristle brush functionality to pick up the digital paint that you've already laid down on the canvas and lets you alter and mix the colours you have on each individual bristle.

Now, in CS6, we have Erodible Tip brushes, which are like real-life pencils, in that the tips wear down as you use them and you need to hit the Sharpen button to get a sharp point again. Your stroke is finer when your pencil is freshly sharpened and rougher as it starts to wear down. Secondly, we now have dedicated Airbrush brushes for spraying paint across your images.

All of these brushes, from CS5 and CS6, have a preview window that pops up when you select the brushes, which gives you a 3D representation of your brush, and as you change its settings the preview is updated, making it easy for you to make real-media comparisons.

> "Your stroke is finer when your pencil is freshly sharpened and rougher as it starts to wear down"

A VISUAL GUIDE TO THE CS6 PAINTING LAYOUT

A handy guide to help you visualise your brush

The preview box displays the exact angle that your brush is tilting so you can see the position and shape that your brush will make on the canvas.

01 Find Erodible Tip brushes

The new Erodible Tip brushes in Photoshop CS6 are easy to find as they look like a pencil in the Brush Presets palette. Pick one to access its options.

02 Brush options

In the Brush palette you can now set up the brush to your liking. You can pick the Shape of the pencil nib, as well as its Size, Softness and Spacing.

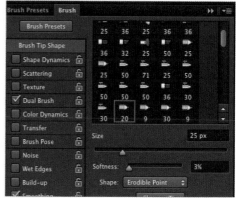

03 Sharpen up

As you draw, the pencil stroke will get rougher and larger, as the nib is wearing down. To sharpen it, hit the Sharpen Tip brush to get a fine point.

Different shapes for Erodible Tips

When you select Erodible Tip brushes, the Shape option gives a drop-down menu with the brush shape presets. Choose from Point, Flat, Round, Square and Triangle.

Different icons

You can easily see the new brushes added in Photoshop CS5 and CS6 as their icons look a little different. The standard brushes are shown as representative brushstrokes, but with the newer brushes you see a picture of the actual brush instead.

Experiment with settings

As you play with the settings for any of the new brush types, then you will see the preview window is updated with your changes, so you can easily set up a brush exactly how you need it.

04 Locate Airbrushes

Just as with the Erodible Tips, the Airbrush tools are also easy to locate, as you will see the little Airbrush nozzle on the brush icon.

05 Set it up

There are loads of different settings associated with the Airbrushes. You can choose how grainy your paint is, how much it splatters, and its size.

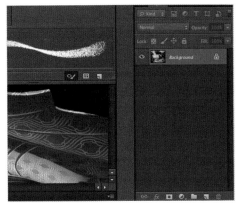

06 Toggle the preview

The preview window to see how your brush setup looks can be turned on and off using the little icon at the bottom of the Brush palette.

Build a better brush

Don't just rely on brushes 'from the box'; create your own custom brushes to suit your painting style

Although Photoshop comes with an array of impressive brushes built in, they're barely the tip of the iceberg; Photoshop's brushes are capable of much more. When you start to alter their settings by clicking on the Brushes tab you'll see just how versatile they can be.

When digitally painting, it's best to work with a graphics tablet. Using a pen stylus will allow you to make the most of Photoshop's brushes with settings like Flow and Opacity.

To customise brushes you'll need to access the Brushes Palette (press F5). The Brushes Palette is where you control every aspect of the brush tool, and although the number of aspects at your control can be a little daunting at first glance, keep persisting and you'll soon be customising brushes like a pro.

You can choose the brush you want to customise by clicking the Brush Presets to bring up a brush stroke thumbnail preview. When you've selected the brush you want, you have a number of options. Clicking on Brush Tip Shape will display the stroke your current brush will make. Here you have the options to change the X and Y axis of the brush head, the Angle, Roundness, Hardness and Spacing.

You can add texture to your brushes, or use Dual Brush to combine two brushes and come up with a completely new third brush. You can even add Scattering to a brush which is great for painting things like leaves and foliage.

"Using a pen stylus will allow you to make the most of Photoshop's brushes"

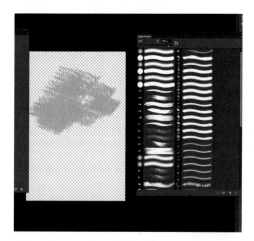

Size
Custom brushes will have their Size Jitter set to 'Pen Pressure', but you can set the Minimum Diameter of the brush head to maintain a brush's appearance.

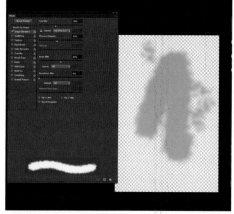

Other Dynamics
Adding the Flow and Opacity Jitter to the settings to Pen Pressure in conjunction with the Size Jitter will make your brushes feel more natural.

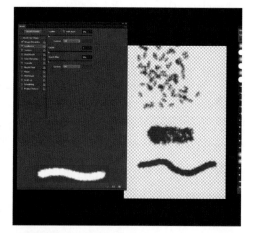

Spacing
Changing the Spacing of a brush tip can drastically alter it. The three strokes here are drawn with the same brush, but the Spacing is 1%, 25% and 100%.

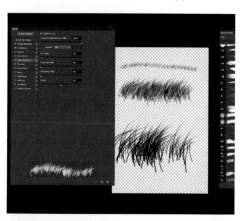

Color Dynamics
Use two different colours in one brush stroke by setting the Foreground/Background Jitter Control to Pen Pressure.

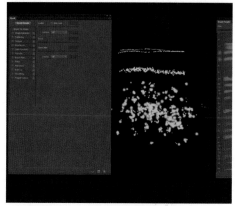

Scattering
Scattering multiplies the number of times the Brush Tip Shape is drawn in a brush stroke and scatters them along the line you've drawn.

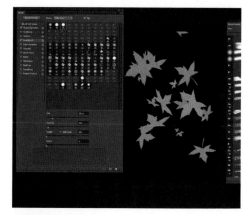

Dual Brush
Dual Brush combines two Brushes together with often unpredictable results. Experimentation is the key here.

QUICK PHOTOSHOP TIPS

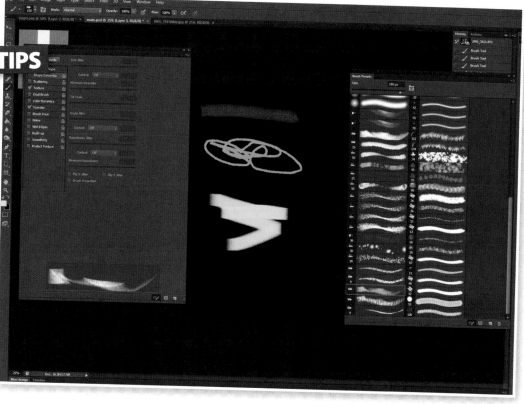

Intuitive brush sizes

Click on the 'Shape Dynamics' tabs and set the Size Jitter to 'Pen Pressure'; your brush size will increase when you apply more pressure to your stylus

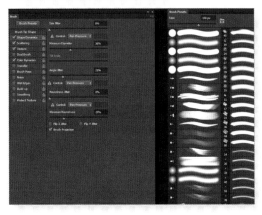

Tablet Options: Other Dynamics/ Transfer

For intuitive brush strokes, set both Flow and Opacity Jitter to 'Pen Pressure'. This will result in the harder you push down on your stylus, the more opaque the brush stroke becomes

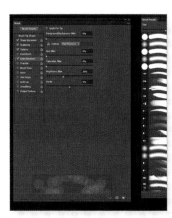

Change colours in one stroke

Set Color Dynamics to 'Pen Pressure' and apply light Pressure to start painting with the background colour, apply more pressure and the colour of the brush stroke blends into the Foreground colour

Alter a brush by tilting your pen

Certain tablets will have the ability to understand how you're tilting your stylus. Setting the Angle Jitter to 'Pen Tilt' takes advantage of this; Photoshop will alter your brush strokes accordingly

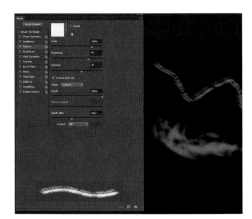

Texture

If you're not so keen on the digital look, make your Brushes look more like natural media by adding a Texture to it that affects the Brush Tip Shape.

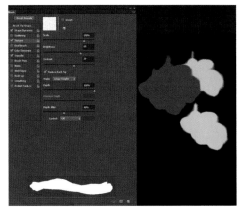

Change Blending Modes

You can set a brush's Blending Mode to Screen to make every stroke lighter than the first, which works great for rendering things like hair or grass.

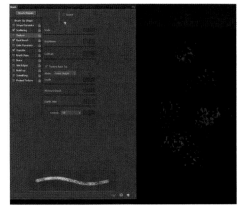

Spatter Effects

Spatter brushes are a great way of adding a messy look. Make sure to alter your brush's Scattering and Angle options for a randomised appearance.

Brushes

Use tools with brushes

A lot of the tools in Photoshop use brushes; here's
our quick guide to the most popular ones

Understanding how Photoshop's brushes work isn't just important to people that want to paint digitally, the knowledge will help you in photo editing and pretty much any Photoshop-related task. All of the tools we look at here can be used with any Brush Tip Shape you have in your Brush Library because they all work with Photoshop's Brush Engine.

No matter which of the Brush Engine-based tools you use, whether it's the Clone Stamp, History Brush or Smudge Tool, you'll be able to alter the options in two specific areas in your Workspace: the Toolbar and the Brushes Palette. The Brushes Palette can be opened by pressing F5 and contains the same brush-editing options regardless of which tool you are currently using.

The Toolbar is positioned directly below the Main Navigation Bar in Photoshop. Unlike the Brushes Palette, the settings available here are tool

specific, you'll get a different selection of settings when the Eraser is selected than you would if using the Blur Tool.

Common elements in the Toolbar that each tool shares are the display of the Brush Tip shape and size and the brush's Blending Mode. There will also be an icon to enable your graphics tablet to override controls set in the Brushes panel.

Opacity and Flow are common settings to see in the Toolbar when using a brush-based tool and are helpful for controlling the strength of a brush's impact if you're using a mouse instead of a pressure-sensitive tablet.

"Opacity and Flow are helpful for controlling a brush's impact"

Popular brushes The various brushes and what they do

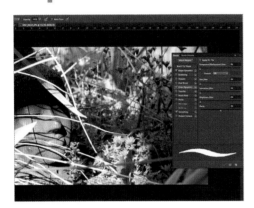

Hard Mix
The Pencil and Brush are almost identical but the Pencil creates hard-edged Aliased strokes and the Brush makes smoother Anti-Aliased brush strokes.

The Clone Stamp
Hit Alt to select an area that will be duplicated when you use the brush elsewhere on the image. Clone from All Layers or just the current Layer.

History Brush
The History Brush lets you fix mistakes and apply Filters; any area you paint on reverts to a previously defined state by using info from the history palette.

Art History Brush
A customisable special effects brush that gives you a pseudo-painterly effect superior to that of using a Filter by dragging your cursor over a photo.

Erasers
Used for both corrections and special effects, changing your brush type and Opacity will give you a range of appearances to remove solid pixels.

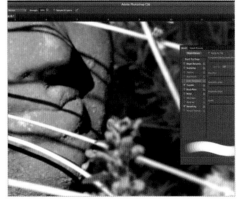

Blur
The Blur tool allows you to blur small areas such as wrinkles or spots. Use with restraint to avoid an obviously over-blurred image.

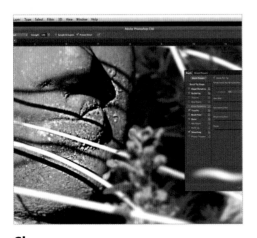

Sharpen
The Sharpen Tool increases the Contrast of any pixels you paint over it with to make the images appear crisper.

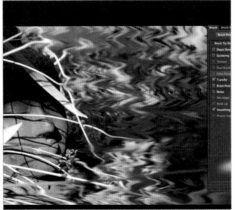

Smudge
The Smudge tool smears your paint across the canvas. The higher the Pressure level, the more of the paint will be removed from the canvas.

Dodge and Burn
Dodge and Burn lighten or darken any area you move the brush over. You can change their Range to affect Highlights, Midtones or Shadows.

Brushes

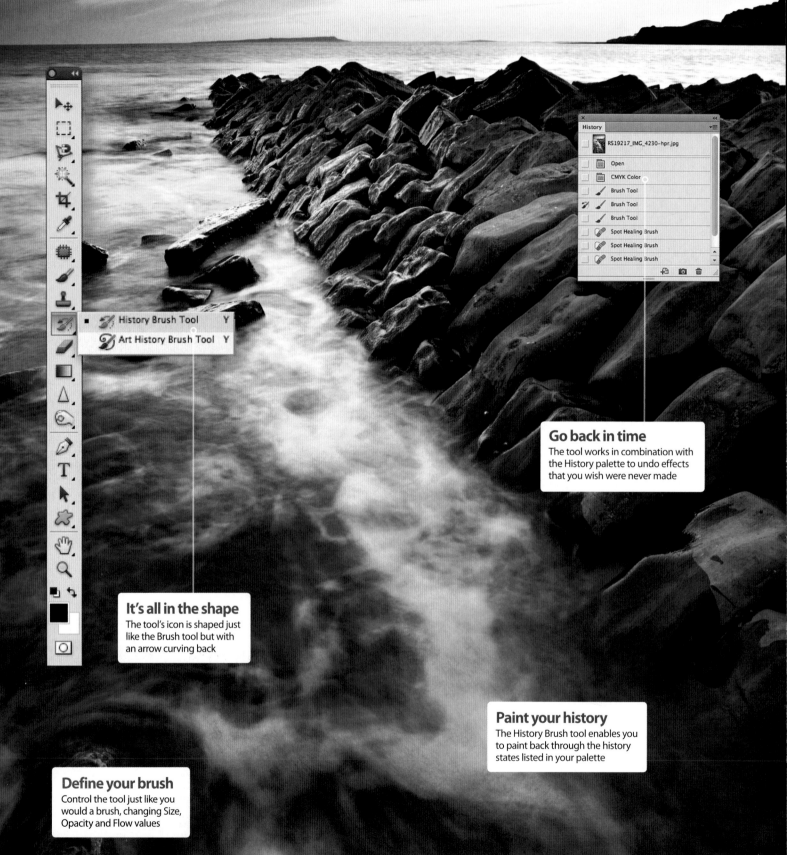

History Brush Tool   Y
Art History Brush Tool   Y

History

RS19217_IMG_4230-hpr.jpg

Open
CMYK Color
Brush Tool
Brush Tool
Brush Tool
Spot Healing Brush
Spot Healing Brush
Spot Healing Brush

Go back in time
The tool works in combination with the History palette to undo effects that you wish were never made

It's all in the shape
The tool's icon is shaped just like the Brush tool but with an arrow curving back

Paint your history
The History Brush tool enables you to paint back through the history states listed in your palette

Define your brush
Control the tool just like you would a brush, changing Size, Opacity and Flow values

The History Brush tool

Learn the creative way to step back through your edits

I t's only human to make mistakes and luckily, when you do them digitally, there's an Undo command to go back in time. Unfortunately, sometimes they can be so far back in your History palette that they are no longer retrievable… or are they? Editing history is much easier with this incredible tool.

"Editing history is much easier with this incredible tool"

The History Brush tool (Y) is a way of undoing edits made to an image that you regret using all the functionality of a brush.

Working with the History palette, the tool can be used to track back to any point in the editing timeline that you choose. And, essentially being a brush, the tool is very adaptable, giving you a lot of freedom over how much and which parts of your image you want to undo.

We take a look at how to use the tool on an image that has had a filter and monochrome effect applied.

Using the History Brush tool Revert back to your original image with a creative effect

01 Apply effect
For this effect we removed colour from our image and applied a filter. Open an image and press Cmd/Ctrl+J to duplicate it onto a new layer. The filter used here is Ocean Ripple, found under Filter>Distort. Set Ripple Size to 6 and Ripple Magnitude to 10 inside the dialog.

02 Remove colour
Any effect will work with the clever tool, but to convert the image to monochrome as in our example, press Cmd/Ctrl+Shift+U. You should see the word Desaturate appear as the current state in your History palette.

03 The History palette
Next to each state in your History palette is a blank box, and the opening state of your image can be found at the very top. Simply click on the box next to the state Ocean Ripple to use it together with the History Brush tool.

04 Select tool
The History Brush tool can be found halfway down the Toolbar and has the shortcut Y. The tool comes with its own settings in the Options bar as well as an array of brush-tip presets for you to choose from. Go for a brush with an interesting pattern for a more creative effect.

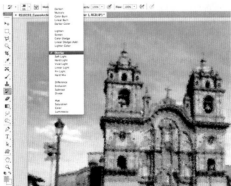

05 Extra control
The Mode drop-down in the Options bar changes the way the tool reacts with the colour and light in your image. For a punchy, high-contrast effect choose Overlay. If you're using a graphics tablet, use the symbol next to Opacity to set the strength of the tool according to the pressure you apply.

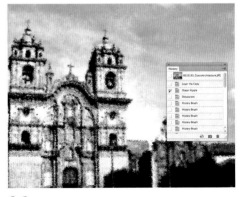

06 Time to paint
Just as you would with a normal Photoshop brush, paint over the main subjects in your image. The effect will reveal the coloured version before the Desaturate command was applied. All that's left is the Ocean Ripple filter. Experiment with brush tips for different styles.

Brushes

Use the History tools in Photoshop

Move parts of your image through time and correct mistakes you hadn't noticed

Want to change history? Meet Photoshop's answer to Doc Brown's DeLorean: the History Brush tool! While not quite as flashy as a time-travelling car, it's a lot more reliable and doesn't require you to have a working flux capacitor!

The History Brush tool is one of the most useful and overlooked image-editing features in Photoshop; it reverts any part of an image back to a previous state without affecting the rest of the image. You can edit your photo as a whole and then use the History Brush to restore your chosen areas back to their original appearance. It has many applications, not only the aforementioned selective image editing. If you've ever had one of those annoying "Uh-oh, I hadn't noticed I'd changed that!" moments, the History Brush tool can be used to correct unintentional changes you may have made

to areas of an image. All you have to do is locate the last point the section was correct in the History palette and set the source by clicking in the small column on the left of the History palette, then 'turn back time' and fix your mistakes by painting the image back to how it used to look with the History Brush tool.

You can brighten or darken with the History Brush by selecting the current state as the source then setting the History brush's Blending mode (in the toolbar) to Screen (to lighten) or Multiply (to darken). The tool will then use the existing information to re-draw a brighter or darker version.

"It's a lot more reliable and doesn't require a working flux capacitor!"

History Options	
☑ Automatically Create First Snapshot	OK
☐ Automatically Create New Snapshot When Saving	Cancel
☑ Allow Non-Linear History	
☐ Show New Snapshot Dialog by Default	
☐ Make Layer Visibility Changes Undoable	

QUICK PHOTOSHOP TIPS

Bring things back quickly

Sometimes it's quicker to mask off the area that you want changes to remain intact and use a large brush to revert the remainder of the image.

Paint from an alternate future!

Ticking 'Allow Non Linear History' in the History palette menu lets you make changes from based upon a state that you have since undone!

Fading through time

You can change the opacity of the strokes you have just applied by going to Edit>Fade immediately after using the History Brush tool.

Use on filters

Useful filters like Dust & Scratches blur an entire image. If you only need a small section changed, use the History Brush to undo the filter on the relevant areas.

01 Apply to a whole image

Open your image and go to Image>Adjustments> Hue Saturation. In the box move the Saturation Slider to the left to desaturate the image.

02 Quickly bring back the subject

Press 'Y' to select the History brush and select a large Airbush with its Opacity set to Pen Pressure in the Brushes tab to bring back most of the subject.

03 Tidy up the edges

Switch to a smaller hard-edged brush to bring back the edges of the subject so the background is still desaturated and the subject is in colour again.

Learn to paint from photos

If you can move a mouse you can create a digital painting – meet the Smudge tool

It appears that even with the great advances in digital art tools, Adobe still seems to have overlooked the 'make a good painting now' filter. So what do you do if you would love to paint but lack the ability or confidence to try it?

The answer lies with the Smudge tool. Available in early versions of Photoshop and Photoshop Elements, this artistic wonder lets you push and, well, smudge pixels about to create a painterly effect. The real boon comes from the fact that you can use a photo for all the shapes and colours, leaving you free to concentrate on moving the tool around for the effect you want.

The actual process is a simple case of clicking and dragging with a mouse. It makes light work of an otherwise fairly difficult look to achieve. The direction you move dictates the direction of the brush mark. To show you how easy it can be, we've created a composition (using basic cutting and pasting skills) and then set the Smudge tool to work. This runs you through moving the tool to get different effects. It is much easier to show than to describe!

"The actual process is a simple case of clicking and dragging"

ORIGINAL

Get painterly with photos
You don't need to be an amazing artist for this to work

01 Create the composition
The Smudge tool (R) can hide a lot of selection sins, so why not have a go at creating your own composition? In this tutorial, we took a base photo and added other elements by selecting with the Lasso tool (L) then copying and pasting. It is by no means pretty but it works!

02 Some essential prep work
Open up the start file from your resource pack. The Smudge tool can be very photo-realistic (see the supplied bonus tutorial) but we are going to use the Cutout filter to help achieve a looser effect. Grab the Lasso tool from the Toolbar and then draw around the sky area.

Brushes

QUICK TIP

Match the resolution

Comping together a start image is a great thing to do, especially as the Smudge tool is very forgiving of messy selections. However, ensure that the images you're pasting into a scene have the same resolution as your final document. If you are pasting something into a document with a larger resolution, it will appear tiny. Go to Image>Image Size and see what it says in the Resolution box. If you need to change it, uncheck the Resample Image box and enter the value you need in Resolution.

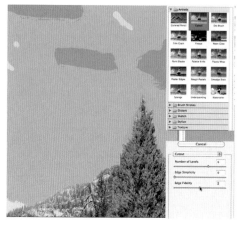

03 Apply filter
Go to Filter>Artistic>Cutout and set Levels to 6, Edge Simplicity to 0 and Edge Fidelity to 2. Deselect and repeat for the next area. See the supplied document for the list of areas and settings used. You can also skip this and use the supplied file.

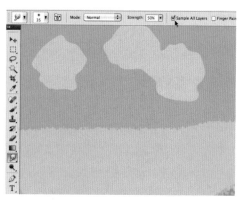

04 Set up the tool
Head to the Toolbar to click on the Smudge tool (it cohabits with the Blur tool). Now head over to the top Options bar and tick the Sample All Layers box. Make sure Finger Painting is deselected. Take note of the Strength setting – this determines how intense the stroke is. We are going to be using 100% throughout.

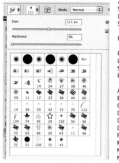

05 Pick the brush
Staying in the Options bar, click on the Brush Preset Picker icon. Click on the small options arrow to see the other preset choices and scoot down to Thick Heavy Brushes. A window will now ask if you want to replace the current brushes. You do, so click OK. Pick the Rough Round Bristle.

06 Start painting!
Create a new layer and call it Sky. Zoom into a view that's comfortable for you and, with a large brush and choppy strokes, move your brush cursor around the canvas, keeping to the form of the objects. You can swoop in towards the middle.

07 The mountain
Make a new layer and call it Mountain. Zoom in and go to the Brush Preset Picker. Pick the Rough Flat Bristle and set a fairly large brush size. Set Strength to 100% and start going over the mountain with diagonal strokes, adjusting the brush size as needed. You can drag the 'paint' to cover any areas missed in the Cutout step.

08 Distant trees
Time for another new layer, this time called Mountain Trees. Be a bit more careful with these and use the Rough Flat Bristle to create the forms of the trees. Click and drag upwards in a straight line to suggest the tops of the trees.

09 Splash about
Another new layer, this time called Water. Staying with the Rough Flat Bristle, move across the water in horizontal strokes. Keep it horizontal to suggest the movement of the water. Start by sweeping along the shoreline and then use smaller strokes for the rest.

10 Sort the conifer

Guess what happens now – that's right, a new layer. Name it Conifer and start smudging over the conifer, adjusting the brush size and following the form. The Rough Flat Bristle still works for this, and is good for dragging out edges for a leafy effect.

11 Rocky outlook

New layer again for the foreground rocks. You know the drill by now – adjust the brush size and follow the objects' forms. Keep the light and shadows as intact as you can, as this is what gives the rocks their mass.

12 The importance of shadow

To stop the rocks looking like they have be plonked into the scene (which, of course, they were), drag out slightly at the edge of the water to give the impression of shadow. This anchors them down and gives a more realistic effect.

13 Floral artistry

The final area is the flowers and grass. Create a new layer for this and use choppy movements to smudge the detail. To suggest grass, use a small brush size then swoop up and out. Look for any areas that are a bit messy from the photo comp. If you see any, just do a general smudge to cover it up.

14 Texture

For the final touch of realism, add in some texture. There are various ways of doing this (the easiest being the Filter>Texture> Texturizer option, but we want to give the impression of buttery oils). Have a peek at the Expert Tip to the right to see what we came up with.

QUICK TIP

Add canvas texture

Add texture to paintings for a final flourish. Duplicate the finished painting and start with 100% for Scaling and 15 for Relief. Use the Eraser tool with the same brush used in the painting. Change the Opacity to 50% and brush over the painting. Try to leave small areas of texture. When you're finished, go to Layer>Flatten Image. You might need to use the Brightness/Contrast command to finish up.

QUICK PHOTOSHOP TIPS

Try to keep in the lines

Although it's true that the Smudge tool can make an art hero out of anyone, there is one absolute, cardinal rule that has to be followed for this to happen. When you are merrily clicking and dragging the brush tip around, follow the form of the object that you are painting over. The Smudge tool has no respect for boundaries and so it will obliterate any definition if you go crazy with the mouse. The good news is that if your paint mark does go a-wandering, you can usually drag back in the opposite direction to fix it (or press Cmd/ Ctrl+U if you notice it immediately).

WRONG   **RIGHT**

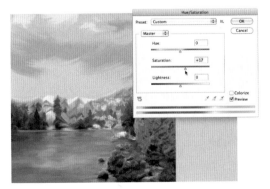

15 Add some zing

One downside of using the Cutout filter is that it does dampen the colours. To fix this, press Cmd/ Ctrl+Opt/Alt+ Shift+E. This creates a single layer but keeps all the others intact. Head to Hue/Saturation and move the Saturation slider to suit.

Filters

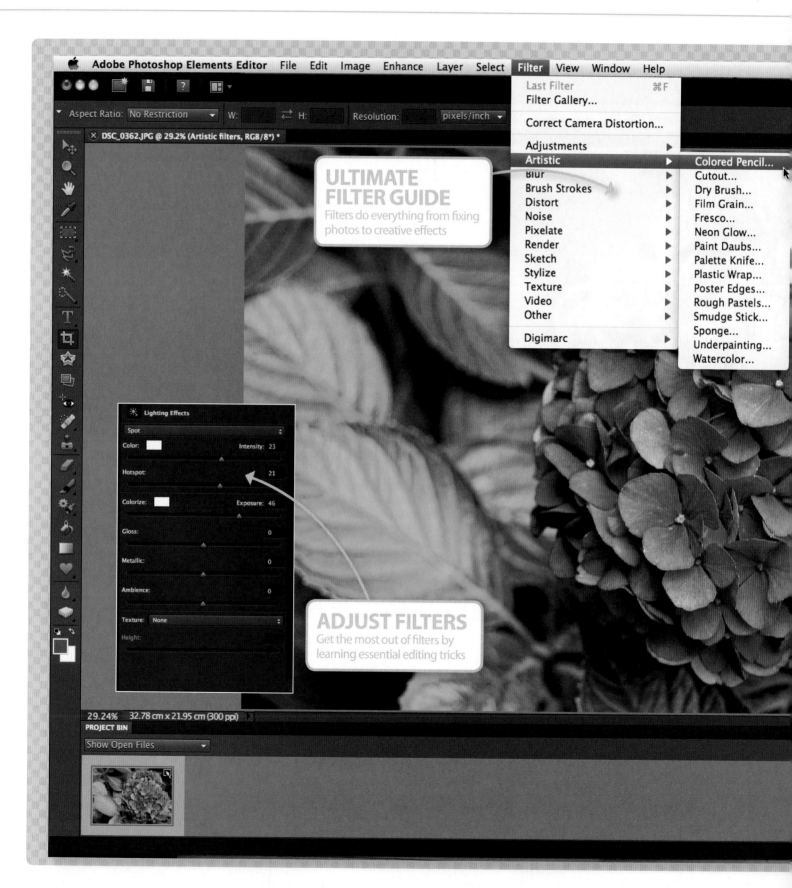

Adobe Photoshop Elements Editor   File   Edit   Image   Enhance   Layer   Select   **Filter**   View   Window   Help

Aspect Ratio: No Restriction   W: H: Resolution: pixels/inch

× DSC_0362.JPG @ 29.2% (Artistic filters, RGB/8*) *

Last Filter   ⌘F
Filter Gallery...

Correct Camera Distortion...

Adjustments ▶
Artistic ▶   Colored Pencil...
Blur ▶   Cutout...
Brush Strokes ▶   Dry Brush...
Distort ▶   Film Grain...
Noise ▶   Fresco...
Pixelate ▶   Neon Glow...
Render ▶   Paint Daubs...
Sketch ▶   Palette Knife...
Stylize ▶   Plastic Wrap...
Texture ▶   Poster Edges...
Video ▶   Rough Pastels...
Other ▶   Smudge Stick...
   Sponge...
Digimarc ▶   Underpainting...
   Watercolor...

ULTIMATE FILTER GUIDE
Filters do everything from fixing photos to creative effects

Lighting Effects

Spot

Color: Intensity: 23

Hotspot: 21

Colorize: Exposure: 46

Gloss: 0

Metallic: 0

Ambience: 0

Texture: None

Height:

ADJUST FILTERS
Get the most out of filters by learning essential editing tricks

29.24%   32.78 cm x 21.95 cm (300 ppi)

PROJECT BIN

Show Open Files

APPLYING FILTER EFFECTS
Learn how to use filters in order to transform your photos

LAYER YOUR FILTER EFFECTS
Build up an array of artistic filters to get an even better outcome

"Spend some time in the Filter Gallery getting to know the options available"

What are filters?

Learn what the filters are and how to use the Filter Gallery dialog box
to preview, control and apply effects quickly and efficiently

Filters are built-in actions that you can apply to an image to create different effects. You can use filters to apply special effects, clean up or retouch your photos in next to no time.

There are a huge number of instances where you can use the Filters, ranging from basic image sharpening or fixing a blurry background to complex filter combinations to create the most intricate effects.

You can find the Filters under the Filter menu in Photoshop. Click on Filter Gallery and a new window will pop up revealing all the filters that are available in your Photoshop version. The Filters are grouped into categories such as Artistic, Distort, Sketch and so forth. Each effect has a specific function, for example under the Distort category you will find the Filters that will create distortions in your image such as waves, ripples and a zigzag.

The Filter Gallery is divided into three panels. On the left you will find the preview window with a magnify tool available to help you preview a filter and see the details of the effect. The centre panel displays all the filters divided by categories and a very helpful thumbnail preview where you can choose the desired effect.

The third panel provides all the controls over the filters, where you can change the settings to control the effect however you wish and view the changes in real-time on the preview window. By clicking on the Add Layer icon allows you to add two or more filters at the same time to create subtle and impressive effects.

"The huge range of Filters are grouped into categories such as Artistic, Distort, Sketch and so on"

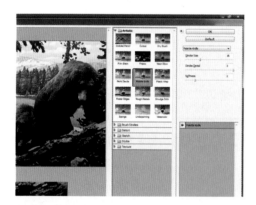

01 Filter thumbnails
Open the Artistic filters and select the Palette Knife filter. This will have its thumbnail highlighted and the result is displayed on the Preview window.

02 Magnify tool
On the bottom-left corner you will find the magnify tool, which is a very handy tool to preview a filter and see the details of the effect.

03 Controls
Each filter has a different sets of controls, you can change the parameters to control the filter and preview the results in the preview window.

04 Layers
Click on the Add Layer icon to add a new effect layer. This allows you to add two or more filters at the same time.

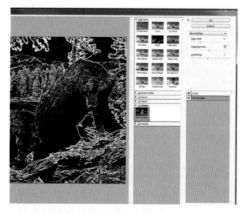

05 Change filter
To change a filter on a layer just select the layer and choose another filter. You can also delete a layer by clicking on the Delete Effect Layer icon.

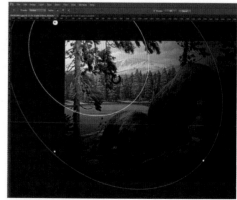

06 Filter menu
Under the Filter menu you will find very powerful filters such as the Lighting Effect filter to create a dramatic scene or set the ambiance for an image.

Filters at a glance

There are over 100 filters in Photoshop, each sectioned into groups. From Artistic filters, where you can achieve pastel or pencil effects to Distort filters, where the filter geometrically distorts an image. Here's a great selection of our favourite filter effects to give you some artistic inspiration.

ARTISTIC

Colored Pencil Dry Brush Poster Edges Rough Pastels Smudge Stick

BRUSH STROKES

Angled Stroke Ink Outlines Spatter Sprayed strokes Sumi-e

DISTORT

Diffuse Glow Glass Spherize Twirl ZigZag

PIXELATE

Color Halftone Crystallize Mezzotint Mosaic Pointillize

SKETCH

Charcoal Halftone Photocopy Reticulation Stamp

TEXTURE

Craquelure Grain Mosaic tiles Stain glass Texturizer

The Artistic filters

If you want to get creative, these effects are the place to start

The Artistic set of filters does as the name would suggest – they give images an artistic effect. Some of these are painterly while others work for a more illustrative feel. There are 15 different options to choose from here (Filter>Artistic), and once you pick one you will open up the Filter Gallery. This is where you control the effect of the filter, with each filter having its own bespoke set of sliders to adjust. The Artistic filters are perfect for getting started in digital art. Maybe you want to make a card for someone or have a family portrait that you would like to print out. The Artistic filters can help with all of this and much, much more, so check out our guide below and give the filters a whirl!

What is a Filter Gallery?
This is the workspace where you will be taken in Photoshop once you have selected your filter. Here you can adjust the settings, preview the image or even change your mind.

Complete curve control Your one-glance guide to the filter choices

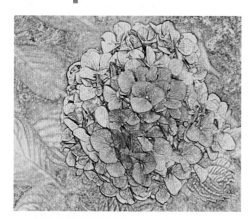

01 Colored Pencil
Keep Pencil Width low but Stroke Pressure and Paper Brightness high. Bear in mind that it uses the Background colour for the paper.

02 Cutout
A fantastic filter for easy illustrations, this simplifies an image into blocks of colour. Use the Number of Levels slider for realism.

03 Dry Brush
This filter only really comes alive if you up the Texture slider until you can see swirls. The higher the brush size, the stronger the effect.

04 Film Grain

This applies a sheet of dots, perfect for a vintage look. Use the Highlight Area to boost the lightest part of the image.

05 Fresco

Another one that stays quiet without much texture. This is good for dramatic or monochrome images as it revels in dark areas.

06 Neon Glow

This uses your Foreground colour and a glow colour to make a psychedelic effect. Control the Glow Size and Glow Brightness to suit.

07 Paint Daubs

With the settings low, this filter barely makes a dent. Up the sliders, though, and your image will look as if paint has been dabbed all over.

08 Palette Knife

This filter breaks the image up into slabs, much as a traditional palette knife does. You can alter the size of these using Stroke Size.

09 Plastic Wrap

A bizarre filter that makes an image look as though it has been vacuum packed. Good for making interesting backgrounds.

10 Poster Edges

Simplifies edges for a graphic feel and creates a speckly texture. The sliders let you decide how dark and how pronounced the texture is.

11 Rough Pastels

Decide how soft the effect is using the Stroke Length and Stroke Detail sliders, and then give the final flourish by adding some texture.

12 Smudge Stick

It's a little bit blotchy and a little bit illustrative. Keep the Highlight Area low and then jiggle between Stroke Length and Intensity.

13 Sponge

Applies a mottled effect. You can set how large this is with Brush Size and then use Definition to set how pronounced it is.

14 Underpainting

There are loads of options within this filter but the effect is essentially the same – blurring! Texture Coverage is good to experiment with.

15 Watercolor

Another 'says what it is' filter, with you controlling the detail, shadows and texture. This filter does tend to darken images.

ORIGINAL

Paint beautiful watercolours

Six steps to beautiful watercolour paintings

Giving photos a real-media effect is a popular technique in both **Photoshop and Photoshop Elements.** Here, you'll learn how to use filters to create a beautiful watercolour painting.

While there's a dedicated filter for this in both programs, using more than one provides a much more realistic final effect. Building up your layers with different artistic filters added to each, you can re-create a great and much more realistic effect.

The trick is to explore and experiment with different filters to see which ones work with each other. Think about how you'd create a watercolour in real life,

for example. Sometimes the pencil underneath is visible. So if you want that look, apply one of the Sketch filters, reduce the opacity of the paint layers and allow some of the sketch work to show through. The Paint Daubs filter is a great starting point for many paint effects. Follow along with our steps here to create a basic but beautiful watercolour painting straight from a photo.

"The trick is to explore and experiment with different filters"

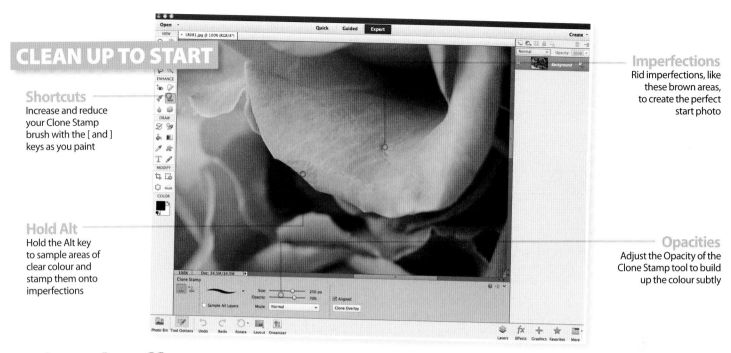

Imperfections
Rid imperfections, like these brown areas, to create the perfect start photo

Shortcuts
Increase and reduce your Clone Stamp brush with the [and] keys as you paint

Hold Alt
Hold the Alt key to sample areas of clear colour and stamp them onto imperfections

Opacities
Adjust the Opacity of the Clone Stamp tool to build up the colour subtly

Painterly effects Turn a photo into a painting

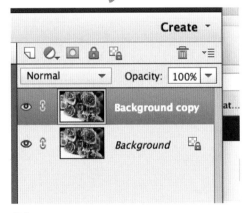

01 Duplicate your layer
Open your photo to begin and, in Expert mode, drag the Background layer to the New Layer icon on the bottom of the Layers Palette.

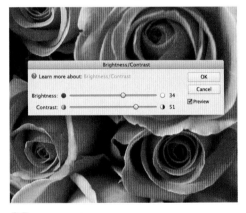

02 Boost the contrast
Click on the Adjustment Layer icon in the Layers Palette. Choose Brightness/Contrast. Boost the Brightness to 34 and push the Contrast to 51.

03 Clear up imperfections
Select the Clone Stamp tool (S). Hold Alt, click on areas where the colour is okay. Let go of Alt and click over the bad areas sampling as you go.

04 Paint Daubs
Choose Filter>Artistic>Paint Daubs. Set the Brush Size to 22, the Sharpness to 23 and change Brush Type to Wide Sharp. Click OK.

05 Add the Watercolor filter
Now head to Filter>Watercolor and set the Brush Detail to 1, Shadow Intensity to 1 and Texture to 2. Hit OK. You've now applied two filters, there's just one more to go!

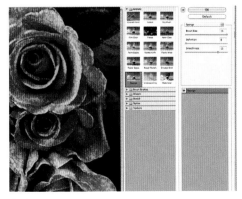

06 Sponge and contrast
The final filter is the Sponge filter. Set the Brush Size to 10, Definition to 0 and Smoothness to 12. Hit OK and boost the contrast in the same way you did in step 2. And that's it! A beautiful effect in six steps.

The Blur filters

Blur doesn't have to be the enemy – see what the Blur filters can do for you!

We are so used to striving for pin-sharp images that it can seem a bit bizarre to suggest blurring an image on purpose, but it can be a useful creative tool, and the Blur filters offer the best way to apply it.

Photographers use blur to draw attention to one area of the image. They call it the depth of field effect, but you can do the same in Photoshop by selecting an area and then blurring it. We show you how to do this below. Blur is also useful for softening edges or applying a soft focus effect. It can be used to soften backgrounds or make colours merge into each other.

There are 11 Blur filters up for grabs, some you get to control, while you get what you're given with others. We have put together a list of what each filter looks like on the right so use that as your start point for experimenting! And if you have never used a Blur filter before, check out the small walkthrough below for adding depth of field.

> "Photographers use blur to draw attention to one area of the image"

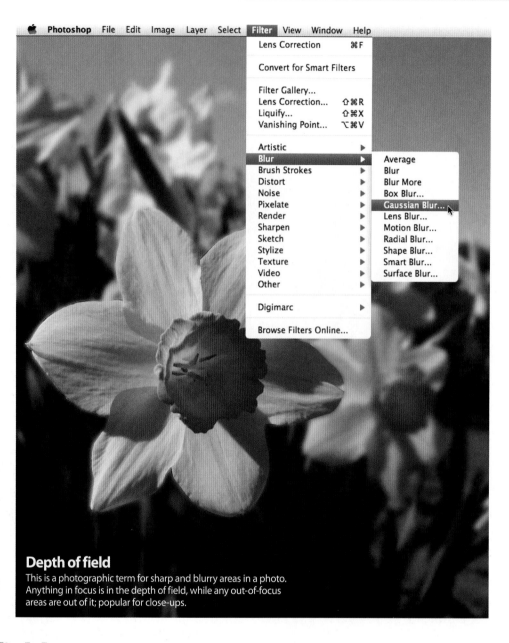

Depth of field
This is a photographic term for sharp and blurry areas in a photo. Anything in focus is in the depth of field, while any out-of-focus areas are out of it; popular for close-ups.

Enhance depth of field
Apply a small amount of blur to draw attention to an object

01 Select an area
Either select the area you want to blur or the object to stay in focus with your tool of choice, then go to Select>Inverse.

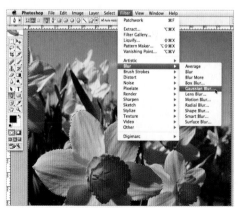

02 Select the blur
Go to Filter>Blur. All of the Blur filters will shoot off to the side – you need to pick Gaussian Blur. Click to activate your edit.

03 Set the blur
Move the Radius slider to increase or decrease the intensity. You can also click the Preview box to see your how your effect looks.

Gaussian Blur
The best all-rounder for blur. Controlled via a slider, it will apply a uniform blur to an image, giving a hazy effect.

Radial Blur
Causes an image to swirl around as if in a vortex. Great for special effects, turning wheels and interesting backgrounds.

Average
This picks the average colour in an image and fills the photo or selection with that colour.

Blur and Blur More
Good for smoothing transitions. Blur applies a small amount while Blur More will apply, er, more!

Box Blur
This keeps the blur contained to the average colour of pixels that are next to each other.

Lens Blur
You can use selections and the Lens Blur filter to give the subtle effect of depth of field.

Motion Blur
Use this to give the impression of speed and movement by blurring the background of your scene.

Shape Blur
A strange one this, as it uses Photoshop's custom shapes to set a blur following that area.

Smart Blur
Three sliders work together to help you achieve a precise blur, a bit like the Smart Sharpen filter.

Surface
If you have noise in an image, this is the filter to go for because it will retain sharp edges.

Filters

Lighting Effects filter

In the dark about this filter's capabilities?
Allow us to light the way for you with
this handy guide

In Photoshop CS6, the Lighting Effects filter has seen some major improvements compared to previous versions. Its interface has seen the biggest change, with a larger and friendlier preview screen. This makes applying lights much easier than before, giving you more control in the style of the effect you need.

In fact, the functionality and power of the Lighting Effects filter, when applied constructively, can provide tremendous results. Couple these with digital photography, and users are presented with a wonderland of creative opportunities. Once you've accessed the dialog box, the Presets drop menu instantly provides you with 17 separate options, counting Default. These include Soft Omni, Flashlight, Flood Light and 2 O'clock Spotlight.

Application is effortless and a live preview is ever-present in the Preview window to monitor treatment. Utilising the control nodes, users can alter the lighting direction and location. This filter also includes a highly efficient set of property options that allow users to measure and edit the intensity of common light effects such as exposure, ambience and the amount of surface reflection. All of these can be deployed to enhance and pinpoint selected image areas.

The key with this filter is in keeping it subtle. A gentle spotlight can really lift your image, but go crazy with too many lights and harsh settings, and you will cheapen your image. Still, a lot of this filter is down to trial and error, and personal preference.

"The Lighting Effects filter has seen some major improvements compared to previous versions"

Save your effects
It's not always easy to remember the exact settings used if you need to repeat an effect. Use the Save option under Presets at the top of the filter to store your personalised effects for a later date.

Add to what's there
You can use Lighting effects with other applications to enhance and create image effects such as moonlight, sunrise and sunset. Try opening a sunny image then duplicating the image. Select the Lighting Effect filter, applying a Spotlight in the appropriate 'o'clock' position. Set this to a yellow tone, set an Orange Properties tone and apply the desired settings. Clicking OK, apply a Soft Light blend mode. Create a new layer and apply an Orange Foreground to Transparent gradient, top to bottom, applying a Linear Burn. Lower Opacity to get the desired effect.

01 Locate filter
The Lighting Effects filter is grouped with Photoshop's Render options. Go into the Filter menu and open this up to begin.

02 Position the light
Use the four dots to change how much area the light source covers. Click and drag outside this area to rotate the angle of the light.

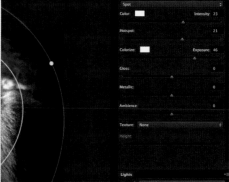

03 Alter Intensity
The Intensity controls how bright the Lighting Effect will be. Use the Color and Hotspot sliders to change the light's overall strength.

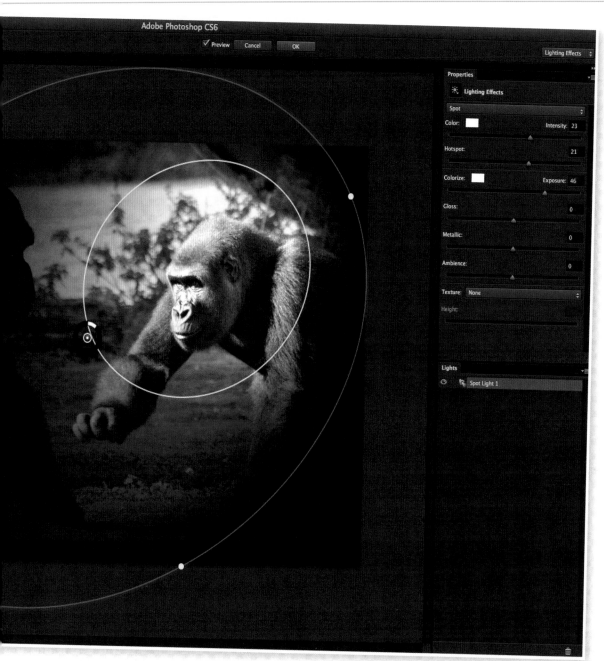

Get exposed
Understanding the functions of the properties is essential. Exposure works by increasing (positive values) or decreasing (negative values) light across the image. A value of 0 has no effect.

Matte or shiny
Gloss determines how much the surface of the image reflects light, from a matte effect (low reflectance) to a shiny effect (high reflectance), much like it does on actual paper surfaces.

Reflect on it
The Metallic slider determines which is more reflective: the light itself or the object on which it's cast.

Ambience
Ambience acts as a light diffuser in your image. It combines with the lighting, so the more negative the value the more it removes, and the more positive the more it uses only the light source.

04 Add colour
To add a splash of colour to tint the light, click on the swatch next to Color. This can match the mood of your image to the subjects involved.

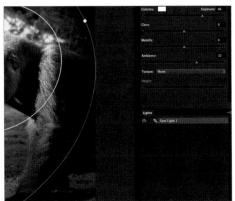

05 Infinite lighting
An Infinite Light adjusts the entire lighting in an image as well as brightness and positioning. Add this using the options under Lights along the top.

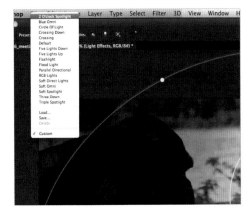

06 Presets
The top left of the filter has preset effects, including omni and directional lighting for more creative styles that can be adapted using the sliders.

Fix noise with the Reduce Noise filter

Discover a clever technique for sorting noise caused by bad lighting conditions or a high ISO

Often when we go out we take along our moderately powerful compact cameras that fit neatly into our pockets or bags, we point and shoot and we come back with hundreds of photos.

Among these we may see one photo that really catches our eye. The trouble is that sometimes due to the nature of digital cameras and the shooting conditions the photo was taken in we may have a great amount of noise. Noise comes in three different flavours – colour noise, luminance noise and JPEG artefacts. Luckily for us we can reduce (although not completely remove) noise using a Photoshop filter called Reduce Noise.

Colour noise can be seen as small red, green and blue dots within our photos. Luminance noise is probably far more recognisable as actual noise – this consists of small black, white and grey dots. JPEG artefacts are blocky and make the image look as though it is low resolution. If you have a more expensive DSLR camera you can combat noise by first shooting in RAW and secondly setting your ISO to a lower number, the results from a DSLR are often very impressive.

Sadly this filter was introduced by Adobe in Photoshop CS2 so users of earlier versions will not be able to use this tutorial. Instead, you could try small amounts on blur on a duplicate layer. We have provided the image that we used here for you to practise on.

"We can reduce noise using Photoshop's Reduce Noise filter"

ORIGINAL

Reduce noise in photos Without losing details or texture

01 Get started
Open your start image. Start things off by duplicating the Background image and naming it 'RGB Noise'. Go to Filter>Noise>Reduce Noise.

02 Set to 0
Make sure you are in Basic mode. Next reduce all the sliders to 0 and make sure Remove JPEG Artifacts has no tick.

03 Reduce RGB noise
Find a spot that has lots of lights. Zoom in to 200% then increase the Reduce Noise slider. We set ours to 50% but this will be different for each photo.

04 Luminance noise
Luminance noise is seen as black, white and grey dots. Copy the 'RGB Noise' layer to a new layer and name it 'Luminance Noise'.

05 Back to the filter
Make sure you are on the new layer and access the Reduce Noise filter. We will now reduce the luminance noise by moving the Strength slider.

06 Strength in numbers
Move the Strength slider gradually up. We have to be careful not to destroy the details, so we also increase the Preserve Details slider.

07 Channel hopping
We can reduce noise further using the filter's Advanced options. Create a copy of the 'Luminance Noise' layer and name it 'Channels'.

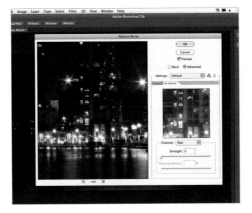

08 And filter once more…
Load the filter again and click Advanced. Click on Per Channel. Now you can edit the noise by channel independently.

09 Final settings
We set Red and Green's Strength to 2 and Preserve Details to 60%, and Blue's Strength to 5 and Preserve Details to 70%.

The Sharpen filters

Blurred images are a common photographic problem, so sharpen up your shaky shots with these filters

We all know that sinking feeling when you realise you've taken a photo and it hasn't come out as crisp as you'd have liked. Well do not fear because, as per usual, Photoshop comes to the rescue. The program ships with a range of Sharpen filters to fix out-of-focus imagery. Unlike other filter sets in Photoshop, the Sharpen filters all seek to do essentially the same thing – increase the sharpness within an image. So why are there five different ones? Well, some of them let you manually input values for varying factors that affect the blur in an image, like the threshold of contrast between pixels or the radius, but this is only really for when you're editing on a more expert level.

Other options within this menu do a sort of mass sharpening and are more useful for newcomers. There's such a variety that you'll probably find your favourite and stick to it, so we won't get too technical! For now, jump on board and let's see how we go about using this useful set of filters.

REDUCE THE BLUR

Sharpen filters
The Sharpen filters are frequently used to fix common blur problems in photographs.

Smart Sharpen
With Smart Sharpen you can edit the amount of sharpening in shadows or highlights, and view your alterations in the preview window.

Unsharp Mask
Despite the misleading name, Unsharp Mask's purpose is also to make an image appear sharper.

Sharpen using Unsharp
This filter is a popular method of emphasising texture and detail

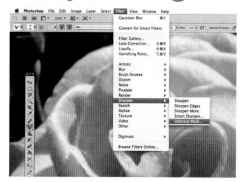

01 New layer
Open the image you want to sharpen. In the Layers palette, drag and drop the Background layer onto the New Layer icon. On the new layer choose Filter>Sharpen>Unsharp Mask. Doing it on a separate layer means you can view your before and after versions (by toggling the eye icon on or off).

02 Adjust the sliders
In the dialog, you'll see a preview window and your image inside. You can adjust how much of the image you see in the preview window by using the + and - keys. This comes in handy for intricate adjustments as you can see exactly what your modifications are doing to the image.

03 Each slider
Use the sliders to adjust the effect. Amount sets how heavily the effect is applied. Radius refers to the strength of the effect, while Threshold alters how much contrast there needs to be between colours for them to be sharpened. Avoid playing with this too much, as it can add unwanted noise.

SHARPEN FILTERS IN FULL

Before   After

Sharpen

This tackles blur by increasing the contrast of adjoining pixels. Click it once to apply, then repeat the action as many times as you need until you reach the desired effect. You can also use the shortcut Cmd/Ctrl+F.

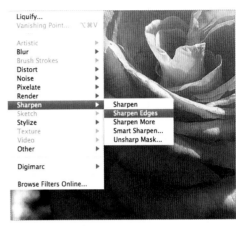

Sharpen Edges

Using this filter sharpens the edges where there are clear colour differences, while keeping the rest of the image smooth. Again, click it once to apply the effect and use Cmd/Ctrl+F to apply it multiple times.

Sharpen More

As the name implies, the Sharpen More filter applies the same effect as Sharpen, but a bit stronger for an even crisper result.

Smart Sharpen

Smart Sharpen is great if all the others are just a tad confusing. It lets you control the amount of sharpening that occurs in the shadows and highlights, and you can adjust the settings manually. Have a look at the step-by-step guide below for more.

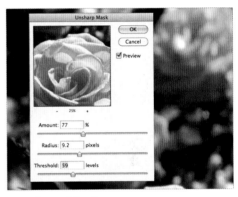

Unsharp Mask

A little confusing because of the name (which derives from a traditional photo technique) the Unsharp Mask lets you adjust the effect with three sliders: Amount, Radius and Threshold.

Get smart with Smart Sharpen Three steps to sharper imagery

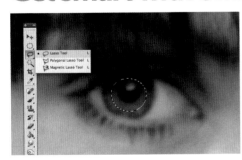

01 Select

To sharpen a selection of an image, pick a selection tool. Here we used the Lasso (L) and drew freehand around the eye. Select it from the Toolbar and click-drag around the area you want, making sure the line meets up so you get a complete selection.

02 Feather

Feathering your selection will make the contrast between what's in the selection and what's outside more subtle. Click on Refine Edge in the Options bar and experiment with the Feather slider. We went with a value of 4px.

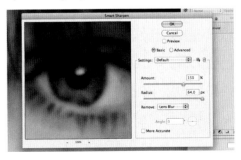

03 Smart Sharpen

Go to Filter>Sharpen>Smart Sharpen and adjust the sliders again until you get the sharpness you need. Be careful not to make the effect too strong and risk increasing noise. Use the preview window to see how your adjustments are looking.

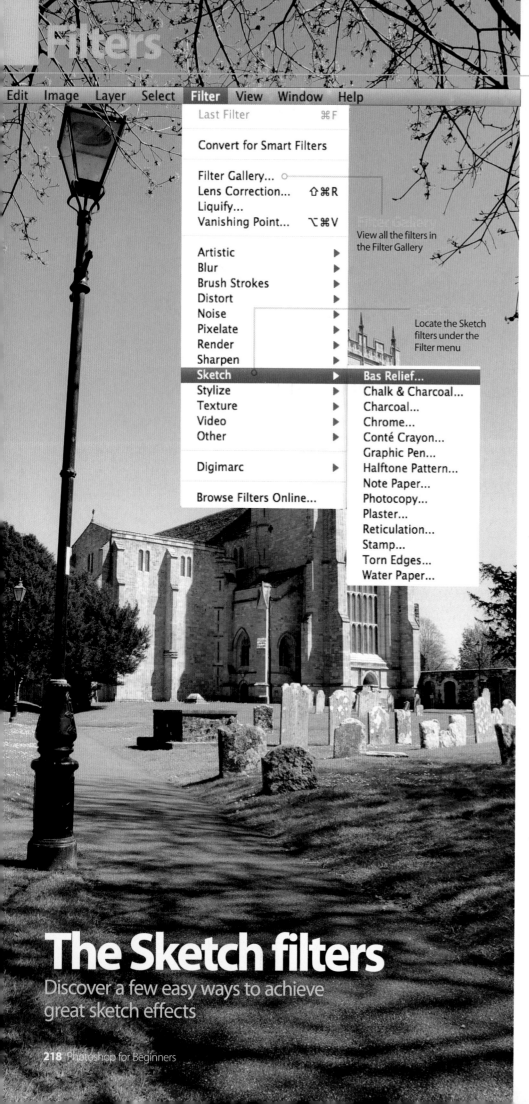

Filters

Edit   Image   Layer   Select   Filter   View   Window   Help

Last Filter	⌘ F
Convert for Smart Filters	
Filter Gallery... ○	
Lens Correction...	⇧ ⌘ R
Liquify...	
Vanishing Point...	⌥ ⌘ V
Artistic	▶
Blur	▶
Brush Strokes	▶
Distort	▶
Noise	▶
Pixelate	▶
Render	▶
Sharpen	▶
Sketch	▶
Stylize	▶
Texture	▶
Video	▶
Other	▶
Digimarc	▶
Browse Filters Online...	

Sketch submenu:
Bas Relief...
Chalk & Charcoal...
Charcoal...
Chrome...
Conté Crayon...
Graphic Pen...
Halftone Pattern...
Note Paper...
Photocopy...
Plaster...
Reticulation...
Stamp...
Torn Edges...
Water Paper...

View all the filters in the Filter Gallery

Locate the Sketch filters under the Filter menu

The Sketch filters

Discover a few easy ways to achieve
great sketch effects

There are times when you want to give an ordinary photo a twist, but don't want to spend hours figuring out how to do so. In come the filters – the Sketch filters this time – to apply a range of different effects based on the traditional method of sketching.

Some of the Sketch filters are based on a traditional sketching tool, like chalk or crayon, whereas others focus on the medium they're sketched on like Torn Edges or Water Paper. The filters use your Foreground and Background colours, so vary them for different effects. As usual, always duplicate your Background layer first so you have your original image intact.

Sketch filters
What each option looks like

Bas Relief
Giving a 3D effect, this filter applies the Foreground and Background colours to simulate the surface texture of the image, with various sliders for detail.

Chalk & Charcoal
Shadows are replaced with black charcoal lines while the highlights and midtones are redrawn with a solid chalk effect in this option for a real-media twist.

Charcoal

Main outlines are emphasised and contrast is heightened, giving the illusion that the image has been drawn in charcoal.

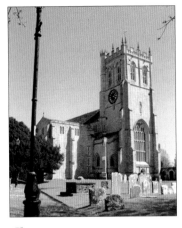

Chrome

Gives the image a chrome effect. Use it on a selection (in this case the path) or the whole document, and experiment with colours.

Conté Crayon

This sketch filter replicates the look of a traditional Conté crayon on a choice of textures. Change the colour swatches for realism.

Graphic Pen

Capture the detail with fine lines, choose their direction, how long the lines are and the Foreground colour for different effects.

Halftone Pattern

Creates a comic-book effect in seconds. With the Foreground white and Background black, apply the filter, then hit Cmd/Ctrl+I and change the blend mode to Linear Light.

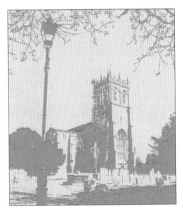

Note Paper

This clever filter achieves a realistic paper effect by combining embossing and texture. Choose warm yellows for the look of aged paper but be careful not to apply it too strongly.

Photocopy

This option reproduces the effect of a realistic photocopy by making the darker areas more outlined while turning midtones to solid black or white. Some detail will be lost.

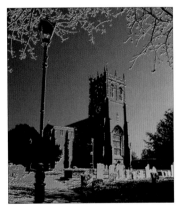

Plaster

Creates the effect of a plaster mould and adds colour based on the Foreground and Background swatches. Darker areas appear raised and light areas indented.

Reticulation

Derived from film photography, Reticulation re-creates the distortion of film emulsion, making the image look shadowy and grainy in certain areas.

Stamp

Best on monochrome images, this creates a rubber-stamp effect, simplifying the image into blocks of white and black with defined outlines.

Torn Edges

Works to reconstruct the image and make it look like it was made from torn pieces of paper. The filter works best with text or high-contrast objects.

Water Paper

Uses painted blotches on a fibrous, damp-looking paper, creating an effect where the colours look as though they've almost run together.

Understand Liquify filters

Learn to use Liquify as a fun way to manipulate your image by pushing, twirling, expanding and more

Ever wanted to turn a picture into goo? Well here's your ticket to pixel melting fun! Liquify is a deluxe filter that has its own set of tools. Go to Filter>Distort>Liquify in Elements (Filter>Liquify in Photoshop), and the selected layer will appear in a large dialog box which serves as a sub-interface for using the Liquify tools. Note: if you're working with an important layer, you may want to duplicate it before editing so you can fall back to the original if needed.

At first you may think that Liquify is only good for creating comedic effects. Sure, you can give your cat a set of bulging animé eyes with the Bloat tool, or be mischievous and start some whirlpools in a serene pond with the Twirl tools. But once you play around with the Liquify tools a little bit more, you're sure to find professional uses that you can make the most of, whatever your background may be.

Photographers can use the Warp and Pucker tools to gently firm someone's figure, or fix an imperfection in an otherwise sound structure. Graphic professionals can create nifty effects like fiery text with the Turbulence tool. On top of all this, traditional artists can scan in their work and use the various tools to alter scale and fine-tune form.

Try one tool, or combine different ones for a multi-faceted edit. As you're warping and stretching your image, you can use the Revert button and the Reconstruct tool to remove any unwanted edits. When you're done, click OK and you'll be brought back to the main Photoshop interface. Your Liquify edits will appear on the selected layer. Give Liquify a try today and see how useful (or just plain fun) it is.

"Try one tool, or combine different ones for a multi-faceted edit"

QUICK PHOTOSHOP TIPS

Tools
Use the top tools to warp your image. Below are the Reconstruct Tool to remove changes, the Zoom Tool to get up close, and the Hand Tool to pan.

Cursor
This shows where your editing will occur. It works like a brush, and you can use the Left and Right Brackets to adjust its size.

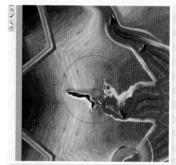
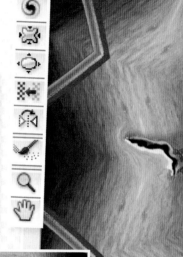

ORIGINAL

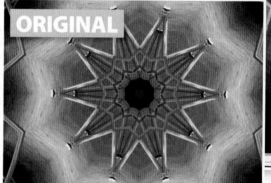

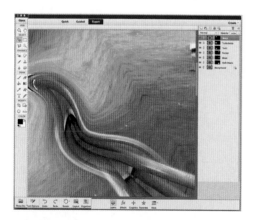

Warp tool
The Warp tool allows you to push pixels as you click and drag with the cursor. Make the brush larger to push around more pixels.

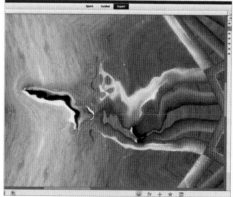

Turbulence tool
This tool scrambles pixels to create churning waves, flickering flames, and similar effects. It's dependent upon the Turbulent Jitter setting.

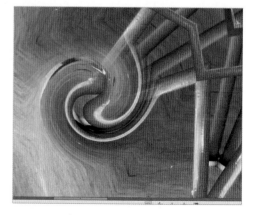

Twirl tools
Use the Twirl Tools to rotate pixels as you hold down the mouse button or drag. Hold Option/Alt to twirl in the opposite direction.

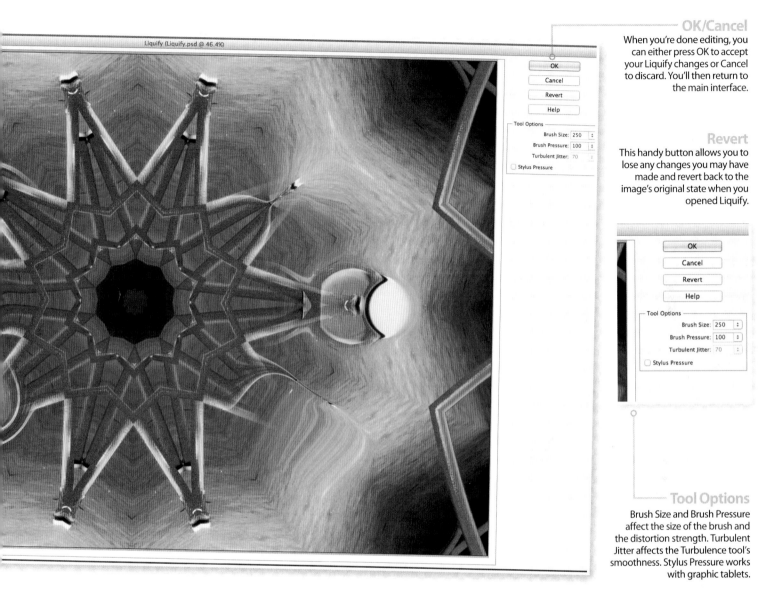

Liquify (Liquify.psd @ 46.4%)

OK
Cancel
Revert
Help

Tool Options

Brush Size: 250
Brush Pressure: 100
Turbulent Jitter: 70

Stylus Pressure

OK/Cancel

When you're done editing, you can either press OK to accept your Liquify changes or Cancel to discard. You'll then return to the main interface.

Revert

This handy button allows you to lose any changes you may have made and revert back to the image's original state when you opened Liquify.

OK
Cancel
Revert
Help

Tool Options

Brush Size: 250
Brush Pressure: 100
Turbulent Jitter: 70

Stylus Pressure

Tool Options

Brush Size and Brush Pressure affect the size of the brush and the distortion strength. Turbulent Jitter affects the Turbulence tool's smoothness. Stylus Pressure works with graphic tablets.

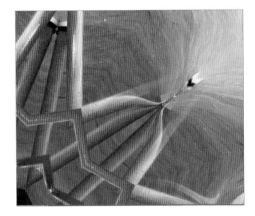

Pucker tool

The Pucker Tool moves pixels towards the brush centre. This can be used to tone down bulbous areas, or to make something small.

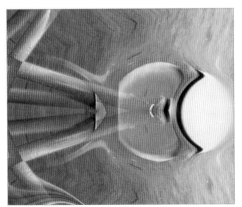

Bloat tool

The opposite of the Pucker tool, the Bloat tool moves pixels away from the centre. Use this tool to enlarge areas and create spherical effects.

Shift Pixels

The Shift Pixels tool moves pixels perpendicularly to the direction to the stroke. Hold down Option/ Alt as you drag to shift in the opposite direction.

Use the Lens Correction filter

Reshape those awkward angles in your photos for improving perspective and removing distortion

Lens correction techniques sort out issues that can occur when taking an image at an angle. It is one of the most common problems in photography. You snap a tall building for example, and when you look at it later, it looks as though the vertical edges of the building are bending inwards. Luckily, because it is such a common problem, Photoshop has the answer within its Filter menu. You can employ some of the following techniques to straighten things out like wonky horizons, or you can increase the perspective for more creative results.

If you're taking a picture straight on, such as a square object requiring perfect right angles, there are a range of tools you can call upon to make these subtle adjustments. The Transform commands, for instance, can be used to reshape subjects on separate layers. But it's the Lens Correction filter in Photoshop that holds the ultimate array of image adjustments. You can correct and apply colour shifts, better known as fringing, which is visible around the edges of brighter subjects in your image and introduce vertical perspective.

We take you through the features of this filter so you can straighten up horizons and add vignette effects to your images. When corrections have been applied we also show you some of our favourite image adjustments to improve colour, brightness and sharpness post-filter. The final results can be a dramatic improvement on what was originally a flat and out-of-shape photo.

We have used quite a dramatic landscape shot to demonstrate this technique, but you can pick up any image with similar problems and see for yourself how easy it is to sort out your image collection's flaws.

"Straighten out wonky horizons or increase the perspective for more creative results"

Basic problems solved We look at the Lens Correction filter

01 Assess the damage
Open the image you eish to correct. In this image the horizon is not straight and due to the earth's curvature, it's also bowed in the centre.

02 Level horizon
Go to Filter>Lens Correction. Uncheck the Grids option and select the Straighten tool. Click and drag along the horizon line to level it out.

03 Reshape curvature
Select the Remove Distortion tool and drag the image from the top edge inwards to bend the horizon until it's flat.

04 Remove fringing
Zoom in to one of the main clouds by the sun; there is a hint of yellow fringing. Under Chromatic Aberration, move the Fix Blue/Yellow slider to -10.

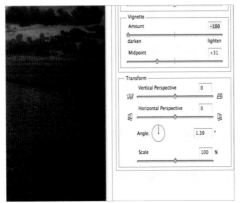

05 More dramatic
The Vignette controls are used to adjust overly light or dark corners of the image. Change Amount to -100 and Midpoint to around +30 for a cool effect.

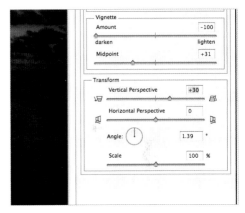

06 Tilt the perspective
The Transform controls in the filter change the vertical and horizontal perspectives of an image. Change the Vertical option to +30 here.

07 Re-assess angles
Click on the Show Grid option to make sure the image's horizon is level. If not, use the Straighten tool to tweak it once more and make it level.

08 Scale up
Some of Photoshop's chequerboard background is visible. Adjust the Scale slider at the bottom of the Transform controls to 120%. Hit OK to apply.

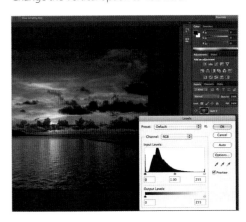

09 Post-filter adjustments
The image's exposure and sharpness can still do with improving, so go to Image>Adjustments>Levels and tweak to suit.

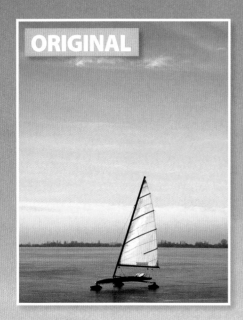

ORIGINAL

Edit colours with Photo Filter

Take a leaf out of traditional photographers' books and use coloured filters

Colour is a vital part of most people's photography and there have been all sorts of inventions to add zing to an image's tones. Traditional photographers have long used coloured filters in front of the camera lens to improve the colour balance and temperature of a photo. This is applied over the entire image or is graduated to concentrate on one area (such as the sky).

The Photoshop equivalent of this is the Photo Filter tool. Found lurking in the Adjustments menu (or Filter>Adjustments if you are using Elements), it enables you to gently coax extra colour out of your image or push things further for more dramatic effects. The easiest application of this tool is to make light work of dodgy white balance by reaching for the Warming Filter (80) or Cooling Filter (80) settings. These fix the two most common balance problems (too blue or too yellow, respectively), but if you have suffered a more unusual blight, just pick a complementary colour to tame things down.

However, we are going to be concentrating on a different aspect of the tool, namely that of editing colours. The beauty of using the Photo Filter over something like Hue/Saturation is that you are provided with a batch of ready-made improvements. This makes it less likely for you to create something that looks fake. The start image for this tutorial is supplied to practise on, or use one of your own snaps.

"It enables you to gently coax extra colour out of your image"

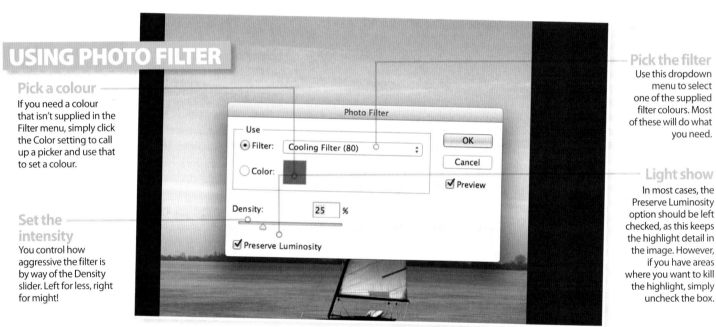

USING PHOTO FILTER

Pick a colour
If you need a colour that isn't supplied in the Filter menu, simply click the Color setting to call up a picker and use that to set a colour.

Set the intensity
You control how aggressive the filter is by way of the Density slider. Left for less, right for might!

Pick the filter
Use this dropdown menu to select one of the supplied filter colours. Most of these will do what you need.

Light show
In most cases, the Preserve Luminosity option should be left checked, as this keeps the highlight detail in the image. However, if you have areas where you want to kill the highlight, simply uncheck the box.

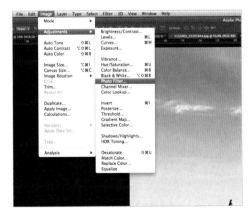

01 Make the adjustment
Go to Image>Adjustments>Photo Filter (Photoshop) or Filter>Adjustments>Photo Filter (Photoshop Elements).

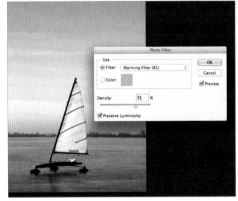

02 Choose a filter
Now you can choose a filter from the drop-down menu. Try a few to see which one looks the best, using Density to control its strength.

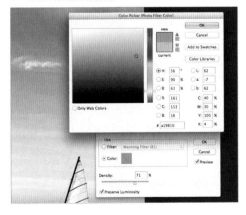

03 Color Picker
If none of the filter presets are exactly what you need, then select the coloured square by clicking on it twice and you can choose your own colour.

Creative projects

FILTERS IN PRACTICE
Utilise filters with other Photoshop techniques for creative results

AMAZING EFFECTS
Discover the tricks behind perfect lighting in photographs

UNREAL EDITS
Give photos an eye-catching twist with amazing editing tricks

"You don't need to be an expert to achieve great creative projects"

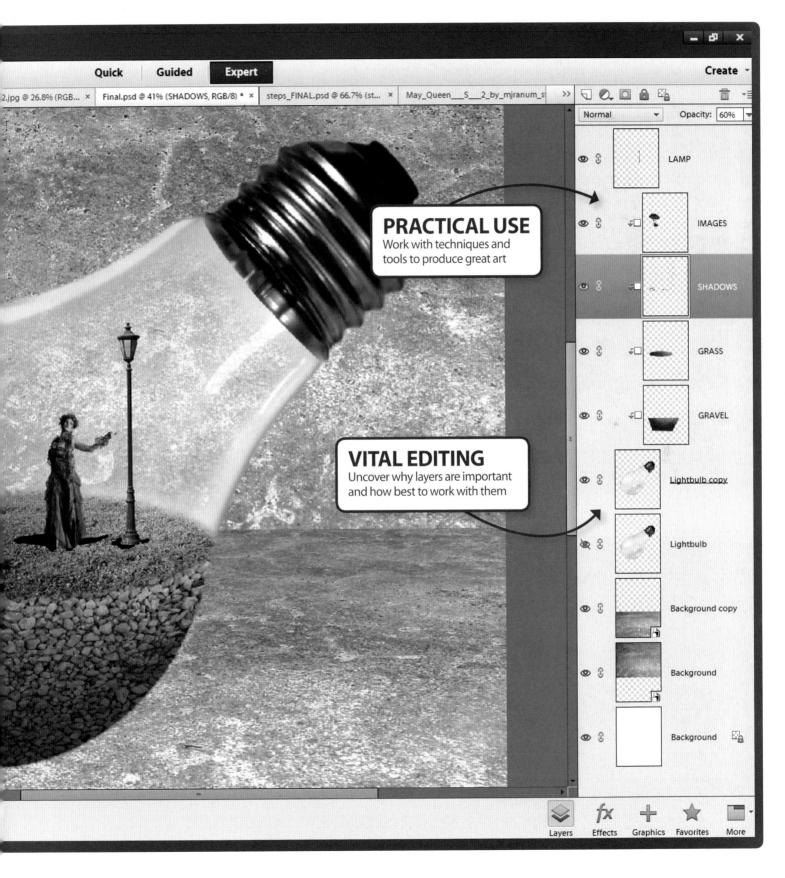

PRACTICAL USE
Work with techniques and tools to produce great art

VITAL EDITING
Uncover why layers are important and how best to work with them

Make a movie poster

Learn how to photo-manipulate a spooky movie poster using advanced techniques

We're going to walk you through the steps for making a spooky, atmospheric movie poster design. You'll be transforming a regular forest backdrop into a scary night scene! You'll also learn to blend images in a non-destructive manner and create awesome, supernatural-looking light effects and more.

You'll even learn how to create the authentic typography seen on most movie posters. We'll be recommending the best free fonts to give your work a professional edge, as well as teaching you some stunning text effects which prove that your typography doesn't have to be boring.

Throughout this tutorial, you'll pick up tricks for working non-destructively by following a professional workflow. This means plenty of adjustment layers, masks and Smart Filters, as well as learning to organise your layers properly.

We look at what makes a good composition, with discussions on key lighting, image placement, perspective and bringing all of these elements together. By the end of this tutorial, you should have mastered a wide range of new techniques and have a better understanding of how to create a professional poster design, with real world applications. So load up Photoshop to get started!

ORIGINALS

"Create a professional poster with real world applications"

Turn photos into promos
Find out how to create your own scary movie posters

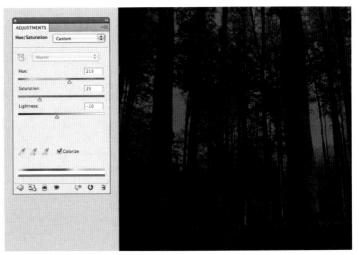

01 Set up your background
Start by creating a new document in Photoshop that is 230mmx300mm at 300ppi. Go to Edit>Place and select the 'forest.jpg' image from your resource pack for this tutorial. Position this inside your document, resizing it in order to fit the canvas.

02 Create a night scene
To convert the forest into a night scene, apply the following adjustment layers and settings: Hue/Saturation with Hue: 215, Saturation: 25 and Lightness: -10 (ensure Colorize is checked); Levels at 15, 0.88, 255; and finally Exposure with Exposure: -2.33, Offset: 0.0026 and Gamma Correction: 0.82.

Creative projects

03 Changing the ground
The ground in the original forest photo doesn't suit our look, so find a suitable alternative. Download the 'hill.jpg' image from the resources for this tutorial and Edit>Place it into the bottom half of the canvas, resizing it to fit.

QUICK TIP

Sourcing photos
The main thing to remember when working with photo manipulations is to choose your image sources wisely. It's much better to spend the extra time finding a collection of images with identical light sources than it is to try and fix incorrect light sources. In this tutorial, the 'monster' had an incorrect light source, so we had to flip him horizontally to match up with the rest of the image by going to Edit>Transform>Flip Horizontally. Not ideal!

04 Add perspective
Use the Perspective Transform tools under to give it a more natural perspective. Squash it to around a quarter of its original height. Then apply a layer mask and use a soft black brush (B) to mask off the sky area of the hill photo.

06 Enter the woman
Find 'woman.jpg' (by Belovodchenko Anton) in your resources and extract her from the background using the Pen tool (P). Paste her into your main document and resize accordingly. Place her centrally on the forest floor.

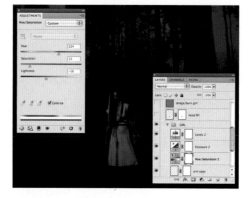

08 More blending
Next we must apply these settings: Hue/Saturation with Hue: 224, Saturation: 15, Lightness: -16 and Colorize ticked; Exposure with Exposure: -1.36, Offset: 0.0026 and Gamma Correction: 1.00; and finally, a Levels adjustment set to 0, 0.84 and 255.

05 Blend elements
Tweak the settings to suit and add a clipping mask to your adjustment layers by Opt/Alt-clicking between them. Create a new layer called Vignette and use a large, soft black brush to paint around the canvas edges and corners.

07 Flip the arm
The woman's right hand is holding something which isn't relevant to the piece. To fix this, apply a layer mask to the woman's layer and mask off her right forearm and hand. Copy and paste her left arm onto a new layer and flip it horizontally.

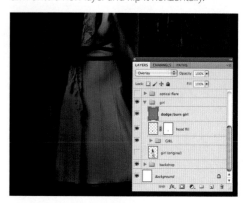

09 Correct lighting
For a believable photo manipulation, the lighting must be correct. The woman needs correcting to fit with the main light source coming from the right. Use the Dodge and Burn tools to add highlights on her right and shadows on her left.

10 Adding light flares

Download the optical flares pack for free from http://tinyurl.com/bcem7kt. Start by applying one of them over the right part of your canvas. This particular flare evokes an eerie and unnatural presence in the forest, and could be an alien ship.

11 Add more lights

Change your optical flare layer's blend mode to Screen to hide the black background. Then add a layer mask and mask off parts of the flare. Repeat Steps 10 and 11 then add more flares over other parts of your image.

12 Dodge and Burn

To bring out the light intensity, we'll use a Dodge/Burn layer. Create a new layer then Edit>Fill with 50% Gray, changing the blend mode to Overlay. Use a soft, low Opacity black brush to Burn (O) your image and white to Dodge it.

13 Adding monsters

To turn up the horror factor in this design, add some monsters hiding in the trees. Download the 'monster.jpg' image from the resources for this tutorial. Place it in your canvas and extract it from its background by using the Pen tool.

14 Blending the monster

To blend the monster, resize it and fit it in between some trees. Mask the bottom and sides, so that it appears to be emerging from the darkness. Apply similar adjustment layers to your woman image to blend the colours with the rest of the image.

15 Adding fog

Now we're going to use some fog to add a spooky atmosphere to our piece. Download the smoke brushes (by Krist Adams, www.kristadams.com) from your resource pack and apply one on a new layer called Fog, using a white Brush.

PEN TOOL CUTOUTS

Extracting subjects from their backgrounds

To use the Pen tool, start by clicking on your subject to create an initial anchor point. Continue to create additional anchor points by clicking around the edge of your subject – in this case, around our poster's monster. If you need to create a curved path line between two anchor points, simply click and drag your newest anchor point in the opposite direction. Once curved, Opt/Alt-click on the anchor point to reset the Pen tool for further straight lines.

"Use some fog to add a spooky atmosphere"

16 Layering the fog

Now reduce the Fog layer's Opacity to 20% to make it appear more natural. Mask off parts of this layer to make the fog appear to swirl around the trees, not just over them. Repeat this technique on several more layers in order to build up a mass of fog going throughout the forest.

17 Poster text

Time for text: type in actor names, the movie title and credits. For the actors, use a clean sans serif font. The title font, Kaushan Script by Pablo Impallari, can be downloaded at tinyurl.com/bqwxbo3. The movie credits are in Uniform Ultra Condensed, free from tinyurl.com/bgoanl2.

18 Title effect

We'll now mimic the visuals of the trees in a creative text effect. Start by duplicating the movie title layer three times, moving them beneath the original. Reduce the Opacity of each to around 50% and apply Filter>Blur>Motion Blur, increasing the strength as you go down the layers.

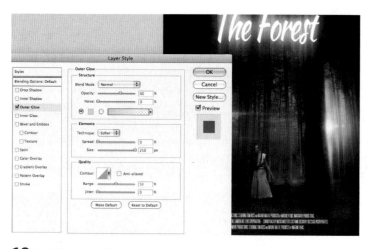

19 Adding a glow

To complete the text effect, add an Outer Glow layer style to the topmost movie title layer (the one without blur). Set the style as follows: blend mode: Normal, Opacity: 60%, Noise: 0%, Color: 7cd2ff, Spread: 0% and Size: 250px.

20 Final adjustments

Add three adjustment layers : a Gradient Map set to black and white, 15% Opacity and the blend mode Overlay; a Vibrance adjustment with Vibrance: 20 and Saturation: 0; and then Levels, set to 0, 0.90, 252 and a layer Opacity of 30%.

DISORGANISED LAYERS

Clipping mask nightmares

It's great to work non-destructively whenever possible, but when you are applying multiple adjustment layers it becomes confusing. In this tutorial, some adjustment layers have a clipping mask applied while others don't. It's important to distinguish between the two otherwise your image will not look right. Remember, when a clipping mask is applied, the adjustment layer only affects the underlying layer. Otherwise, it affects all layers below it.

The exceptions in this tutorial are the adjustment layers applied to the woman. Since we duplicated her arm onto a new layer, we had to apply adjustments to just her and the new arm layer. You can place both the woman and arm layers within a layer group and change the group's blend mode to Normal, then apply adjustment layers without a clipping mask. They should only affect the two layers inside this new group.

Photograph your own model

Build up your own library of photos using these camera techniques

If you own a camera and know someone who's up for having their picture taken, then why not incorporate them into your Photoshop compositions?

The trick is to make life easier when you're editing the image in Photoshop later. There are techniques for controlling a camera's flash that will prevent over-exposure, and being wary of the backdrop can make or break an image.

Take this poster design, for example, where we need a clean edge around the person. Backgrounds of a singular colour mean that tools such as the Quick Selection and Magic Wand will instantly find edges, and create clean cutouts ready for adding into a design.

QUICK TIP

Move parts of the background
Use the Refine Radius tool (in Refine Edge) to remove parts of the background between hairs.

TOM ROSS

MAXINE MALEK

The Forest

THE FOREST MOVIE PRODUCTIONS. STARRING TOM ROSS AND MAXINE MALEK. PRODUCED BY IMAGINE FILMS, IMAGINARY PRODUCTIONS.
DIRECTED BY: GREAT DESIGNERS EVERYWHERE. CAMERA BY: LENS CORPORATION. – SOUNDTRACK BY MUSIC MASTERS. COSTUME DESIGN BY DRESSAGE INCORPORATED.
THE FOREST MOVIE PRODUCTIONS. STARRING TOM ROSS AND MAXINE MALEK. PRODUCED BY IMAGINE FILMS.

ORIGINAL

01 Lens setup

When taking a photo of a person to use in Photoshop, it's best to shoot them against a plain white wall or background. This makes cutting them out much easier later on. Set your lens to 50mm for minimal distortion.

02 Flash diversion

If you're using flash, bounce the light off the ceiling for a softer lighting effect, or place a piece of paper over the flash itself. Use a fast shutter speed such as 1/250s to reduce blurring, and set the ISO to 400 or less.

03 Mask layer

In Photoshop, if the background is white then the Quick Selection tool will do a good job of selecting it. After that, press Cmd/Ctrl+Shift+I and add a new layer mask. Go to Layer>Duplicate Layer and set Document to your main composition file.

Hugh Jackson

Harriet Jackson

Micky Davis

Jenny Davis

Hayley Jackson

Melora Smith & Hunter Jackson

Alyshia Davis

Michael Smith & Tanya Dayley

Michael Jr.

Darryl Davis

Uncle Bob

D.J. Smith

Mary Smith

Magda Smith & George Davis

Jeremy Jones

Mitch Smith & Sara Summers

Misha Smith & Albert Jones

Martha & Mitchell Smith

Create a modern family tree

Thrill your loved ones with a freshly modern take on the traditional family tree

Need something special to give out at the next family get-together? Surprise your relatives with a slick family tree!

To set the stage, we'll use some ellipses for rolling hills, a light blur image as the basis for the aurora-like backdrop, and a simple tree adorned with layer styles. Adventurous Photoshop users can use the Pen tool to craft their own tree. For silhouettes, we'll use shape files courtesy of http://all-silhouettes. com. These are vector shapes which can be brought into play using the Custom Shape tool (Photoshop users: be sure to choose Shape Layers in the Options bar), and they're all supplied in your resource pack. We'll use them to represent various family members. We also provide a frame and tips for using actual photos if you want to make a more personalised keepsake.

To turbocharge the colours in our piece, we'll use the Color Balance and Hue/Saturation adjustments along with a Color Fill set to Linear Dodge. Some dabs with a sparkle brush will make a nice mystic substitute for leaves.

Photoshop users: it's advised to group all your related layers for easier asset management later in the process.

> "To turbocharge colours, use the Color Balance and Hue/Saturation adjustments along with a Color Fill set to Linear Dodge"

Illustrate your family tree
Get creative and make a 21st-Century design

01 Light blur
Create a new document at 235 x 300mm, 300ppi and with a transparent background. Go to File>Place and add 'Blur.jpg' to the top of the canvas. Don't worry about the empty space at the bottom – we'll fill it soon.

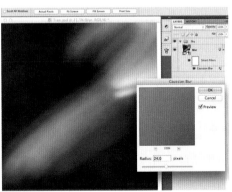

02 Gaussian blur
Go to Filter>Blur>Gaussian Blur and apply a 24 pixel blur. This will make it more suitable as a background element, reducing its detail but retaining colour and flow. Let's have a bit more of a play with it.

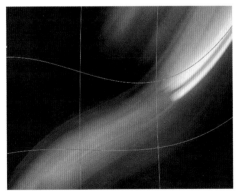

03 Warp the surface
Press Cmd/Ctrl+T to bring up Free Transform. Click the Warp button in the Options bar to bring up the Warp mode, which makes the layer a malleable surface. Manipulate the mesh to give a more dynamic, wavy effect to the blur.

Creative projects

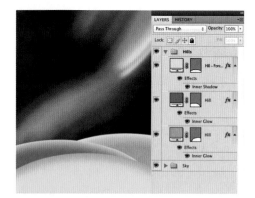

04 Rolling hills
Use the Ellipse tool (U) to create three hill shapes at the bottom. We used the colours #b9a151, #497441 and #dfddac (foreground). Apply soft Inner Glows to the two background hills and a soft Inner Shadow to the one in the foreground.

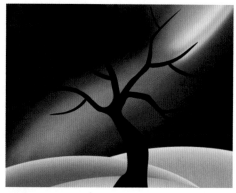

05 Plant the tree
Now it's time to introduce the ancestral tree. Go to File>Place and add 'Tree.png'. Place it so that it is planted in the foreground hill. For an ancestral tree, it sure is homely. Let's have a go at dressing it up with some styles.

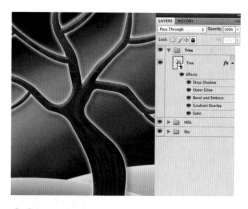

06 Style the tree
Open the Styles Palette. From the palette menu, choose Load Styles and locate 'Tree.asl'. With the tree layer still selected, click the new preset. You can examine and fiddle with the styles if you would like to.

07 Colour glare
Click the Create New Fill Layer button in the Layers palette to add a Color fill layer using #f006ff. Set the blend mode to Linear Dodge and drop Opacity to 90%. Paint the mask with black to remove everything except the upper-right tree area.

08 Silhouettes
There are many online resources for custom shapes in the CSH format. Go ahead and search for family silhouettes to import, or download the same ones we used from the supplied resources. If you'd like to use photos, consult the Expert tip to the left.

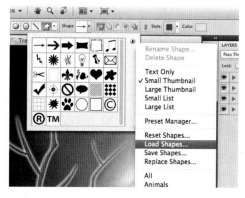

09 Load shapes
Select the Custom Shape tool (U) and expand the preset drop-down in the Options bar. Use the Load Shapes option from the fly-out menu to import the appropriate CSH files. Set the foreground colour to white.

Photo frame
Use real family photos to make a more personalised piece. You can create a frame using the various Shape tools, then dress the elements with Layer Styles. Make an inner shape to use as a clipping mask first. Position your photo above the mask, then Opt/Alt-click between the layers to place it within the shape. You can use 'Frame.psd' as a template ('Frame_Elements.psd' for Elements users). Customise it then merge the layers (Cmd/Ctrl+Opt/Alt+Shift+E).

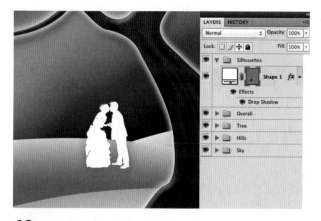

10 Add the first shapes
Select one of the silhouette shapes you loaded from your Custom Shape presets. Photoshop users: select Shape layers from the Options bar. On the canvas, hold Shift as you click and drag out your shape. Add a soft Drop Shadow.

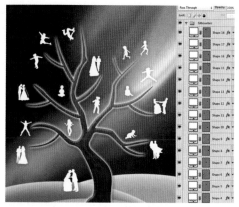

11 Add the other shapes
Now add the rest of the silhouette shapes to your composition. Be sure to create a new layer for each, and remember to hold Shift as you drag them out, keeping them in proportion.

12 Write the names

Use the Type tool (T) in order to add in names for each family member (we have used Verdana). Then add drop shadows to help distinguish them from the background.

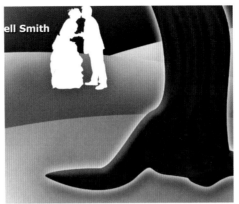

13 Cast shadows

On a new layer below the tree, use a soft, round brush with black at 15% Opacity in order to create some shadows under the tree, and under the matriarch/patriarch.

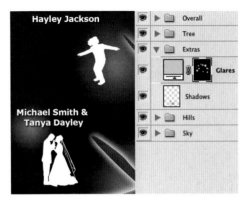

14 Add glares

Click the Create New Fill Layer icon in the Layers palette to add a Color fill layer using #b4df6a. Drop the layer's Opacity to 50%. Fill the mask with black, then paint dabs with a soft(ish), white brush at 100% Opacity to add glares throughout.

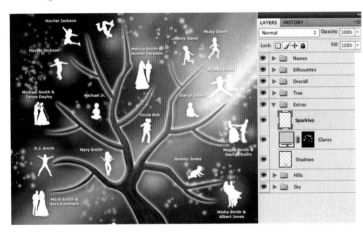

15 Make it sparkle

Load 'Sparkle.abr' from the Brush palette menu (Brush Presets in CS5+). Dial Brush Opacity up to 40%. Set the foreground color to #ffffff and the background to #9ef847. On a new layer, dab throughout the composition.

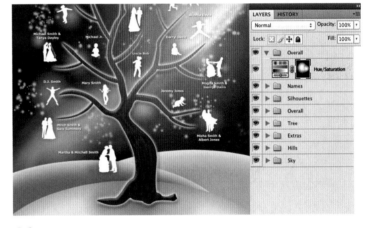

16 Saturate the image

Click the New Adjustment Layer icon and choose Hue/Saturation. Increase Saturation to +39. Paint black in the mask with a soft, round brush to remove the effect from everywhere else except from the centre.

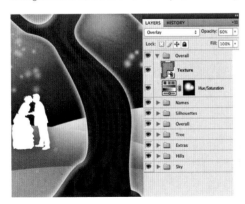

17 Place a texture

Now go to File>Place and then add 'Texture.jpg'. This old envelope scan will introduce just a little bit of a tinge of overall texture. Make sure you also set the blend mode to Overlay and drop Opacity to 60%.

18 Add a vignette

Apply a black Color Fill layer. Fill the mask with black, set the foreground color to white, then come back with a soft, white brush at 20% Opacity to paint around the edges. This will darken the perimeter, drawing viewers' eyes inward.

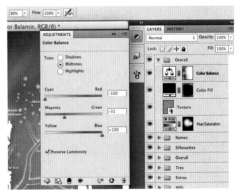

19 Color Balance to finish

Click the New Adjustment Layer icon and choose Color Balance. For Midtones, set the sliders (from top to bottom) to -100, -31 and 100. Paint black in the mask with a soft, round brush to restore some of the original colour. And you're done!

Creative projects

Design a bank note

If you had a currency what would it look like?

Some graphics, when designed in Photoshop, give us the opportunity to practise a lot of techniques and processes along the way. Designing your own bank note can be fun as well as useful. The process can open up the door to the many different options Photoshop has to offer, such as blend modes, custom shapes, adjustment layers, gradients and much more.

To begin this project we'll pull in two textures to create the base paper for your bank note. These textures will also give your bank note an old and distressed look. Next we'll add a gradient to the paper to spice up the colours before playing with a Hue/Saturation adjustment layer. We'll then experiment with a mixture of different custom shapes to add decorative elements to the bank note. Text can then be applied before moving to the final touches.

You don't have to follow the tutorial to the letter. If you're feeling creative, go ahead and experiment with different decorative elements or even use your own imagery on the bank note, such as family photos, buildings or birds. There are no right or wrong ways to approach this design project, so have fun and enjoy learning some new techniques along the way.

> "Experiment with different decorative elements or even use your own imagery on the note"

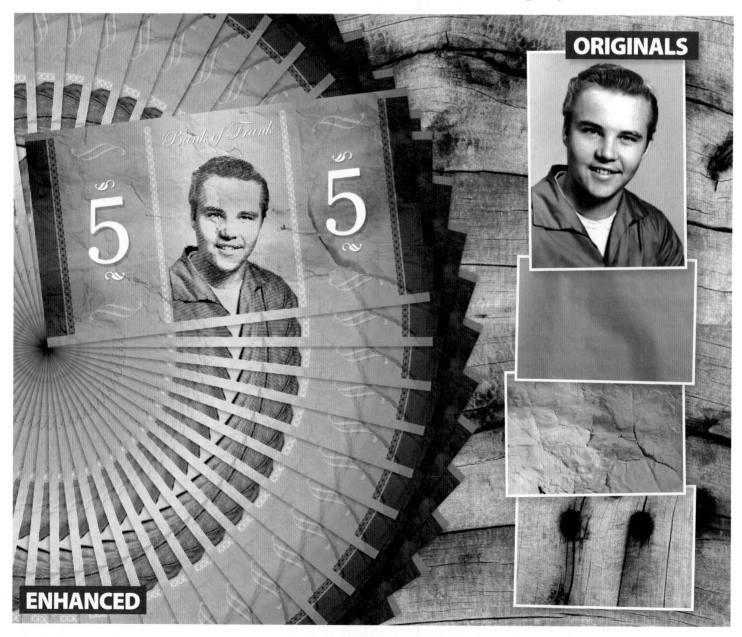

ORIGINALS

ENHANCED

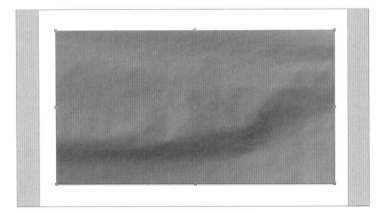

01 Open up the first texture

First of all you need to create a new document by going Cmd/Ctrl+N and make sure it is 235mm wide and 300mm high. Drag the first texture ('texture1. jpg') into your spread, and then resize (Cmd/Ctrl+T) it to roughly the shape of a bank note.

02 Insert the second texture

Open 'texture2.jpg', reduce its size and place it above texture1. Cmd/Ctrl-click texture1's thumbnail to get a selection, then hit Cmd/Ctrl+Shift+I to inverse this and cut (Cmd/Ctrl+X) the overlapping area. Reduce the texture's Opacity to around 40%.

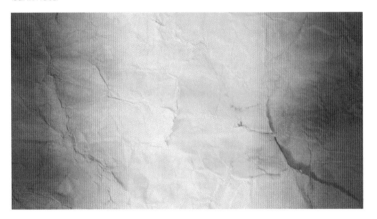

03 Add a gradient

Cmd/Ctrl-click a layer to create a new selection. Go to Layer>New Fill Layer> Gradient. Click the Blue, Red, Yellow preset, change the left and right-most tones to #8e08eb, the middle one to #e9ffb3 then blend mode to Overlay.

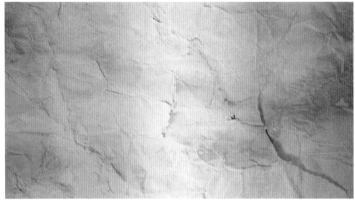

04 Use Hue/Saturation

To change the colour slightly, as well as to tone down the saturation, apply a Hue/Saturation adjustment by going to Layer>New Adjustment Layer>Hue/ Saturation. Adjust the Hue to +30 and reduce the Saturation to -80.

05 Paste in your portrait

Open 'portrait.jpg', hit Cmd/Ctrl+A to select all, Cmd/Ctrl+C to copy, move to your main bank note document and hit Cmd/Ctrl+V to paste it. Then go to Image>Mode> Grayscale. When the dialog appears, select Discard. Go to Image>Mode>Bitmap and change the Method to Halftone Screen.

06 Tweak the frequency

Depending on the resolution of your image, you'll need to alter the frequency. Here we used 30. Change the Shape to Line and press OK. This should achieve a halftone-pint effect, which will give the impression the photo has been printed onto the note. Now change this layer's mode to Color Burn.

Creative projects

QUICK TIP

Custom shapes

Photoshop comes with many built-in custom shapes, but you can dramatically increase your arsenal by downloading more from the web. There are many excellent ornamental and decorative shapes out there to choose from. Once the custom shape file has downloaded (.CHS), you can load it into Photoshop by simply double-clicking it. Play around with these shapes by adding more to your bank note. Test out various sizes, colours, opacities and blend modes to get a good result.

07 Show me the money

As this is an imaginary bank note, you don't necessarily need a currency symbol, unless you'd like to invent one of your own. Create a new layer (Cmd/Ctrl+N) and add your value with the Horizontal Type tool (T).

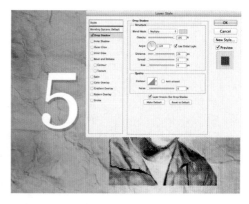

08 Arrange the bank notes

Double-click on your text layer and add a Drop Shadow with the 24px Distance, 0px Spread and 0px Size. Change the colour to #cad7b0 and increase the Opacity to 100%. Duplicate the layer and position the numbers either side.

09 Create the dividers

Next we'll add some custom shape elements to the bank note. Hit Shift+U until you have the Custom Shape tool selected, then open the picker at the top and select All from the fly-out menu. Pick Leaf Ornament 2 and place four on your note.

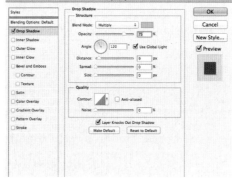

10 Resize to fit your note

Flip the top two elements so they face the opposite direction (Edit>Transform>Flip Horizontal). Now add a Drop Shadow to the elements using the same colour as previous, but this time with 9px Distance, 0px Spread and 0px Size.

11 Position two rectangles

Now you need to find and place the custom shape Ornament 1 onto your bank note. Change its colour to #c6d0d0 and add a black Drop Shadow with a 42% Opacity, 4px Distance, 0px Spread and 0px Size.

12 Create the dividers

Now duplicate (Layer>Duplicate Layer) the element four times and place accordingly. Flip each one so the middle swoops point towards the centre, then merge them together by highlighting, Ctrl/right-clicking and selecting Merge Layers.

13 Resize to fit your note

Next you can apply some text to the note. Here we've decided to add the name of the bank above the portrait in a classic font, Edwardian Script ITC. You can play around here by adding more text to the note as you see fit.

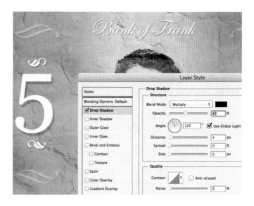

14 Position two rectangles

Because the text that has been added to the note is white, you will want it to stand out by using more shadow. Apply another black Drop Shadow with a 42% Opacity, 4px Distance, 0px Spread and 0px Size.

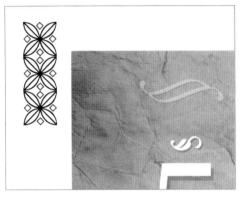

15 Create the dividers

Next you need to create four dividers to separate the portrait and the numbers. Drag in the custom shape Ornament 8 to your canvas, duplicate it roughly 30 times and position each one underneath the last to create a long divider.

16 Resize to fit your note

Merge the Ornament 8 custom shape layers and resize the divider to fit your bank note. Duplicate the divider four times and position them accordingly. Alter the middle two dividers to white by adding a Color Overlay in the Layer Styles menu.

17 Position two rectangles

Next, with the Rectangular Marquee tool (M), you need to create two equal-sized rectangles either side of the black dividers. Fill the selection with black and then change the layer's blend mode to Soft Light.

18 Show me the money

Now the bank note is finished, highlight all of the layers (excluding the white Background) and merge them together. Now Duplicate the layer multiple times and rotate each one to create a fan.

19 Arrange the bank notes

For the final result you can duplicate the bank note multiple times to replicate a full 360-degree fan of money. You can then add a wood texture ('wood.jpg') on a new layer underneath the fan. This gives the impression that the money is resting on a table and frames it well.

EXPERIMENTAL EDITING IS KEY

Find inspiration to achieve a unique design

There's no right or wrong way to approach this design, the possibilities are limitless. Just about every aspect of the note in this tutorial can be altered to produce your very own unique result. Just a bit of research into existing currency and you'll soon notice that the designs are incredibly varied, from complex to simple to asymmetrical to symmetrical.

As well as experimenting with the range of custom shapes available, try inserting more text in different fonts and sizes. Also try adding in more imagery, such as building or birds, or anything that takes your fancy.

Creative projects

Make a magical flying carpet

Climb aboard as we take a magical voyage, turning a
frumpy rug into a flying carpet with the Warp command

Time to take flight! A little girl will be our intrepid navigator, leading us onward and upward to new and exciting techniques. In an ironic and pleasantly jarring reversal, we'll place clouds below a normally grounded rug with some special editing skills, lending a high-altitude and vertigo-inducing atmosphere to our creation.

The flying carpet will be comprised of a rug stock image and a tassel that is duplicated several times. These elements will be arranged and individually warped in order to bring them to supernatural life and provide a billowing sense of motion. We will also add some eye-catching extras such as a motion-blur effect, a mystic glow and a wake of sparkling stars. In order to really solidify the enchanted mood, we will use a series of adjustment layers and blend in some old writing, suggestive of an ancient appeal to the wind spirits.

For readers with Elements or Photoshop versions lacking the necessary features (or even for those who may want to skip creating the magic carpet), we've included a ready-to-fly magic carpet file on the disc.

> "Elements will be arranged and individually warped to bring them to supernatural life"

ORIGINAL

01 Open the mundane rug

Open 'Start.psd', go to File>Place and insert the 'Rug.jpg' supplied file. Scale these down slightly before confirming. Users with Elements or versions prior to CS2 can open 'StartCarpet.psd' and skip straight to Step 4.

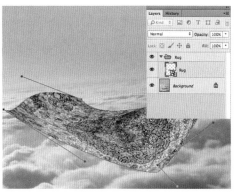

02 Set the rug to flight

Hit Cmd/Ctrl+T to access Free Transform, then select the Warp mode button in the options bar. Try to manipulate the Warp Grid and the control point handles in the corners to make the carpet look like it's flying.

03 Apply the tassels

Add a new layer below the rug and insert 'Tassel. png'. Position this at a corner of the rug, hit Cmd/ Ctrl+T and select the Warp button. Use the Warp Grid and handles to give the tassel a dynamic pose. Now repeat for the other three tassels.

04 Seeing double

Cmd/Ctrl-click the rug and tassel layers, then click-drag to the Create a New Layer icon to make a duplicate. Hit Cmd/Ctrl+E to merge into one layer, then drag below the rug/tassel layers.

05 Use a little blur

Go to Filter>Blur>Motion Blur, set the Distance to 240 pixels and align the Angle to the action. Add a layer mask with a black Foreground and use a soft 80% Opacity brush to remove surplus areas.

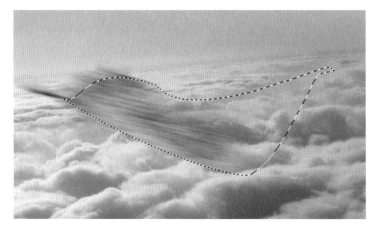

06 Select areas of the rug

Cmd/Ctrl-click the rug's thumbnail to make a selection, then click the eyeball icons for the rug and tassel layers. This toggles their Visibility so we can work beneath them easier.

07 Make a white base

Insert a new layer, set the Foreground to white and use the Paint Bucket tool to fill the selection by clicking within the marching ants. Now hit Cmd/Ctrl+D to turn off the selection.

Creative projects

QUICK TIP

Smart warping

It's wise to convert a layer to a Smart Object before applying Warp. Why? So that you can resume where you left off at any time and re-edit things, just like you can revisit a Smart Filter and fiddle with its settings. To convert a standard layer into a Smart Object, simply Ctrl/right-click on it and choose Convert to Smart Object. Now you can go to Edit>Transform>Warp or Free Transform (Cmd/Ctrl+T) and click the Warp mode button in the following options.

08 Include some smudge

Select the Smudge tool, choose a small soft brush at 90% Opacity, then click-drag outwards on the white base in order to create tentacle-like protrusions. We will turn these into a magical glow in the next step.

09 Cast a mystic glow

To replicate the glow, go to Filter>Blur> Gaussian Blur. Set the Radius to 25 pixels, then click OK. Duplicate the layer by hitting Cmd/Ctrl+J, then toggle the Visibility back on for the previously hidden rug and tassel layers.

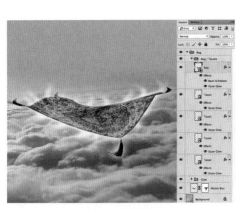

10 Adjust layer styles

Add Outer Glow layer styles to the rug and tassels in the image through the fx button which you can locate in the Layers palette, then simply use a slight Bevel & Emboss on the rug (use the Inner Bevel).

11 The fearless pilot

Insert 'Girl.png', scale it down and position it in the cockpit – or rather on top of the rug – before confirming. If you'd like to use your own model, or provide a co-pilot, extract a model from your own photo and add it to the composition.

12 Place some shadow

Add a new layer above the rest and set the Foreground to black. Now apply a soft round brush at 10% Opacity to bring in some shadows around the girl's feet and the rug beneath her. Repeat this for any additional passengers.

13 Tweak the pilot

Cmd/Ctrl-click the girl layer's thumbnail and repeat for any other passengers. Click the eyeball to toggle the Visibility, insert a layer below the girl and set Foreground to white. Use the Paint Bucket tool to fill the selection, then hit Cmd/Ctrl+D.

14 Apply more smudges

Hit Cmd/Ctrl+J in order to duplicate the white base layer, then select the Smudge tool. Choose a small soft brush at 90% Opacity, then click-drag out to create some more tentacle-like protrusions, like in Step 8.

15 Blur the lines again

Go to Filter>Blur>Motion Blur, set the Distance to 540 pixels and then adjust the Angle so that it aligns with the action. Now you can turn the Visibility back on for the girl's and any other passengers' layers.

16 She's an angel!
Now let's give the girl a more ethereal look. Add a layer mask with the icon in the Layers palette, set the Foreground to black and use a soft round brush at 50% Opacity to carefully paint out some of girl's edges.

17 Get some sparkles
Select the Brush tool and insert 'Sparkle.abr' from the Presets menu. Set the Foreground to white and the Background to #dccddd. Now paint at 100% to add a sparkle trail. The following steps will be added to the top of the stacking order.

18 Play with the Levels
Click the Create New Adjustment Layer button in the Layers palette and choose Levels. Now enter these settings below the Histogram (from left to right): 30, 1.35 and 230. This should brighten the overall image.

19 Replicate an ancient sprawl
Place 'Scrawl.jpg' from the supplied resources and then set the blend mode to Overlay. Add a layer mask, set the Foreground to black, and then use a soft brush at 80% Opacity to paint away some of the layer.

20 Color Balance adjustment layer
Click the Create New Adjustment Layer button, but this time choose Color Balance. Set the Midtones (from top to bottom): -90, -15 and +65. Now fill the mask with black, set the Foreground to white, then paint in the centre-left area.

21 Darken the edges
Add a new layer and then set the blend mode to Overlay. With black as the Foreground colour, use a soft round brush at around 2,000px and 50% Opacity in order to paint around the edges.

QUICK TIP

Reusable assets
We've included a ready-to-fly magic carpet ('CarpetComplete.psd') for those users who don't have the necessary features to create it from the base rug and tassel photos. This can be imported into the main composition via File>Place, or you can open it and drag its contents into another document. This same concept can be used to create a library of assets, ready to deploy at any time. These could be branding elements, template components, robot parts, or anything that you need to reuse frequently. Make sure these elements are at a good enough resolution for your projects.

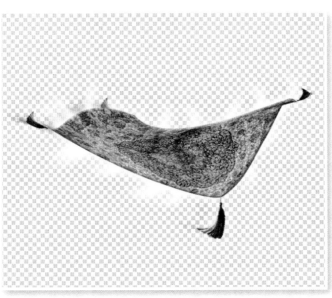

22 Finish with some fills
To finish, click the Create New Fill Layer button in the Layers palette and choose Solid Color. Pick #76700c, change the blend mode to Color Burn and the Opacity to 40%. Set the Foreground to black, and paint out some of the central area.

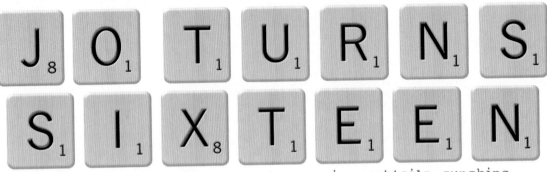

JO TURNS SIXTEEN

Super Sweet 16th. with: tea. cakes. music. cocktails. sunshine.

tweet to woo!

BIRTHDAY PARTY

12th May

5pm to 12pm

The Beach Club

You coming?

R.S.V.P.................

Design a party invitation

Make your party amazing before it's even started with bespoke party invitations that'll impress your guests

ORIGINALS

Everyone wants to have the perfect party with all their family and friends. One of the first steps is to have the best invitation to give your guests a small insight into what they can expect when they attend. But instead of buying the usual generic invitations, why not use your creativity to design your own personalised invites?

If it's a birthday party, why not include family photos or baby pictures to convey growth and dynasty? Maybe you're organising a wedding and want to create invites, so you could use photos to illustrate small details like flowers and hearts. Perhaps you're planning a space party for your son. You could use the Pen tool to draw rockets and plants, then edit a photo of your son to capture his love of space. The possibilities are endless and you can pretty much design any form of invite you have in mind, just by using the simple tools Photoshop has to offer. You can have as much fun with this project as you'll at your party or event.

> "Give your guests a small insight into what they can expect when they attend your party"

Get the party started
Harness Photoshop's selection tools, adjustments and more

01 Crop the image
Open your image and apply the Crop tool (C) to gradually adjust and make it a square. You can hold down the Shift key to ensure that your square is symmetrical. Now hit Enter and duplicate your image by hitting Cmd/Ctrl+J.

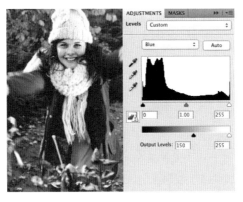

02 Create a vignette effect
Now you can add a simple vintage filter to give your image more of a Polaroid feel. For a start you can go to Layer>New Adjustment Layer>Levels. From the RGB panel, select Blue and set the value of the Output Levels to 150.

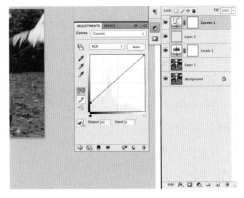

03 Establish depth
Create a new layer and fill it with a light beige (#f2d4b1). Then set the blend mode to Multiply. After, go to Layer>New Adjustment Layer>Curves and make a point at the bottom left hand corner, make the Output to 40.

Creative projects

QUICK TIP

Pre-plan your design

Pre-planning what you're going to create is always a key step within your process. By doing this you aren't going into the project blind and you'll have a rough idea of what you aim to create. Sketch out a few options before you head to the computer and hand-draw what you want to achieve digitally, such as the bunting or any other elements you may want to add. You don't have to stick to your initial design, as your ideas may change as you progress.

04 Continue the adjustment

Carrying on with the Adjustment, create another point that is slightly higher than the first point on your curve Adjustment, and this time change the Output to 75 and then Input to 70.

05 The final variation

Finally, create a third point towards the top right hand corner of your Curve Adjustment and then change the variations of the Output to 190 and the Input to 190, also. You will notice you have given your image a nice little filter to it.

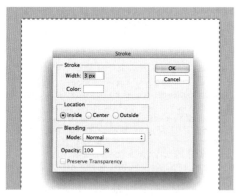

06 Complete the Polaroid style

Create a new document (Cmd/Ctrl+N) and make it 1,025 x 1,197px with the Background Contents set to white. Hit Cmd/Ctrl+A to select your layer. Go to Edit>Stroke, set Location to Inside and Stroke Width to 3px. Now paste in your vintage filter effect.

07 Tweak the result

Use the Magic Wand (W) to select the outside of the image, then Ctrl/right-click and click Select Inverse. Go to Edit>Stroke, select Outside for Location and set a Width of 3px. Create a folder on your desktop called 'Polaroids' and save this image.

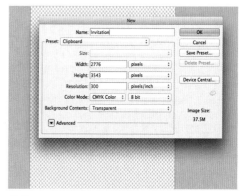

08 Set up another document

Open another new document, making it 2,776 x 3,543px, and set the Background Contents to Transparent. This will be the main document for your invitation. Now it is time to create the lovely bunting.

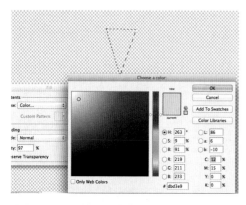

09 Draw the bunting

Use the Pen Path tool (P) in order to create an isosceles triangle, add a new layer, go to Path and pick Make a Selection. Grab the Magic Wand, Ctrl/right-click in order to Select Inverse and fill (Edit>Fill) your shape.

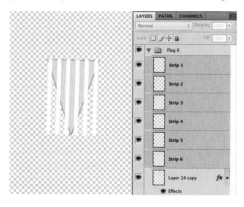

10 Build the patterns

Go to Layer>Layer Style>Blending Options> Stroke, change the Stroke to a darker colour than your triangle and make the Size 5px. On a new layer, use the Rectangular Marquee tool to create a thin rectangle and fill this with white.

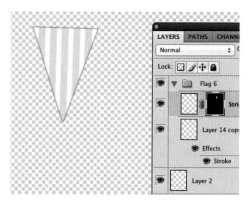

11 Mask elements together

Select the shape of the triangle using the Magic Wand tool, click the stripe layer and then add a vector mask. You can now repeat Steps 9 to 11 in order to create different colours and patterns for your bunting.

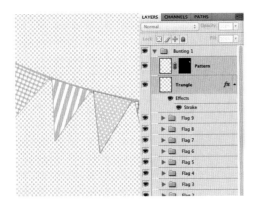

12 Compact the flags

Apply the Pen tool to create the shape for the string, align the flags together and use Free Transform to move and rotate each flag. Now tidy up your layers by adding a new group for each of your flags.

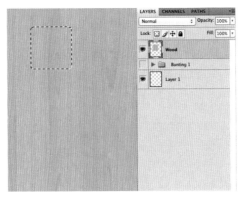

13 Build Scarbble pieces

Hide your bunting, create a new layer, paste in a wood texture and draw a rectangle using the Rounded Rectangle tool with a Radius of 0.1. Go to Paths>Make Selection and add a vector mask to make the wood into a rounded rectangle.

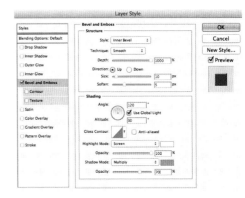

14 Achieve a simple 3D effect

Go to Layer>Layer Style>Bevel and Emboss. Keep the default settings but change the Depth to 1,000%, Size to 10px, Soften to 5px and set the Highlight Mode to 100% Opacity. Make Shadow Mode a dark beige and set the Opacity to 70%.

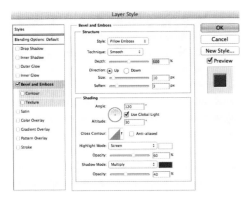

15 Deboss letters and numbers

Go to Layer> Layer Style >Bevel and Emboss. Set these variables: Style: Pillow Emboss; Depth: 500%; Size: 10%; Soften: 3%; Highlight Mode: Opacity at 60%; Shadow Mode to Multiply, dark beige and a 40% Opacity.

16 Add borders and a backdrop

Hide your Scrabble layers and fill your first layer with a Background tone via Edit>Fill. To create the border, make a new layer and use the Pen tool to form its shape. Go to Paths>Make Selection, then fill it with a colour similar to the background.

QUICK TIP

Using hand-rendered type

Hand-rendered type is, funnily enough, a group of fonts drawn by hand. Instead of adding digital fonts onto your invitation, why not write the text yourself by hand? The combination of digital and traditional application could add depth and originality to your final creation. This will truly make your invitation an original creative piece, as no one else has your exact handwriting. Plus, writing each individual invitation will give them a personal feel. Also, why not hand-draw the little extra illustrations, such as swirls?

17 Piecing together

At this point you have created everything you need to comprise your invitation. Now experiment with the positioning of your letter bricks, buntings and Polaroid. Use Free Transform (Cmd/Ctrl+T) to make moving your components easier.

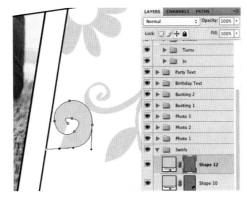

18 Bring in final touches

Begin to apply the text by using the Type tool. Add new layers for each illustration and then apply the Pen to create your shapes. This time use the Shape Layer option and pick your tone before you start drawing.

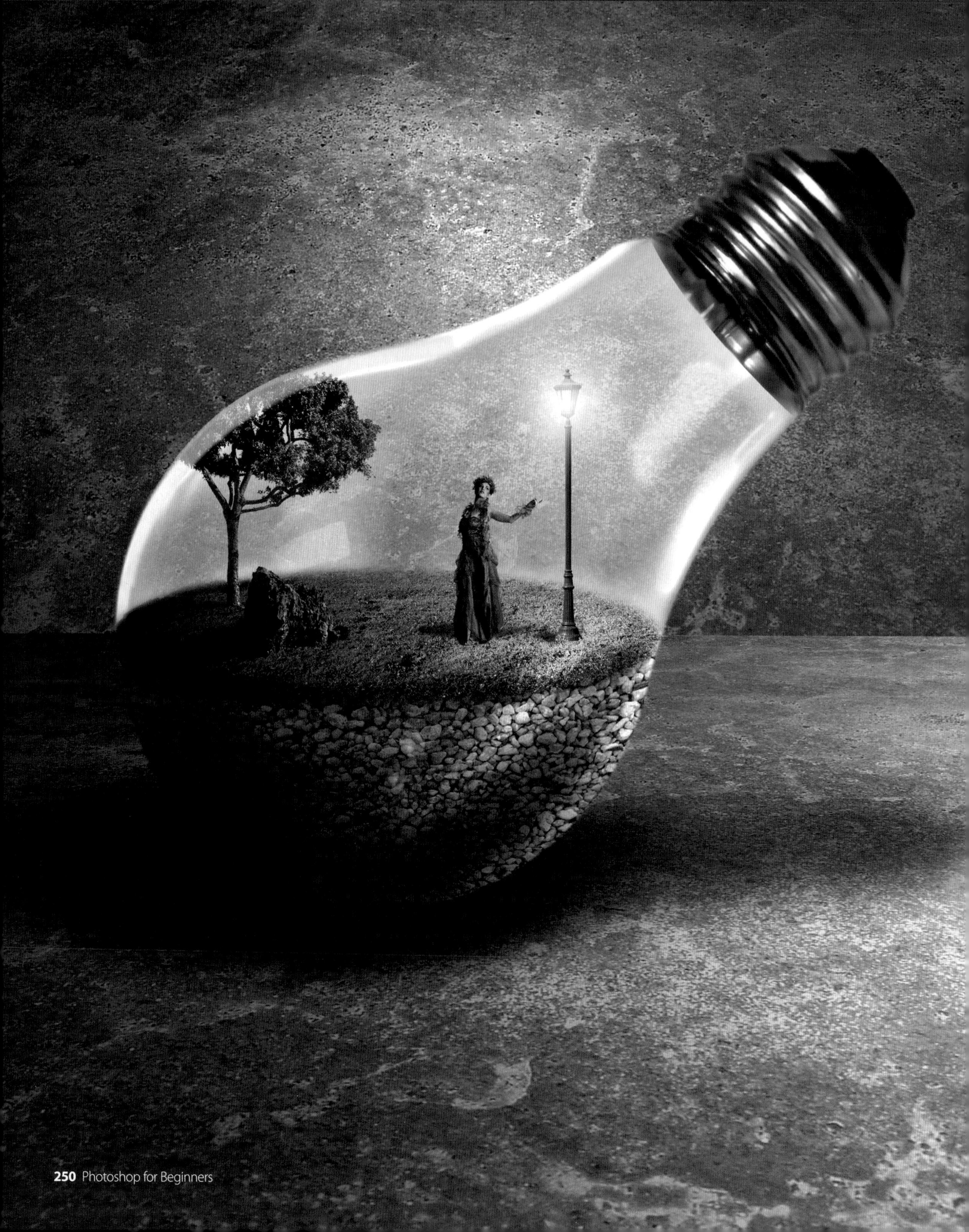

Compose surreal artwork

Learn how to create a bizarre composite using several techniques and filters in Photoshop Elements

You can achieve amazingly surreal photomanipulations in Photoshop Elements using the right tools and techniques.

Here we'll teach you how to work with several images and manipulate them into place before editing the image using filters and brushes.

We'll start by working with the Free Transform tool to learn how to resize, skew and rotate your elements. We'll then work with several layers and filters to produce this composition. Another great tool you will learn is the Magic Extractor, which will help us make accurate selections. This tool is only available in Photoshop Elements, but you can achieve a similar effect using the Quick Eraser tool (E) or the Quick Selection tool (W) in Photoshop CS versions. We'll also explore how to use the Lighting Effects filter to apply shadows and inject more dramatic lighting in your scene.

You will find all the images and files that you need to get you started supplied on the disc, so don't hesitate to open the PSDs to check how all of the layers are distributed.

"Explore how to use the Lighting Effects filter to apply shadows and inject more dramatic lighting into your scene"

Build an abstract scene
Delve into your imagination to produce a bizarre photo composite

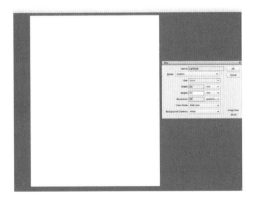

01 Set up your document
Begin by creating a new blank file. Hit Cmd/Ctrl+N to open the New dialog box, name your project 'Lightbulb', then set the Width to 235mm, the Height to 300mm and the Resolution to 300. Confirm this by clicking OK.

02 Place the background
Go to File>Place and select 'Background.jpeg'. Duplicate this (Cmd/Ctrl+J) and rename it 'Background_copy'. Move (V) this layer down, tweak the perspective (via Cmd/Ctrl+T), hold Cmd/Ctrl and drag the handles to skew the image.

03 Place the lightbulb image
Place 'Lightbulb.png'. Click Constrain Proportions on the Tool Options, set the Width to 60%, change the Angle to (-)10 degrees and click the green check mark. Duplicate the layer, name it 'Lightbulb_copy' and turn the layer visibility off.

Creative projects

QUICK TIP

Clipping mask

A clipping mask is a group of layers to which a mask is applied. The clipping mask enables you to cover the image below the base layer, which defines the visible borders of the entire group. For example, if you have text and you want to apply an image to create a nice texture, the clipping mask is the easiest way to achieve this effect. To add a clipping mask, hold down Opt/Alt, position the pointer on the line dividing the two layers and click.

04 Add a clipping mask

Ctrl/right-click on the Lightbulb_copy layer and choose Simplify. Insert 'GRAVEL.jpeg', resize the image (W: 45, H:25), hold Cmd/Ctrl and skew things a little. Now hold Opt/Alt, position the pointer between the Gravel and the Lightbulb and click.

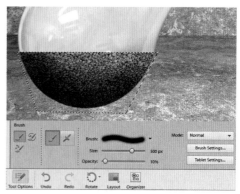

05 Apply the Brush tool

Keep the Gravel layer selected, Ctrl/right-click and hit Simplify (for CS choose Rasterize instead). Grab a soft brush (B), set the Size to 500px and the Opacity to 10%. Apply around the image in order to create shadows.

06 Use the Elliptical Marquee tool

Open 'LANDSCAPE.jpeg', grab the Elliptical Marquee tool (M), set the Feather to 25 pixels, add an Ellipse, then copy/paste (Cmd/Ctrl+C and V) into a layer and rename it 'Grass'. Hit Cmd/Ctrl+T, hold Alt/Opt and resize the image.

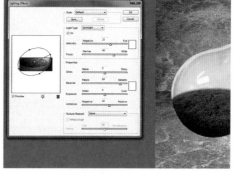

07 Boost the light

Hold Opt/Alt again, position the pointer between the Grass and the Gravel layer, then create a clipping mask. Go to Filter>Render>Lighting Effects and set the Light Type to Spotlight. Set the Intensity to 25, Focus to 40 and Ambience to 20.

08 Insert more images

Go to File>Place, then select 'TREE.png', 'Rock.png' and 'LAMP.png'. Now open the Free Transform tool to resize and move the images around the composition. Hold Shift, select the Tree and Rock layers and then hit Cmd/Ctrl+E to merge.

09 Break out the magic!

Open 'Woman.jpeg' from your disc (courtesy of Marcus Ranum) and go to Image>Magic Extractor (or Magic Eraser). Apply a red Foreground brush on areas you want to keep and a blue Background on areas you want to remove.

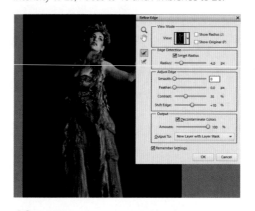

10 Refine your selections

Go to Select>Refine Edge, check Smart Radius, and change the Radius to 4px, Contrast to 35%, Shift Edge to +10% and Decontaminate Colors to 100%. Next Ctrl/right -click, select Apply Layer Mask and then paste.

11 Erase some areas

Select Lightbulb_copy, grab the Eraser tool (E), pick a large soft brush at around 200px, then set the Opacity to around 30%. Slowly erase inside the lightbulb without going over the borders and just reveal the background.

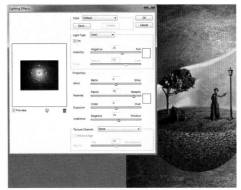

12 Bring in some shadows
Add a new layer below the Images layer and name it 'Shadows'. Apply a hard brush at 10px while zoomed in, then go to Filter>Blur>Gaussian Blur, set the Radius to 5px and make sure you change the Opacity to 60%.

13 Enhance the lights
Select the Background_copy layer and Ctrl/right-click in order to Simplify (or click Rasterize). Go to Filter>Render>Lighting Effect, choose Spotlight, and then change the Intensity to 25 and Ambience to 10.

14 Increase the blur
Select the Lightbulb layer, hit Cmd/Ctrl+U and set the Lightness to -100. Use Free Transform to scale the image, then apply a 40px Gaussian Blur. Select the Eraser tool with 30% Opacity to erase the back portion of the image, then set the Opacity to 80%.

15 Merge your layers
Select the Woman layer, hold Shift, select the Lightbulb_copy layer and hit Cmd/Ctrl+E to merge. Pick the Burn tool (O), set the Exposure to 20% and apply around this to bring in more shadows.

16 Finish with a lens flare
Select and merge all the layers (Cmd/Ctrl+E), then hold Cmd/Ctrl, click the merged layer and go to Image>Crop. Go to Filter>Render>Lens Flare, set Brightness to 50% and pick Lens Type 105mm Prime.

THE DEPTH OF FIELD EDIT
Use Foreground and Background brushes to enhance the effect

01 Apply the Magic Extractor
The Magic Extractor is a great tool to make accurate selections in Photoshop Elements. Click the Foreground Brush tool and draw multiple lines to mark the area you want to select.

02 Pick the Background Brush
Select the Background Brush tool in the dialog box, and then paint across all the colours and textures you don't want to select.

03 Navigate your canvas
To help get a more-accurate selection, use the Zoom or Hand tool to magnify and find your way around the image.

04 Preview the selection
Click Preview to see the current selection or hit X to switch between the preview selection area and the original photo. The Magic Extractor is a handy tool to select complex objects.

Glossary

Glossary of key terms

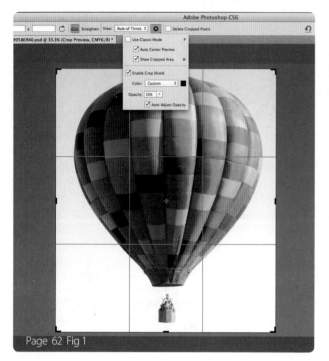

Page 62 Fig 1

Page 188 Fig 2

Page 128 Fig 3

Adjustment layers

These are non-destructive layers that enable you to make changes to your image, without affecting your original. You can also go back to adjustment layers and change the settings at a later date.

Artifact

We use this term when images are saved as JPEGs or shot in low light with noise. Artifacts are unwanted elements that appear when heavy compression or editing has occurred.

Background layer

This is the original layer that you open in Photoshop. By default this layer is locked to protect it from changes, double-click on the layer to turn it into a regular, editable layer.

Blending mode

The blending mode options in the Layers palette determine how the pixels in the layer interact with the pixels in the layers below it.

Brush Preset

Photoshop comes with Presets for brushes meaning that different combinations of size and thickness, have been stored for you to use. Create your own if you find a brush setup that works for you. (Fig 2).

Camera Raw

This is Photoshop's built-in RAW-processing plug-in, which enables you to open photographs that have been shot in the RAW format, rather than JPEG.

Clipboard

This is where file elements are stored if you cut or copy from one image to another. If the Clipboard gets too full, then you might find that it starts to slow processing.

Clone

The technique of taking a clean area from a photograph and applying it over a flawed area of an image. This is done with the Clone Stamp tool. Click on the clean area while pressing Opt/Alt to 'source' the sample, then paint over the flaw.

CMYK

This stands for Cyan, Magenta, Yellow and Black, which is a common Image Mode for printing. Photoshop Elements does not support CMYK images. Most printers will convert RGB images into CMYK for printing, but if you have Photoshop you may want to work in CMYK so you can see how the final image will look more accurately. Some filters and adjustments only work in RGB.

Colour cast

When an unwanted colour is 'cast' over your photograph. The Color Balance command can fix this.

Contrast

The difference between light and dark areas in any given image, can be altered using Levels and Curves, as well as the Brightness/Contrast command.

Crop

This is the act of trimming an image, discarding unwanted pixels from the final composition. (Fig 1).

DPI

This stands for Dots Per Inch and it is a measure of printer resolution. Use higher DPI settings for better prints. We recommend working at 300dpi where possible.

Duotone

This is the term for a greyscale image that uses two colour inks to tint photos. Not available in Elements.

Exposure

The amount of light in which a photograph is taken. Fix both underexposure (too dark) and overexposure (too light) in Photoshop.

Page 104 Fig 4

Feathering

When you make selections, the Feather command softens the edge so that it blends more naturally into the background.

Filters

Preset controls that give special effects to your photos. There are loads built into Photoshop and Photoshop Elements.

Flatten

Flatten individual layers into one, keeping file sizes down. Bear in mind that you will lose all separate layers so you won't be able to go back and change things later on.

Gaussian Blur

One of the Blur filters in Photoshop. This is one of the most common blurs and it softens through a 'bell-shaped' distribution of colour and tone.

Gradient

A smooth transition effect from one colour to another.

Grayscale

This removes all colour from an image, using just black, white and grey on one channel. There are several ways to transform an image to black and white.

Highlights

This refers to the brightest elements of any given image.

Histogram

A graph that shows how the pixels are distributed in an image. The horizontal axis shows the 'levels' from the darkest to brightest pixels (0-255), whereas the vertical axis shows how many pixels are at each level. Aim for an even distribution of tones.

History

Your commands are saved as History States, so that you can use the History palette to backtrack if something goes wrong.

Image Mode

This is the name given to image modes, such as RGB, CMYK, etc. This can be changed by going to Image>Mode.

JPEG

This is the most common file format used by digital cameras and it does compress image information to keep file sizes down.

Layer

Overlay different images or elements over one another. (Fig 4).

Layer group

Collect layers into groups when working with multiple layers to stay organised. Group all layers that relate to the same thing.

Layer masks

Layer masks let you control how much of one layer shows through to the one below it. You paint directly on to the mask in white or black in order to reveal or hide.

Levels

This is a feature that helps you control the colour and tone in your images.

Midtone

This is the term for the area of tones that fall between the brightest and darkest pixels.

Noise

This is an artifact that shows up as grain on your photos. Most common when images have been compressed, or shot in low light. It can be removed easily.

Opacity

This is the control used in the Layers palette or in the top options bar for most tools, which determines how 'visible' or 'transparent' an effect is.

Pixel

These are the tiny, rectangular points of colour that a digital image is composed of.

PPI

This stands for Pixels Per Inch, which is a measure of image resolution used by cameras and computers.

PSD

This is Photoshop's very own file format and it can be used to save multiple layers.

Quick Mask

This – as the name suggests – is an extremely quick way of masking areas in an image in order to form a selection.

Red eye

This is a very common flaw found in digital portrait photographs, which is caused by the use of camera flash.

Resolution

This is a measure of clarity and sharpness in an image. The higher the resolution, the better-quality the image, and print size.

RGB

This is the Red, Green, Blue image makeup that is used by computer screens.

Saturation

This is the strength of a colour and it can be altered in the Hue/ Saturation options.

Selection

A Selection, as it suggests, is the name given when you isolate a certain part of any image.

Shadows

The darkest elements in an image.

Sharpening

This is the process of enhancing details in an image. Be very careful when sharpening, as too much of it can lead to noise. (Fig 3).

Swatches

This is a selection of preset colours that you are able to pick from within Photoshop. You are also able to create or download more if you need to.

TIFF

This is a file format that is often used for printing. It is compressed in such a manner that it does not affect the image quality, be aware that it can lead to bigger file sizes.

Transform

This is the set of controls that enables you to distort, skew, scale, and so on, an image, as you wish.

Unsharp Mask

A popular filter in Photoshop that is used for sharpening, because it increases the detail in images.

On your free disc

Essential creative resources for Photoshop projects

There's much more to this bookazine than the pages within, as it also comes with a fantastic free CD packed full of features. We have the essential tutorial files that you need to get cracking with many of the tutorials that we have featured, including start images, textures and more. There are also five video tutorials, two premium fonts from Typodermic Fonts, 19 retro filter actions from SparkleStock, and four premium text styles from Ultimate Bundles, so you can really get creative. This should all help you get to grips with the basic tools and techniques in both Photoshop and Photoshop Elements.

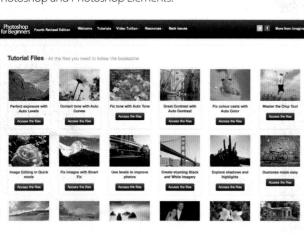

Video tutorials

There are four video tutorials from Santo Romano; two on the use of layers when creating a basic composition, and two on accessing and applying layer styles. There is also a video tutorial from Andrei Oprinca on digital painting effects. Watch and learn.

Tutorial files

Free with this book are a range of start images that you can use in your personal projects and follow along with the tutorials in the book. We have everything from animals and people, to macros and landscapes. You can access these by going to the Tutorials option on the main disc interface.

Actions
Check out the 19 retro Photoshop actions provided by SparkleStock, and inject a little more creativity into your Photoshop projects.